The Instinct of Workmanship and the State of the Industrial Arts

The Instinct of Workmanship and the State of the Industrial Arts

THORSTEIN VEBLEN

COSIMO CLASSICS

NEW YORK

The Instinct of Workmanship and the State of the Industrial Arts

For information, address:

Cosimo, P.O. Box 416
Old Chelsea Station
New York, NY 10113-0416

or visit our website at:
www.cosimobooks.com

The Instinct of Workmanship and the State of the Industrial Arts was originally published in 1914.

Library of Congress Cataloging-in-Publication Data
A catalog record for this book is available from the Library of Congress

Cover design by www.kerndesign.net

ISBN:1-59605-893-5

CONTENTS

THE INSTINCT OF WORKMANSHIP

CHAPTER I

INTRODUCTORY

FOR mankind as for the other higher animals, the life of the species is conditioned by the complement of instinctive proclivities and tropismatic aptitudes with which the species is typically endowed. Not only is the continued life of the race dependent on the adequacy of its instinctive proclivities in this way, but the routine and details of its life are also, in the last resort, determined by these instincts. These are the prime movers in human behaviour, as in the behaviour of all those animals that show self-direction or discretion. Human activity, in so far as it can be spoken of as conduct, can never exceed the scope of these instinctive dispositions, by initiative of which man takes action. Nothing falls within the human scheme of things desirable to be done except what answers to these native proclivities of man. These native proclivities alone make anything worth while, and out of their working emerge not only the purpose and efficiency of life, but its substantial pleasures and pains as well.

Latterly the words "instinct" and "instinctive" are no longer well seen among students of those biological sciences where they once had a great vogue. Students who occupy themselves with the psychology of animal behaviour are cautiously avoiding these expressions, and in this caution they are doubtless well advised. For such use the word appears no longer to be serviceable as a technical term. It has lost the requisite sharp definition and consistency of connotation, apparently through disintegration under a more searching analysis than the phenomena comprised under this concept had previously been subjected to. In these biological sciences interest is centering not on the question of what activities may be set down to innate propensity or predisposition at large, but rather on the determination of the irreducible psychological—and, indeed, physiological—elements that go to make up animal behaviour. For this purpose "instinct" is a concept of too lax and shifty a definition to meet the demands of exact biological science.

For the sciences that deal with the psychology of human conduct a similarly searching analysis of the elementary facts of behaviour is doubtless similarly desirable; and under such closer scrutiny of these facts it will doubtless appear that here, too, the broad term "instinct" is of too unprecise a character to serve the needs of an exhaustive psychological analysis. But the needs of an inquiry into the nature and causes of the growth of institutions are not precisely the same as those of such an exhaustive psychological analysis. A genetic inquiry into institutions will address itself to the growth of habits and conventions, as conditioned by the material environment and by the innate and persistent propensities of human nature; and for these propensities, as they take effect in the give and take of cultural growth, no better designation than the time-worn "instinct" is available.

In the light of recent inquiries and speculations it is scarcely to be questioned that each of these distinguishable propensities may be analysed into simpler constituent elements, of a quasi-tropismatic or physiological nature; [1] but in the light of every-day experience and common notoriety it is at the same time not to be questioned that these simple and irreducible psychological elements of human behaviour fall into composite functional groups, and so make up specific and determinate propensities, proclivities, aptitudes that are, within the purview of the social sciences, to be handled as irreducible traits of human nature. Indeed, it would appear that it is in the particular grouping and concatenation of these ultimate psychological elements into characteristic lines of interest and propensity that the nature of man is finally to be distinguished from that of the lower animals.

These various native proclivities that are so classed together as "instincts" have the characteristic in common that they all and several, more or less imperatively, propose an objective end of endeavour. On the other hand what distinguishes one instinct from another is that each sets up a characteristic purpose, aim, or object to be attained, different from the objective end of any other instinct. Instinctive action is teleological, consciously so, and the teleological scope and aim of each instinctive propensity differs characteristically from all the rest. The several instincts are teleological categories,

[1] Cf. Jacques Loeb, *Comparative Physiology of the Brain and Comparatvie Psychology*, ch. i.

and are, in colloquial usage, distinguished and classed on the ground of their teleological content. As the term is here used, therefore, and indeed as it is currently understood, the instincts are to be defined or described neither in mechanical terms of those anatomical or physiological aptitudes that causally underlie them or that come into action in the functioning of any given instinct, nor in terms of the movements of orientation or taxis involved in the functioning of each. The distinctive feature by the mark of which any given instinct is identified is to be found in the particular character of the purpose to which it drives.[1] "Instinct," as contra-distinguished from tropismatic action, involves consciousness and adaptation to an end aimed at.

It is, of course, not hereby intended to set up or to prescribe a definition of "instinct" at large, but only to indicate as closely as may be what sense is attached to the term as here used. At the same time it is believed that this definition of the concept does violence neither to colloquial usage nor to the usage of such students as have employed the term in scientific discussion, particularly in discussion of the instinctive proclivities of mankind. But it is not to be overlooked that this definition of the term may be found inapplicable, or at least of doubtful service, when applied to those simpler and more immediate impulses that are sometimes by tradition spoken of as "instinctive," even in human behaviour,—impulses that might with better effect be designated

[1] Cf. W. James, *Principles of Psychology*, ch. xxiv and xxv, where, however, the difference between tropism and instinct is not kept well in hand,—the tropisms having at that date not been subjected to inquiry and definition as has been true since then; William McDougall, *Introduction to Social Psychology*, ch. i.

"tropismatic." In animal behaviour, for instance, as well as in such direct and immediate impulsive human action as is fairly to be classed with animal behaviour, it is often a matter of some perplexity to draw a line between tropismatic activity and instinct. Notoriously, the activities commonly recognised as instinctive differ widely among themselves in respect of the degree of directness or immediacy with which the given response to stimulus takes place. They range in this respect all the way from such reactions as are doubtfully to be distinguished from simple reflex action on the one hand, to such as are doubtfully recognised as instinctive because of the extent to which reflection and deliberation enter into their execution on the other hand. By insensible gradation the lower (less complex and deliberate) instinctive activities merge into the class of unmistakable tropismatic sensibilities, without its being practicable to determine by any secure test where the one category should be declared to end and the other to begin.[1] Such quasi-tropismatic activities may be rated as purposeful by an observer, in the sense that they are seen to further the life of the individual agent or of the species, while there is no consciousness of purpose on the part of the agent under observation; whereas "instinct," in the narrower and special sense to which it seems desirable to restrict the term for present use, denotes the conscious pursuit of an objective end which the instinct in question makes worth while.

The ends of life, then, the purposes to be achieved, are assigned by man's instinctive proclivities; but the ways

[1] Loeb, *Comparative Physiology of the Brain*, pp. 177–178.

and means of accomplishing those things which the instinctive proclivities so make worth while are a matter of intelligence. It is a distinctive mark of mankind that the working-out of the instinctive proclivities of the race is guided by intelligence to a degree not approached by the other animals. But the dependence of the race on its endowment of instincts is no less absolute for this intervention of intelligence; since it is only by the prompting of instinct that reflection and deliberation come to be so employed, and since instinct also governs the scope and method of intelligence in all this employment of it. Men take thought, but the human spirit, that is to say the racial endowment of instinctive proclivities, decides what they shall take thought of, and how and to what effect.

Yet the dependence of the scheme of life on the complement of instinctive proclivities hereby becomes less immediate, since a more or less extended logic of ways and means comes to intervene between the instinctively given end and its realisation; and the lines of relation between any given instinctive proclivity and any particular feature of human conduct are by so much the more devious and round-about and the more difficult to trace. The higher the degree of intelligence and the larger the available body of knowledge current in any given community, the more extensive and elaborate will be the logic of ways and means interposed between these impulses and their realisation, and the more multifarious and complicated will be the apparatus of expedients and resources employed to compass those ends that are instinctively worth while.

This apparatus of ways and means available for the

pursuit of whatever may be worth seeking is, substantially all, a matter of tradition out of the past, a legacy of habits of thought accumulated through the experience of past generations. So that the manner, and in a great degree the measure, in which the instinctive ends of life are worked out under any given cultural situation is somewhat closely conditioned by these elements of habit, which so fall into shape as an accepted scheme of life. The instinctive proclivities are essentially simple and look directly to the attainment of some concrete objective end; but in detail the ends so sought are many and diverse, and the ways and means by which they may be sought are similarly diverse and various, involving endless recourse to expedients, adaptations, and concessive adjustment between several proclivities that are all sufficiently urgent.

Under the discipline of habituation this logic and apparatus of ways and means falls into conventional lines, acquires the consistency of custom and prescription, and so takes on an institutional character and force. The accustomed ways of doing and thinking not only become an habitual matter of course, easy and obvious, but they come likewise to be sanctioned by social convention, and so become right and proper and give rise to principles of conduct. By use and wont they are incorporated into the current scheme of common sense. As elements of the approved scheme of conduct and pursuit these conventional ways and means take their place as proximate ends of endeavour. Whence, in the further course of unremitting habituation, as the attention is habitually focussed on these proximate ends, they occupy the interest to such an extent as commonly to throw their own ulterior purpose into the background and often let it be lost sight of; as may happen, for instance, in the acquisition and use of money. It follows that in much of human conduct these proximate ends alone are present in consciousness as the object of interest and the goal of endeavour, and certain conventionally accepted ways and means come to be set up as definitive principles of what is right and good; while the ulterior purpose of it all is only called to mind occasionally, if at all, as an afterthought, by an effort of reflection.[1]

Among psychologists who have busied themselves with these questions there has hitherto been no large measure of agreement as to the number of specific instinctive proclivities that so are native to man; nor is there any agreement as to the precise functional range and content ascribed to each. In a loose way it is apparently taken for granted that these instincts are to be conceived as discrete and specific elements in human nature, each working out its own determinate functional content without greatly blending with or being diverted by the working of its neighbours in that spiritual complex into which they all enter as constituent elements.[2] For the purposes of an exhaustive psychological analysis it is doubtless expedient to make the most of such discreteness as is observable among the instinctive proclivities. But for an inquiry into the scope and method of their working-out in the growth of institutions it is perhaps even more to the purpose to take note of how and with

[1] Cf. Graham Wallas, *Human Nature in Politics*, especially ch. i.

[2] Cf., e. g., James, *Principles of Psychology*, ch. xxiv; William McDougall, *Introduction to Social Psychology*, ch. iii.

what effect the several instinctive proclivities cross, blend, overlap, neutralise or reënforce one another.

The most convincing genetic view of these phenomena throws the instinctive proclivities into close relation with the tropismatic sensibilities and brings them, in the physiological respect, into the same general class with the latter.[1] If taken uncritically and in general terms this view would seem to carry the implication that the instincts should be discrete and discontinuous among themselves somewhat after the same fashion as the tropismatic sensibilities with which they are in great measure bound up; but on closer scrutiny such a genetic theory of the instincts does not appear to enforce the view that they are to be conceived as effectually discontinuous or mutually exclusive, though it may also not involve the contrary,—that they make a continuous or ambiguously segmented body of spiritual elements. The recognised tropisms stand out, to all appearance, as sharply defined physiological traits, transmissible by inheritance intact and unmodified, separable and unblended, in a manner suggestively like the "unit characters" spoken of in latter day theories of heredity.[2]

[1] Loeb, *Comparative Physiology of the Brain*, especially ch. xiii.

[2] It is of course only as physiological traits that the tropisms are conceived not to overlap, blend or interfere, and it is likewise only in respect of their physiological discontinuity that the like argument would bear on the instincts. In respect of their expression, in the way of orientation, movement, growth, secretion, and the like, the tropismatic response to dissimilar stimuli is often so apparently identical that expert investigators have at times been at a loss to decide to which one of two or several recognised tropismatic sensibilities a given motor response should be ascribed. But in respect of their ultimate physiological character, the intimate physiological process by which the given sensibility takes effect, the response due to different tropismatic sensibilities appears in each case

While the instinctive sensibilities may not be explained as derivatives of the tropisms, there is enough of similarity in the working of the two to suggest that the two classes of phenomena must both be accounted for on somewhat similar physiological grounds. The simple and more narrowly defined instinctive dispositions, which have much of the appearance of immediate reflex nervous action and automatically defined response, lend themselves passably to such an interpretation,—as, for example, the gregarious instinct, or the instinct of repulsion with its accompanying emotion of disgust. Such as these are shared by mankind with the other higher animals on a fairly even footing; and these are relatively simple, immediate, and not easily sophisticated or offset by habit. These seem patently to be of much the same nature as the tropismatic sensibilities; though even in these simpler instinctive dispositions the characteristic quasi-tropismatic sensibility distinctive of each appears to be complicated with obscure stimulations of the nerve centres arising out of the functioning of one or another of the viscera. And what is true of the simpler instincts in this respect should apply to the vaguer and more complex instincts also, but with a larger allowance for a more extensive complication of visceral and organic stimuli.

Whether these subconscious stimulations of the nerve centres through the functioning of the viscera are to be conceived in terms of tropismatic reaction is a difficult question which has had little attention hitherto. But in any case, whatever the expert students of these phenomena may have to say of this matter, the visceral or or-

to be distinctive and not to blend with any other response to a different stimulus, with which it may happen to synchronise.

ganic stimuli engaged in any one of the instinctive sensibilities are apparently always more than one and are usually somewhat complex. Indeed, while it seems superficially an easy matter to refer any one of the simple instincts directly to some certain one of the viscera as the main or primary source from which its appropriate stimulation comes to the nerve centres, it is by no means easy to decide what one or more of the viscera, or of the other organs that are not commonly classed as viscera, will have no part in the matter.

It results that, on physiological grounds, the common run of human instincts are not to be conceived as severally discrete and elementary proclivities. The same physiological processes enter in some measure, though in varying proportions, into the functioning of each. In instinctive action the individual acts as a whole, and in the conduct which emerges under the driving force of these instinctive dispositions the part which each several instinct plays is a matter of more or less, not of exclusive direction. They must therefore incontinently touch, blend, overlap and interfere, and can not be conceived as acting each and several in sheer isolation and independence of one another. The relations of give and take among the several instinctive dispositions, therefore—of inosculation, "contamination" and cross purposes—are presumably slighter and of less consequence for the simpler and more apparently tropismatic impulses while on the other hand the less specific and vaguer instinctive predispositions, such as the parental bent or the proclivity to construction or acquisition, will be so comprehensively and intricately bound in a web of correlation and inter-dependence—will so unremittingly contaminate, offset or fortify one another, and have each so large and yet so shifting a margin of common ground with all the rest—that hard and fast lines of demarcation can scarcely be drawn between them. The best that can practically be had in the way of a secure definition will be a descriptive characterisation of each distinguishable propensity, together with an indication of the more salient and consequential ramifications by which each contaminates or is contaminated by the working of other propensities that go to make up that complex of instinctive dispositions that constitutes the spiritual nature of the race. So that the schemes of definition that have hitherto been worked out are in great part to be taken as arrangements of convenience, serviceable apparatus for present use, rather than distinctions enforced at all points by an equally sharp substantial discreteness of the facts.[1]

This fact, that in some measure the several instincts spring from a common ground of sentient life, that they each engage the individual as a whole, has serious consequences in the domain of habit, and therefore it counts for much in the growth of civilisaticn and in the everyday conduct of affairs. The physiological apparatus engaged in the functioning of any given instinct enters in part, though in varying measure, into the working of some or of any other instinct; whereby, even on physiological grounds alone, the habituation that touches the functioning of any given instinct must, in a less degree but pervasively, affect the habitual conduct of the same agent when driven by any other instinct. So that on this view the scope of habit, in so far as it bears on the

[1] Cf., e. g., McDougall, *Introduction to Social Psychology*, ch. i–iii.

instinctive activities, is necessarily wider than the particular concrete line of conduct to which the habituation in question is due.

The instincts are hereditary traits. In the current theories of heredity they would presumably be counted as secondary characteristics of the species, as being in a sense by-products of the physiological activities that give the species its specific character; since these theories in the last resort run in physiological terms. So the instinctive dispositions would scarcely be accounted unit characters, in the Mendelian sense, but would rather count as spiritual traits emerging from a certain concurrence of physiological unit characters and varying somewhat according to variations in the complement of unit characters to which the species or the individual may owe his constitution. Hence would arise variations of individuality among the members of the race, resting in some such manner as has just been suggested on the varying endowment of instincts, and running back through these finally to recondite differences of physiological function. Some such account of the instinctive dispositions and their relation to the physical individual seems necessary as a means of apprehending them and their work without assuming a sheer break between the physical and the immaterial phenomena of life.

Characteristic of the race is a degree of vagueness or generality, an absence of automatically determinate response, a lack of concrete eventuality as it might be called, in the common run of human instincts. This vague and shifty character of the instincts, or perhaps rather of the habitual response to their incitement, is to be taken in connection with the breadth and variability of their physiological ground as spoken of above. For the long-term success of the race it is manifestly of the highest value, since it leaves a wide and facile margin of experimentation, habituation, invention and accommodation open to the sense of workmanship. At the same time and by the same circumstance the scope and range of conventionalisation and sophistication are similarly flexible, wide and consequential. No doubt the several racial stocks differ very appreciably in this respect.

The complement of instinctive dispositions, comprising under that term both the native propensity and its appropriate sentiment, makes up what would be called the "spiritual nature" of man—often spoken of more simply as "human nature." Without allowing it to imply anything like a dualism or dichotomy between material and immaterial phenomena, the term "spiritual" may conveniently be so used in its colloquial sense. So employed it commits the discussion to no attitude on the question of man's single or dual constitution, but simply uses the conventional expression to designate that complement of functions which it has by current usage been employed to designate.

The human complement of instincts fluctuates from one individual to another in an apparently endless diversity, varying both in the relative force of the several instinctive proclivities and in the scheme of co-ordination, coalescence or interference that prevails among them. This diversity of native character is noticeable among all peoples, though some of the peoples of the lower cultures show a notable approach to uniformity of type, both physical and spiritual. The diversity is particularly marked among the civilised peoples, and perhaps in a peculiar degree among the peoples of Europe and her colonies. The extreme diversity of native character, both physical and spiritual, noticeable in these communities is in all probability due to their being made up of a mixture of racial stocks. In point of pedigree, all individuals in the peoples of the Western culture are hybrids, and the greater number of individuals are a mixture of more than two racial stocks. The proportions in which the several transmissible traits that go to make up the racial type enter into the composition of these hybrid individuals will accordingly vary endlessly. The number of possible permutations will therefore be extremely large; so that the resulting range of variation in the hybrids that so result from the crossing of these different racial stocks will be sufficiently large, even when it plays within such limits as to leave the generic human type intact. From time to time the variation may even exceed these limits of human normality and give a variant in which the relative emphasis on the several constituent instinctive elements is distributed after a scheme so far from the generically human type as to throw the given variant out of touch with the common run of humanity and mark him as of unsound mind or as disserviceable for the purposes of the community in which he occurs, or even as disserviceable for life in any society.

Yet, even through these hybrid populations there runs a generically human type of spiritual endowment. prevalent as a general average of human nature throughout, and suitable to the continued life of mankind in society. Disserviceably wide departures from this generically human and serviceable type of spiritual endowment will tend constantly to be selectively eliminated from the race, even where the variation arises from hybridism. The like will hold true in a more radical fashion as applied to any variants that may arise through a Mendelian mutation.

So that the numerous racial types now existing represent only such mutants as lie within the limits of tolerance imposed by the situation under which any given mutant type has emerged and survived. A surviving mutant type is necessarily suited more or less closely to the circumstances under which it emerged and first made good its survival, and it is presumably less suited to any other situation. With a change in the situation, therefore, such as may come with the migration of a given racial stock from one habitat to another, or with an equivalent shifting growth of culture or change of climate, the requirements of survival are likely to change. Indeed, so grave are the alterations that may in this way supervene in the current requirements for survival, that any given racial stock may dwindle and decay for no other reason than that the growth of its culture has come to subject the stock to methods of life widely different from those under which its type of man originated and made good its fitness to survive. So, in the mixture of races that make up the population of the Western nations a competitive struggle for survival has apparently always been going on among the several racial stocks that enter into the hybrid mass, with varying fortunes according as the shifting cultural demands and opportunities have favoured now one, now another type of man. These cultural conditions of survival in the racial struggle for existence have varied in the course of centuries, and with grave consequences for the life-history of the race and of its culture; and they are perhaps changing more substantially and rapidly in the immediate present than at any previous time within the historical period. So that, for instance, the continued biological success of any given one of these stocks in the European racial mixture has within a moderate period of time shifted from the ground of fighting capacity, and even in a measure from the ground of climatic fitness, to that of spiritual fitness to survive under the conditions imposed by a new cultural situation, by a scheme of institutions that is insensibly but incessantly changing as it runs.[1]

These unremitting changes and adaptations that go forward in the scheme of institutions, legal and customary, unremittingly induce new habits of work and of thought in the community, and so they continually instil new principles of conduct; with the outcome that the same range of instinctive dispositions innate in the population will work out to a different effect as regards the demands of race survival. To all appearance, what counts first in this connection toward the selective survival of the several European racial stocks is their relative fitness to meet the material requirements of life,—their economic fitness to live under the new cultural limitations and with the new training which this altered cultural situation gives. But the fortunes of the Western

[1] Cf., e. g., Otto Ammon, *Die Gesellschaftsordnung;* G. Vacher de Lapouge, *Les sélections sociales*, and *Race et milieu social*, especially "Lois fondamentales de l'Anthroposociologie."

civilisation as a cultural scheme, apart from the biological survival or success of any given racial constituent in the Western peoples, is likewise bound up with the viability of European mankind under these institutional changes, and dependent on the spiritual fitness of inherited human nature successfully and enduringly to carry on the altered scheme of life so imposed on these peoples by the growth of their own culture. Such limitations imposed on cultural growth by native proclivities ill suited to civilised life are sufficiently visible in several directions and in all the nations of Christendom.

What is known of heredity goes to say that the various racial types of man are stable; so that during the life-history of any given racial stock, it is held, no heritable modification of its typical make-up, whether spiritual or physical, is to be looked for. The typical human endowment of instincts, as well as the typical make-up of the race in the physical respect, has according to this current view been transmitted intact from the beginning of humanity,—that is to say from whatever point in the mutational development of the race it is seen fit to date humanity,—except so far as subsequent mutations have given rise to new racial stocks, to and by which this human endowment of native proclivities has been transmitted in a typically modified form. On the other hand the habitual elements of human life change unremittingly and cumulatively, resulting in a continued proliferous growth of institutions. Changes in the institutional structure are continually taking place in response to the altered discipline of life under changing cultural conditions, but human nature remains specifically the same.

The ways and means, material and immaterial, by which the native proclivities work out their ends, therefore, are forever in process of change, being conditioned by the changes cumulatively going forward in the institutional fabric of habitual elements that governs the scheme of life. But there is no warrant for assuming that each or any of these successive changes in the scheme of institutions affords successively readier, surer or more facile ways and means for the instinctive proclivities to work out their ends, or that the phase of habituation in force at any given point in this sequence of change is more suitable to the untroubled functioning of these instincts than any phase that has gone before. Indeed, the presumption is the other way. On grounds of selective survival it is reasonably to be presumed that any given racial type that has endured the test of selective elimination, including the complement of instinctive dispositions by virtue of which it has endured the test, will on its first emergence have been passably suited to the circumstances, material and cultural, under which the type emerged as a mutant and made good its survival; and in so far as tne subsequent growth of institutions has altered the available scope and method of instinctive action it is therefore to be presumed that any such subsequent change in the scheme of institutions will in some degree hinder or divert the free play of its instinctive proclivities and will thereby hinder the direct and unsophisticated working-out of the instinctive dispositions native to this given racial type.

What is known of the earlier phases of culture in the life-history of the existing races and peoples goes to say that the initial phase in the life of any given racial type, the phase of culture which prevailed in its environment when it emerged, and under which the stock first proved its fitness to survive, was presumably some form of savagery. Therefore the fitness of any given type of human nature for life after the manner and under the conditions imposed by any later phase in the growth of culture is a matter of less and less secure presumption the farther the sequence of institutional change has departed from that form of savagery which marked the initial stage in the life-history of the given racial stock. Also, presumably, though by no means assuredly, the younger stocks, those which have emerged from later mutations of type, have therefore initially fallen into and made good their survival under the conditions of a relatively advanced phase of savagery,—these younger races should therefore conform with greater facility and better effect to the requirements imposed by a still farther advance in that cumulative complication of institutions and intricacy of ways and means that is involved in cultural growth. The older or more primitive stocks, those which arose out of earlier mutations of type and made good their survival under a more elementary scheme of savage culture, are presumably less capable of adaptation to an advanced cultural scheme.

But at the same time it is on the same grounds to be expected that in all races and peoples there should always persist an ineradicable sentimental disposition to take back to something like that scheme of savagery for which their particular type of human nature once proved its fitness during the initial phase of its life-history. This seems to be what is commonly intended in the cry, "Back to Nature!" The older known racial stocks, the offspring of earlier mutational departures from the initially generic human type, will have been selectively adapted to more archaic forms of savagery, and these show an appreciably more refractory penchant for elementary savage modes of life, and conform to the demands and opportunities of a "higher" civilisation only with a relatively slight facility, amounting in extreme cases to a practical unfitness for civilised life. Hence the "White Man's burden" and the many perplexities of the missionaries.

Under the Mendelian theories of heredity some qualification of these broad generalisations is called for. As has already been noted above, the peoples of Europe, each and several, are hybrid mixtures made up of several racial stocks. The like is true in some degree of most of the peoples outside of Europe; particularly of the more important and better known nationalities. These various peoples show more or less distinct and recognisable national types of physique—or perhaps rather of physiognomy—and temperament, and the lines of differentiation between these national types incontinently traverse the lines that divide the racial stocks. At the same time these national types have some degree of permanence; so much so that they are colloquially spoken of as types of race. While no modern anthropologist would confuse nationality with race, it is not to be overlooked that these national hybrid types are frequently so marked and characteristic as to simulate racial characters and perplex the student of race who is intent on identifying the racial stocks out of which any one of these hybrid populations has been compounded. Presumably these national and local types of physiognomy and temperament are to be rated as hybrid types that have been fixed by selective breeding, and for an explanation of this phenomenon recourse is to be taken to the latterday theories of heredity.

To any student familiar with the simpler phenomena of hybridism it will be evident that under the Mendelian rules of hybridisation the number of biologically successful—viable—hybrid forms arising from any cross between two or more forms may diverge very widely from one another and from either of the parent types. The variation must be extreme both in the number of hybrid types so constructed and in the range over which the variation extends,—much greater in both respects than the range of fluctuating (non-typical) variations obtainable under any circumstances in a pure-bred race, particularly in the remoter filial generations. It is also well known, by experiment, that by selective breeding from among such hybrid forms it is possible to construct a composite type that will breed true in respect of the characters upon which the selection is directed, and that such a "pure line" may be maintained indefinitely, in spite of its hybrid origin, so long as it is not crossed back on one or other of the parent stocks, or on a hybrid stock that is not pure-bred in respect of the selected characters.

So, if the conditions of life in any community consistently favour a given type of hybrid, whether the favouring conditions are of a cultural or of a material nature, something of a selective trend will take effect in such a community and set toward a hybrid type which shall meet these conditions. The result will be the establishment of a composite pure line showing the advantageous traits of physique and temperament, combined with a varying complement of other characters that have no such selective value. Traits that have no selective value in the given case will occur with fortuitous freedom, combining in unconstrained diversity with the selectively decisive traits, and so will mark the hybrid derivation of this provisionally established composite pure line. With continued intercrossing within itself any given population of such hybrid origin as the European peoples, would tend cumulatively to breed true to such a selectively favourable hybrid type, rather than to any one of the ultimate racial types represented by the parent stocks out of which the hybrid population is ultimately made up. So would emerge a national or local type, which would show the selectively decisive traits with a great degree of consistency but would vary indefinitely in respect of the selectively idle traits comprised in the composite heredity of the population. Such a composite pure line would be provisionally stable only; it should break down when crossed back on either of the parent stocks. This "provisionally stable composite pure line" should disappear when crossed on pure-bred individuals of one or other of the parent stocks from which it is drawn,—pure-bred in respect of the allelomorphic characters which give the hybrid type its typical traits.

But whatever the degree of stability possessed by these hybrid national or local types, the outcome for the present purpose is much the same; the hybrid populations afford a greater scope and range of variation in their human nature than could be had within the limits of any pure-bred race. Yet, for all the multifarious diversity of racial and national types, early and late, and for all the wide divergence of hybrid variants, there is no difficulty about recognising a generical human type of spiritual endowment, just as the zoölogists have no difficulty in referring the various races of mankind to a single species on the ground of their physical characters. The distribution of emphasis among the several instinctive dispositions may vary appreciably from one race to another, but the complement of instincts native to the several races is after all of much the same kind, comprising substantially the same ends. Taken simply in their first incidence, the racial variations of human nature are commonly not considerable; but a slight bias of this kind, distinctive of any given race, may come to have decisive weight when it works out cumulatively through a system of institutions, for such a system embodies the cumulative sophistications of untold generations during which the life of the community has been dominated by the same slight bias.[1]

Racial differences in respect of these hereditary spiritual traits count for much in the outcome, because in the last resort any race is at the mercy of its instincts. In the course of cultural growth most of those civilisations or peoples that have had a long history have from time to time been brought up against an imperative call to revise their scheme of institutions in the light of their native instincts, on pain of collapse or decay; and they have chosen variously, and for the most part blindly, to live or not to live, according as their instinctive bias

[1] The all-pervading modern institution of private property appears to have been of such an origin, having cumulatively grown out of the self-regarding bias of men in their oversight of the community's material interests.

has driven them. In the cases where it has happened that those instincts which make directly for the material welfare of the community, such as the parental bent and the sense of workmanship, have been present in such potent force, or where the institutional elements at variance with the continued life-interests of the community or the civilisation in question have been in a sufficiently infirm state, there the bonds of custom, prescription, principles, precedent, have been broken—or loosened or shifted so as to let the current of life and cultural growth go on, with or without substantial retardation. But history records more frequent and more spectacular instances of the triumph of imbecile institutions over life and culture than of peoples who have by force of instinctive insight saved themselves alive out of a desperately precarious institutional situation, such as now (1913) faces the peoples of Christendom.

Chief among those instinctive dispositions that conduce directly to the material well-being of the race, and therefore to its biological success, is perhaps the instinctive bias here spoken of as the sense of workmanship. The only other instinctive factor of human nature that could with any likelihood dispute this primacy would be the parental bent. Indeed, the two have much in common. They spend themselves on much the same concrete objective ends, and the mutual furtherance of each by the other is indeed so broad and intimate as often to leave it a matter of extreme difficulty to draw a line between them. Any discussion of either, therefore, must unavoidably draw the other into the inquiry to a greater or less extent, and a characterisation of the one will involve some dealing with the other.

As the expression is here understood, the "Parental Bent" is an instinctive disposition of much larger scope than a mere proclivity to the achievement of children.[1] This latter is doubtless to be taken as a large and perhaps as a primary element in the practical working of the parental solicitude; although, even so, it is in no degree to be confused with the quasi-tropismatic impulse to the procreation of offspring. The parental solicitude in mankind has a much wider bearing than simply the welfare of one's own children. This wider bearing is particularly evident in those lower cultures where the scheme of consanguinity and inheritance is not drawn on the same close family lines as among civilised peoples, but it is also to be seen in good vigour in any civilised community. So, for instance, what the phrase-makers have called "race-suicide" meets the instinctive and unsolicited reprobation of all men, even of those who would not conceivably go the length of contributing in their own person to the incoming generation. So also, virtually all thoughtful persons,—that is to say all persons who hold an opinion in these premises,—will agree that it is a despicably inhuman thing for the current generation wilfully to make the way of life harder for the next generation, whether through neglect of due provision for their subsistence and proper training or through wasting their heritage of resources and opportunity by improvident greed and indolence. Providence is a virtue only so far as its aim is provision for posterity.

It is difficult or impossible to say how far the current

[1] Cf. McDougall, *Social Psychology*, ch. x.

solicitude for the welfare of the race at large is to be credited to the parental bent, but it is beyond question that this instinctive disposition has a large part in the sentimental concern entertained by nearly all persons for the life and comfort of the community at large, and particularly for the community's future welfare. Doubtless this parental bent in its wider bearing greatly reënforces that sentimental approval of economy and efficiency for the common good and disapproval of wasteful and useless living that prevails so generally throughout both the highest and the lowest cultures, unless it should rather be said that this animus for economy and efficiency is a simple expression of the parental disposition itself. It might on the other hand be maintained that such an animus of economy is an essential function of the instinct of workmanship, which would then be held to be strongly sustained at this point by a parental solicitude for the common good.

In making use of the expression, "instinct of workmanship" or "sense of workmanship," it is not here intended to assume or to argue that the proclivity so designated is in the psychological respect a simple or irreducible element; still less, of course, is there any intention to allege that it is to be traced back in the physiological respect to some one isolable tropismatic sensibility or some single enzymotic or visceral stimulus. All that is matter for the attention of those whom it may concern. The expression may as well be taken to signify a concurrence of several instinctive aptitudes, each of which might or might not prove simple or irreducible when subjected to psychological or physiological analysis. For the present inquiry it is enough to note that in human behaviour this disposition is effective in such consistent, ubiquitous and resilient fashion that students of human culture will have to count with it as one of the integral hereditary traits of mankind.[1]

As has already appeared, neither this nor any other instinctive disposition works out its functional content in isolation from the instinctive endowment at large.

[1] Latterly the question of instincts has been a subject of somewhat extensive discussion among students of animal behaviour, and throughout this discussion the argument has commonly been conducted on neurological, or at the most on physiological ground. This line of argument is well and lucidly presented in a volume recently published (*The Science of Human Behavior*, New York, 1913) by Mr. Maurice Parmalee. The book offers an incisive critical discussion of the Nature of Instinct (ch. xi) with a specific reference to the instinct of workmanship (p. 252). The discussion runs, faithfully and competently, on neurological ground and reaches the outcome to be expected in an endeavour to reduce instinct to neurological (or physiological) terms. As has commonly been true of similar endeavours, the outcome is essentially negative, in that "instinct" is not so much explained as explained away. The reason of this outcome is sufficiently evident; "instinct," being not a neurological or physiological concept, is not statable in neurological or physiological terms. The instinct of workmanship no more than any other instinctive proclivity is an isolable, discrete neural function; which, however, does not touch the question of its status as a psychological element. The effect of such an analysis as is offered by Mr. Parmalee is not to give terminological precision to the concept of "instinct" in the sense assigned it in current usage, but to dispense with it; which is an untoward move in that it deprives the student of the free use of this familiar term in its familiar sense and therefore constrains him to bring the indispensable concept of instinct in again surreptitiously under cover of some unfamiliar term or some terminological circumlocution. The current mechanistic analyses of animal behaviour are of great and undoubted value to any inquiry into human conduct, but their value does not lie in an attempt to make them supersede those psychological phenomena which it is their purpose to explain. That such supersession of psychological phenomena by the mechanistic formulations need nowise follow and need not be entertained appears, e. g., in such work as that of Mr. Loeb, referred to above, *Comparative Physiology of the Brain and Comparative Psychology*.

The instincts, all and several, though perhaps in varying degrees, are so intimately engaged in a play of give and take that the work of any one has its consequences for all the rest, though presumably not for all equally. It is this endless[1] complication and contamination of instinctive elements in human conduct, taken in conjunction with the pervading and cumulative effects of habit in this domain, that makes most of the difficulty and much of the interest attaching to this line of inquiry.

There are few lines of instinctive proclivity that are not crossed and coloured by some ramification of the instinct of workmanship. No doubt, response to the direct call of such half-tropismatic, half-instinctive impulses as hunger, anger, or the promptings of sex, is little if at all troubled with any sentimental suffusion of workmanship; but in the more complex and deliberate activities, particularly where habit exerts an appreciable effect, the impulse and sentiment of workmanship comes in for a large share in the outcome. So much so, indeed, that, for instance, in the arts, where the sense of beauty is the prime mover, habitual attention to technique will often put the original, and only ostensible, motive in the background. So, again, in the life of religious faith and observance it may happen now and again that theological niceties and ritual elaboration will successfully, and in great measure satisfactorily, substitute themselves for spiritual communion; while in the courts of law a tenacious following out of legal technicalities will not infrequently defeat the ends of justice.

[1] Endless in the sense that the effects of such concatenation do not run to a final term in any direction.

As the expression is here understood, all instinctive action is intelligent in some degree; though the degree in which intelligence is engaged may vary widely from one instinctive disposition to another, and it may even fall into an extremely automatic shape in the case of some of the simpler instincts, whose functional content is of a patently physiological character. Such approach to automatism is even more evident in some of the lower animals, where, as for instance in the case of some insects, the response to the appropriate stimuli is so far uniform and mechanically determinate as to leave it doubtful whether the behaviour of the animal might not best be construed as tropismatic action simply.[1] Such tropismatic directness of instinctive response is less characteristic of man even in the case of the simpler instinctive proclivities; and the indirection which so characterises instinctive action in general, and the higher instincts of man in particular, and which marks off the

[1] Many students of animal behaviour are still, as psychologists generally once were, inclined to contrast instinct with intelligence, and to confine the term typically to such automatically determinate action as takes effect without deliberation or intelligent oversight. This view would appear to be a remnant of an earlier theoretical position, according to which all the functions of intelligence were referred to a distinct immaterial entity, entelechy, associated in symbiosis with the physical organism. If all such preconceptions of a substantial dichotomy between physiological and psychological activity be abandoned it becomes a matter of course that intellectual functions themselves take effect only on the initiative of the instinctive dispositions and under their surveillance, and the antithesis between instinct and intelligence will consequently fall away. What expedients of terminology and discrimination may then be resorted to in the study of those animal instincts that involve a minimum of intellect is of course a question for the comparative psychologists. Cf., for instance, C. Lloyd Morgan, *Introduction to Comparative Psychology* (2nd edition, 1906) ch. xii, especially pp. 206–209, and *Habit and Instinct*, ch. i and vi.

instinctive dispositions from the tropisms, is the indirection of intelligence. It enters more largely in the discharge of some proclivities than of others; but all instinctive action is intelligent in some degree. This is what marks it off from the tropisms and takes it out of the category of automatism.[1]

Hence all instinctive action is teleological. It involves holding to a purpose. It aims to achieve some end and involves some degree of intelligent faculty to compass the instinctively given purpose, under surveillance of the instinctive proclivity that prompts the action. And it is in this surveillance and direction of the intellectual processes to the appointed end that the instinctive dispositions control and condition human conduct; and in this work of direction the several instinctive proclivities may come to conflict and offset, or to concur and reënforce one another's action.

The position of the instinct of workmanship in this complex of teleological activities is somewhat peculiar, in that its functional content is serviceability for the ends of life, whatever these ends may be; whereas these ends to be subserved are, at least in the main, appointed and made worth while by the various other instinctive dispositions. So that this instinct may in some sense be said to be auxiliary to all the rest, to be concerned with the ways and means of life rather than with any one given ulterior end. It has essentially to do with proximate rather than ulterior ends. Yet workmanship is none the less an object of attention and sentiment in its own right. Efficient use of the means at hand and adequate management of the resources available for the purposes of life

[1] Cf. H. S. Jennings, *Behavior of the Lower Animals*, ch. xii, xx, xxi.

is itself an end of endeavour, and accomplishment of this kind is a source of gratification.

All instinctive action is intelligent and teleological. The generality of instinctive dispositions prompt simply to the direct and unambiguous attainment of their specific ends, and in his dealings under their immediate guidance the agent goes as directly as may be to the end sought,—he is occupied with the objective end, not with the choice of means to the end sought; whereas under the impulse of workmanship the agent's interest and endeavour are taken up with the contriving of ways and means to the end sought.

The point of contrast may be unfamiliar, and an illustration may be pertinent. So, in the instinct of pugnacity and its attendant sentiment of anger [1] the primary impulse is doubtless to a direct frontal attack, assault and battery pure and simple; and the more highly charged the agent is with the combative impulse, and the higher the pitch of animation to which he has been wrought up, the less is he inclined or able to take thought of how he may shrewdly bring mechanical devices to bear on the object of his sentiment and compass his end with the largest result per unit of force expended. It is only the well-trained fighter that will take without reflection to workmanlike ways and means at such a juncture; and in case of extreme exasperation and urgency even such a one, it is said, may forget his workmanship in the premises and throw himself into the middle of things instead of resorting to the indirections and leverages to which his workmanlike training in the art of fighting has habituated him. So, again, the immediate prompt-

[1] See McDougall, *Introduction to Social Psychology*, ch. iii and x.

ings of the parental bent urge to direct personal intervention and service in behalf of the object of solicitude. In persons highly gifted in this respect the impulse asserts itself to succour the helpless with one's own hands, to do for them in one's own person not what might on reflection approve itself as the most expedient line of conduct in the premises, but what will throw the agent most personally into action in the case. Notoriously, it is easier to move well-meaning people to unreflecting charity on an immediate and concrete appeal than it is to secure a sagacious, well sustained and well organised concert of endeavour for the amelioration of the lot of the unfortunate. Indeed, refinements of workmanlike calculation of causes and effects in such a case are instinctively felt to be out of touch with the spirit of the thing. They are distasteful; not only are they not part and parcel of the functional content of the generous impulse, but an undue injection of these elements of workmanship into the case may even induce a revulsion of feeling and defeat its own intention.

The instinct of workmanship, on the other hand, occupies the interest with practical expedients, ways and means, devices and contrivances of efficiency and economy, proficiency, creative work and technological mastery of facts. Much of the functional content of the instinct of workmanship is a proclivity for taking pains. The best or most finished outcome of this disposition is not had under stress of great excitement or under extreme urgency from any of the instinctive propensities with which its work is associated or whose ends it serves. It shows at its best, both in the individual workman's technological efficiency and in the growth of technological proficiency and insight in the community at large, under circumstances of moderate exigence, where there is work in hand and more of it in sight, since it is initially a disposition to do the next thing and do it as well as may be; whereas when interest falls off unduly through failure of provocation from the instinctive dispositions that afford an end to which to work, the stimulus to workmanship is likely to fail, and the outcome is as likely to be an endless fabrication of meaningless details and much ado about nothing. On the other hand, in seasons of great stress, when the call to any one or more of the instinctive lines of conduct is urgent beyond measure, there is likely to result a crudity of technique and presently a loss of proficiency and technological mastery.

It is, further, pertinent to note in this connection that the instinct of workmanship will commonly not run to passionate excesses; that it does not, under pressure, tenaciously hold its place as a main interest in competition with the other, more elemental instinctive proclivities; but that it rather yields ground somewhat readily, suffers repression and falls into abeyance, only to reassert itself when the pressure of other, urgent interests is relieved. What was said above as to the paramount significance of the instinct of workmanship for the life of the race will of course suffer no abatement in so recognising its characteristically temperate urgency. The grave importance that attaches to it is a matter of its ubiquitous subservience to the ends of life, and not a matter of vehemence.

The sense of workmanship is also peculiarly subject to bias. It does not commonly, or normally, work to an independent, creative end of its own, but is rather concerned with the ways and means whereby instinctively given purposes are to be accomplished. According, therefore, as one or another of the instinctive dispositions is predominant in the community's scheme of life or in the individual's every-day interest, the habitual trend of the sense of workmanship will be bent to one or another line of proficiency and technological mastery. By cumulative habituation a bias of this character may come to have very substantial consequences for the range and scope of technological knowledge, the state of the industrial arts, and for the rate and direction of growth in workmanlike ideals.

Changes are going forward constantly and incontinently in the institutional apparatus, the habitual scheme of rules and principles that regulate the community's life, and not least in the technological ways and means by which the life of the race and its state of culture are maintained; but changes come rarely—in effect not at all—in the endowment of instincts whereby mankind is enabled to employ these means and to live under the institutions which its habits of life have cumulatively created. In the case of hybrid populations, such as the peoples of Christendom, some appreciable adaptation of this spiritual endowment to meet the changing requirements of civilisation may be counted on, through the establishment of composite pure lines of a hybrid type more nearly answering to the later phases of culture than any one of the original racial types out of which the hybrid population is made up. But in so slow-breeding a species as man, and with changes in the conditions of life going forward at a visibly rapid pace, the chance of an adequate adaptation of hybrid human nature to new conditions seems doubtful at the best. It is also to be noted that the vague character of many of the human instincts, and their consequent pliability under habituation, affords an appreciable margin of adaptation within which human nature may adjust itself to new conditions of life. But after all has been said it remains true that the margin within which the instinctive nature of the race can be effectively adapted to changing circumstances is relatively narrow—narrow as contrasted with the range of variation in institutions—and the limits of such adaptation are somewhat rigid. As the matter stands, the race is required to meet changing conditions of life to which its relatively unchanging endowment of instincts is presumably not wholly adapted, and to meet these conditions by the use of technological ways and means widely different from those that were at the disposal of the race from the outset. In the initial phases of the life-history of the race, or of any given racial stock, the exigencies to which its spiritual (instinctive) nature was selectively required to conform were those of the savage culture, as has been indicated above,—presumably in all cases a somewhat "low" or elementary form of savagery. This savage mode of life, which was, and is, in a sense, native to man, would be characterised by a considerable group solidarity within a relatively small group, living very near the soil, and unremittingly dependent for their daily life on the workmanlike efficiency of all the members of the group. The prime requisite for survival under these conditions would be a propensity unselfishly and impersonally to make the most of the material means at hand and a penchant for turning all resources of knowledge and material to account to sustain the life of the group.

At the outset, therefore, as it first comes into the life-history of any one or all of the racial stocks with which modern inquiry concerns itself, this instinctive disposition will have borne directly on workmanlike efficiency in the simple and obvious sense of the word. By virtue of the stability of the racial type, such is still its character, primarily and substantially, apart from its sophistication by habit and tradition. The instinct of workmanship brought the life of mankind from the brute to the human plane, and in all the later growth of culture it has never ceased to pervade the works of man. But the extensive complication of circumstances and the altered outlook of succeeding generations, brought on by the growth of institutions and the accumulation of knowledge, have led to an extension of its scope and of its canons and logic to activities and conjunctures that have little traceable bearing on the means of subsistence.

CHAPTER II

CONTAMINATION OF INSTINCTS IN PRIMITIVE TECHNOLOGY

ALL instinctive behaviour is subject to development and hence to modification by habit.[1] Such impulsive action as is in no degree intelligent, and so suffers no adaptation through habitual use, is not properly to be called instinctive; it is rather to be classed as tropismatic. In human conduct the effects of habit in this respect are particularly far-reaching. In man the instincts appoint less of a determinate sequence of action, and so leave a more open field for adaptation of behaviour to the circumstances of the case. When instinct enjoins little else than the end of endeavour, leaving the sequence of acts by which this end is to be approached somewhat a matter of open alternatives, the share of reflection, discretion and deliberate adaptation will be correspondingly large. The range and diversity of habituation is also correspondingly enlarged.

In man, too, by the same fact, habit takes on more of a cumulative character, in that the habitual acquirements of the race are handed on from one generation to the next, by tradition, training, education, or whatever general term may best designate that discipline of habitu-

[1] Cf. M. F. Washburn, *The Animal Mind*, ch. x, xi, where the simpler facts of habituation are suggestively presented in conformity with current views of empirical psychology.

ation by which the young acquire what the old have learned. By similar means the like elements of habitual conduct are carried over from one community or one culture to another, leading to further complications. Cumulatively, therefore, habit creates usages, customs, conventions, preconceptions, composite principles of conduct that run back only indirectly to the native predispositions of the race, but that may affect the working-out of any given line of endeavour in much the same way as if these habitual elements were of the nature of a native bias.

Along with this body of derivative standards and canons of conduct, and handed on by the same discipline of habituation, goes a cumulative body of knowledge, made up in part of matter-of-fact acquaintance with phenomena and in greater part of conventional wisdom embodying certain acquired predilections and preconceptions current in the community. Workmanship proceeds on the accumulated knowledge so received and current, and turns it to account in dealing with the material means of life. Whatever passes current in this way as knowledge of facts is turned to account as far as may be, and so it is worked into a customary scheme of ways and means, a system of technology, into which new elements of information or acquaintance with the nature and use of things are incorporated, assimilated as they come.

The scheme of technology so worked out and carried along in the routine of getting a living will be serviceable for current use and have a substantial value for a further advance in technological efficiency somewhat in proportion as the knowledge so embodied in technological practice is effectually of the nature of matter-of-fact. Much of the information derived from experience in industry is likely to be of this matter-of-fact nature; but much of the knowledge made use of for the technological purpose is also of the nature of convention, inference and authentic opinion, arrived at on quite other grounds than workmanlike experience. This alien body of information, or pseudo-information, goes into the grand total of human knowledge quite as freely as any matter of fact, and it is therefore also necessarily taken up and assimilated in that technological equipment of knowledge and proficiency by use of which the work in hand is to be done.

But the experience which yields this useful and pseudo-useful knowledge is got under the impulsion and guidance of one and another of the instincts with which man is endowed, and takes the shape and color given it by the instinctive bias in whose service it is acquired. At the same time, whatever its derivation, the knowledge acquired goes into the aggregate of information drawn on for the ways and means of workmanship. Therefore the habits formed in any line of experience, under the guidance of any given instinctive disposition, will have their effect on the conduct and aims of the workman in all his work and play; so that progress in technological matters is by no means an outcome of the sense of workmanship alone.

It follows that in all their working the human instincts are in this way incessantly subject to mutual "contamination," whereby the working of any one is incidentally affected by the bias and proclivities inherent in all the rest; and in so far as these current habits and customs in this way come to reënforce the predispositions comprised under any one instinct or any given group of instincts, the bias so accentuated comes to pervade the habits of thought of all the members of the community and gives a corresponding obliquity to the technological groundwork of the community. So, for instance, addiction to magical, superstitious or religious conceptions will necessarily have its effect on the conceptions and logic employed in technological theory and practice, and will impair its efficiency by that much. A people much given to punctilios of rank and respect of persons will in some degree carry these habitual predilections over into the field of workmanship and will allow considerations of authenticity, of personal weight and consequence, to decide questions of technological expediency; so that ideas which have none but a putative efficiency may in this way come in for a large share in the state of the industrial arts. A people whose culture has for any reason taken on a pronounced coercive (predatory) character, with rigorous class distinctions, an arbitrary governmental control, formidable gods and an authoritative priesthood, will have its industrial organisation and its industrial arts fashioned to meet the demands and the logic of these institutions. Such an institutional situation exerts a great and pervasive constraint on the technological scheme in which workmanship takes effect under its rule, both directly by prescribing the things to do and the time, place and circumstance of doing them, and indirectly through the habits of thought induced in the working population living under its rule. Innovation, the utilisation of newly acquired technological insight, is greatly hindered by such institutional requirements that are enforced by other impulses than the sense of workmanship.

In the known lower cultures such institutional complications as might be expected greatly to hinder or deflect the sense of workmanship are commonly neither large, rigorous nor obvious. Something of the kind there apparently always is, in the way, for instance, of the customary prerogatives and perquisites of the older men, as well as their tutelary oversight of the younger generation and of the common interests of the group.[1] When this rule of seniority is elaborated into such set forms as the men's (secret) societies, with exacting initiatory ceremonies and class tabus,[2] its effect on workday life is often very considerable, even though the community may show little that can fairly be classed as autocracy, chieftainship, or even aristocratic government. In many or all of these naïve and early developments of authority, and perhaps especially in those cultures where the control takes this inchoate form of a customary "gerontocracy,"[3] its immediate effect is that an abiding sense of authenticity comes to pervade the routine of daily life, such as effectually to obstruct all innovation, whether in the ways and means of work or in the conduct of life more at large. Control by a gerontocracy appears to reach its best development and to run with the fullest consistency and effect in communities where an appreciable degree of predatory exploit is habitual, and the inference is ready, and at least plausible, that this institution is sub-

[1] Cf., e. g., Spencer and Gillen, *Native Tribes of Central Australia;* Seligmann, *The Veddas.*

[2] Hutton Webster, *Primitive Secret Societies*, especially ch. iii and iv.

[3] J. G. Frazer, *Early History of the Kingship*, ch. iv, p. 107.

stantially of a predatory origin, that the principles (habits of thought) on which it rests are an outgrowth of pugnacity, self-aggrandisement and fear. Under favouring conditions of friction and jealousy between groups these propensities will settle into institutional habits of authority and deference, and so long as the resultant exercise of control is vested by custom in the class of elders the direct consequence is a marked abatement of initiative throughout the community and a consequent appearance of conservatism and stagnation in its technological scheme as well as in the customary usages under whose guidance the community lives.[1] So these instinctive propensities which have no primary significance in the way of workmanship may come to count very materially in shaping the group's technological equipment of ideas and in deflecting the sense of workmanship from the naïve pursuit of material efficiency.

The rule of the elders appears to have been extremely prevalent in the earlier phases of culture. So much so that it may even be set down as the most characteristic trait of the upper savagery and of the lower barbarism; whether it takes the elaborately institutionalised form of a settled gerontocracy, as among the Australian blacks, with sharply defined class divisions and perquisites and a consistent subjection of women and children; or the looser customary rule of the Elders, with a degree of deference and circumspection on the part of the younger generation and an uncertain conventional inferiority of women and children, as seen among the pagans of the

[1] E. g., some native tribes of Australia; cf. Spencer and Gillen, *The Native Tribes of Central Australia*, especially ch. i.

Malay peninsula,[1] the Eskimo of the Arctic seaboard,[2] the Mincopies of the Andamans,[3] or, on a somewhat higher level, the Pueblo Indians of the American Southwest.[4] Illustrative instances of such an inchoate organisation of authority are very widely distributed, but the communities that follow such a naïve scheme of life are commonly neither large, powerful, wealthy, nor much in the public eye. The presumption is that the sense of authenticity which pervades these and similar cultures, amounting to a degree of tabu on innovation, has had much to do with the notably slow advance of technology among savage peoples. Such appears presumably to have been the prevalent run of the facts throughout the stone age in all quarters of the Earth.

It is not altogether plain just what are the innate predispositions chiefly involved in this primitive social control which at its untroubled best develops into a "gerontocracy." There can apparently be little question but that its prime motive force is the parental bent, expressing itself in a naïve impulsive surveillance of the common interests of the group and a tutelage of the incoming generation. But here as in other social relations the self-regarding sentiments unavoidably come into play; so that (*a*) the tutelage of the elders takes

[1] Skeat and Blagden, *Pagan Races of the Malay Peninsula.*

[2] J. Murdoch, "The Point Barrow Eskimo," *Report of the Bureau of American Ethnology,* 1887–1888; F. Boas, "The Central Eskimo," *Ibid,* 1884–1885.

[3] E. H. Man, "On the Aboriginal Inhabitants of the Andaman Islands," *J. A. I.*, vol. xii.

[4] *Reports, Bureau of American Ethnology,* numerous papers by different writers, perhaps especially Mrs. Stevenson, "The Sia," 11th Report (1889–1890).

something of an authoritative tone and blends self-aggrandisement with their quasi-parental solicitude, giving an institutional outcome which makes the young generation subservient to the elders, ostensibly for the mutual and collective good of both parties to the relation; (*b*) if predatory or warlike exploit in any degree becomes habitual to the community the sentiment of self-aggrandisement gets the upper hand, and subservience to the able-bodied elders becomes the dominant note in this relation of tutelage, and their parental interest in the welfare of the incoming generation in a corresponding degree goes into abeyance under the pressure of the appropriate sentiments of pugnacity and self-seeking, giving rise to a coercive régime of a more or less ruthless character; (*c*) correlatively, along with unwearying insistence on their own prerogatives and collective discretion, on the part of the elders, there goes, on the part of the community at large, a correspondingly habitual acceptance of their findings and the precedents they have established, resulting in a universal addiction to the broad principles of unmitigated authenticity, with no power anywhere capable of breaking across the accumulated precedents and tabus. Even the ruling class of elders, being an unwieldy deliberative body or executive committee, is held by parliamentary inertia, as well as by a circumspect regard for their prescriptive rights, to a due observance of the customary law. The force of precedent is notoriously strong on the lower levels of culture. Under the rule of the elders deference to precedent grows into an inveterate habit in the young, and when presently these come to take their turn as discretionary elders the habit of deference to the precedents established by those who have gone before still binds them, and the life and thought of the community never escape the dead hand of the parent.

When worked out into an institution of control in this way, and crossed with the other instinctive propensities that go to make governmental authority, it is apparently unavoidable that the parental bent should suffer this curious inversion. In the simplest and unsophisticated terms, its functional content appears to be an unselfish solicitude for the well-being of the incoming generation—a bias for the highest efficiency and fullest volume of life in the group, with a particular drift to the future; so that, under its rule, contrary to the dictum of the economic theorists, future goods are preferred to present goods [1] and the filial generation is given the

[1] Current economic theory commonly proceeds on the "hedonistic calculus", so called, (cf. Jeremy Bentham, Introduction to the *Principles of Morals and Legislation*) or the "hedonic principle", as it has also been called, (cf. Pantaleoni, *Pure Economics*, ch. i). This "principle" affords the major premise of current theory. It postulates that individual self-seeking is the prime mover of all economic conduct. There is some uncertainty and disagreement among latterday economists as to the precise terms proper to be employed to designate this principle of conduct and its working-out; in the apprehension of later speculators Bentham's "pleasure and pain" has seemed too bald and materialistic, and they have had recourse to such less precise and definable terms as "gratification," "satisfactions," "sacrifice," "utility" and "disutility," "psychic income," etc., but hitherto without any conclusive revision of the terminology. These differences and suggested innovations do not touch the substance of the ancient postulate. Proceeding on this postulate the theoreticians have laid down the broad proposition that "present goods are preferred to future goods"; from which arise many meticulous difficulties of theory, particularly in any attempt to make the deliverances of theory square with workday facts. The modicum of truth contained in this proposition would appear to be better expressed in the formula: "Prospective security is preferred to prospective risk;" which seems to

preference over the parental generation in all that touches their material welfare. But where the self-regarding sentiments, self-complacency and self-abasement, come largely into play, as they are bound to do in any culture that partakes appreciably of a predatory or coercive character, the prerogatives of the ruling class and the principles of authentic usage become canons of truth and right living and presently take precedence of workmanlike efficiency and the fulness of life of the group. It results that conventional tests of validity presently accumulate and increasingly deflect and obstruct the

be nearly all that is required either as a generalisation of the human motives in the case or as a premise for the theoretical refinements aimed at, whereas the dictum that "present goods are preferred to future goods" must, on reflection, commend itself as substantially false. By and large, of course, goods are not wanted except for prospective use—beyond the measure of that urgent current consumption that plays no part in the theoretical refinements for which the dictum is invoked. It will immediately be apparent on reflection that even for the individual's own advantage "present goods are preferred to future goods" only where and in so far as property rights are secure, and then only for future use. It is for productive use in the future, or more particularly for the sake of prospective revenue to be drawn from wealth so held, by lending or investing it, that such a preference becomes effective. Apart from this pecuniary advantage that attaches to property held over from the present to the future there appears to be no such preference even as a matter of individual self-seeking, and where such pecuniary considerations are not dominant there is no such preference for "present goods." It is present "wealth," not present "goods," that is the object of desire; and present wealth is desired mainly for its prospective advantage. It is well known that in communities where there are habitually no business-like credit extensions or investments for profit, savings take the form of hoarding, that is, accumulation for future use in preference to present consumption. There might be some division of opinion as to the character of the prospective use for which goods are sought, but there can be little question that much, if not most, of this prospective use is not of a self-regarding character and is not sought from motives of sensuous gain.

naïve pursuit of workmanlike efficiency, in large part by obscuring those matters of fact that lend themselves to technological insight.

But like other innate predispositions the parental bent continually reasserts itself in its native and untaught character, as an ever resilient solicitude for the welfare of the young and the prospective fortunes of the group. As such it constantly comes in to reënforce the instinct of workmanship and sustain interest in the direct pursuit of efficiency in the ways and means of life. So closely in touch and so concurrent are the parental bent and the sense of workmanship in this quest of efficiency that it is commonly difficult to guess which of the two proclivities is to be credited with the larger or the leading part in any given line of conduct; although taken by and large the two are after all fairly distinct in respect of their functional content. This thorough and far-going concurrence of the two may perhaps be taken to mean that the instinct of workmanship is in the main a propensity to work out the ends which the parental bent makes worth while.

It seems to be these two predispositions in conjunction that have exercised the largest and most consistent control over that growth of custom and conventional principles that has standardised the life of mankind in society and so given rise to a system of institutions. This control bears selectively on the whole range of institutions created by habitual response to the call of the other instincts and has the effect of a "common-sense" surveillance which prevents the scheme of life from running into an insufferable tangle of grotesque extravagances. That their surveillance has not always been decisive need scarcely be specifically called to mind; human culture in all ages presents too many imbecile usages and principles of conduct to let anyone overlook the fact that disserviceable institutions easily arise and continue to hold their place in spite of the disapproval of native common sense. The selective control exercised over custom and usage by these instincts of serviceability is neither too close nor too insistent. Wide, even extravagant, departures from the simple dictates of this native common sense occur even within the narrow range of the domestic and minor civil institutions, where these two common-sense predispositions should concur to create a prescriptive usage looking directly to the continuation and welfare of the race. Considerations, or perhaps rather conventional preconceptions, running on other grounds, as, for instance, on grounds of superstition or religion, of propriety and gentility, of pecuniary or political expediency, have come in for a large share in ordering the institutions of family and neighbourhood life. Yet doubtless it is the parental bent and the sense of workmanship in concurrence that have been the primary and persistent factors in (selectively) shaping the household organisation among all peoples, however great may have been the force of other factors, instinctive and habitual, that have gone to diversify the variegated outcome.

It appears, then, that so long as the parental solicitude and the sense of workmanship do not lead men to take thought and correct the otherwise unguarded drift of things, the growth of institutions—usage, customs, canons of conduct, principles of right and propriety, the course of cumulative habituation as it goes forward under the driving force of the several instincts native to man,—will commonly run at cross purposes with serviceability and the sense of workmanship.[1]

That such should be the case lies in the nature of things, as will readily appear on reflection. Under given circumstances and under the impulsion of a given instinctive propensity a given line of behaviour becomes habitual and so is installed by use and wont as a principle of conduct. The principle or canon of conduct so gained takes its place among the habitual verities of life in the community and is handed on by tradition. Under further impulsion of the same and other instinctive propensities, and under altered circumstances, conduct in other, unrelated lines will be referred to this received principle as a bench-mark by which its goodness is appraised and to which all conduct is accommodated, giving a result which is related to the exigencies of the case only at the second remove and by channels of habit which have only a conventional relevancy to the case. The farther this manner of crossing and grafting of habitual elements proceeds in the elaboration of principles and usage, the

[1] Traditionally a theoretical presumption has been held to the contrary. It has been taken for granted that the institutional outcome of men's native dispositions will be sound and salutary; but this presumption overlooks the effects of complication and deflection among instincts, due to cumulative habit. The tradition has come down as an article of uncritical faith from the historic belief in a beneficent Order of Nature; which in turn runs back to the early-modern religious conception of a Providential Order instituted by a shrewd and benevolent Creator; which rests on an anthropomorphic imputation of parental solicitude and workmanship to an assumed metaphysical substratum of things. This traditional view therefore is substantially theological and has that degree of validity that may be derived from the putative characteristics of any anthropomorphic divinity.

larger will be the mass and the graver will be the complication of materially irrelevant considerations present in any given line of conduct, the more extensive and fantastic will be the fabric of conventionalities which come to condition the response to any one of the innate human propensities, and the more "irrelevant, incompetent and impertinent" will be the line of conduct prescribed by use and wont. Except by recourse to the sense of workmanship there is no evading this complication of ineptitudes and irrelevancies, and such recourse is not easily had. For the bias of settled habit goes to sustain the institutional fabric of received sophistications, and these sophistications are bound in such a network of give and take that a disturbance of the fabric at any point will involve more or less of a derangement throughout.

This body of habitual principles and preconceptions is at the same time the medium through which experience receives those elements of information and insight on which workmanship is able to draw in contriving ways and means and turning them to account for the uses of life. And the conventional verities count in this connexion almost wholly as obstructions to workmanlike efficiency. Worldly wisdom, insight into the proprieties and expediencies of human intercourse, the scheme of tabus. consanguinities, and magical efficacies, yields very little that can effectually be turned to account for technological ends. The experience gained by habituation under the stress of these other proclivities and their derivative principles is necessarily made use of in workmanship, and so enters into the texture of the technological system, but a large part of it is of very doubtful value for the purpose. Much of this experience runs at cross purposes with workmanship, not only in that the putative information which this experience brings home to men has none but a putative serviceability, but also in that the habit of mind induced by its discipline obscures that insight into matter of fact that is indispensable to workmanlike efficiency.

But the most obstructive derangement that besets workmanship is what may be called the self-contamination of the sense of workmanship itself. This applies in a peculiar degree to the earlier or more elementary phases of culture, but it holds true only with lessening force throughout the later growth of civilisation. The hindrance to technological efficiency from this source will often rise to large proportions even in advanced communities, particularly where magical, religious or other anthropomorphic habits of thought are prevalent. The difficulty has been spoken of as anthropomorphism, or animism,—which is only a more archaic anthropomorphism. The essential trait of anthropomorphic conceptions, so far as bears on the present argument, is that conduct, more or less fully after the human fashion of conduct, is imputed to external objects; whether these external objects are facts of observation or creatures of mythological fancy. Such anthropomorphism commonly means an interpretation of phenomena in terms of workmanship, though it may also involve much more than this, particularly in the higher reaches of mythmaking. But the simpler anthropomorphic or animistic beliefs that pervade men's every-day thinking commonly amount to little if anything more than the naïve imputation of a workmanlike propensity in the observed facts. External objects are believed to do things; or rather it is believed that they are seen to do things.

The reason of this imputation of conduct to external things is simple, obvious, and intimate in all men's apprehension; so much so, indeed, as not readily to permit its being seen in perspective and appreciated at anything like its effectual force. All facts of observation are necessarily seen in the light of the observer's habits of thought, and the most intimate and inveterate of his habits of thought is the experience of his own initiative and endeavours. It is to this "apperception mass" that objects of apperception are finally referred, and it is in terms of this experience that their measure is finally taken. No psychological phenomenon is more familiar than this ubiquitous "personal equation" in men's apprehension of whatever facts come within their observation.

The sense of workmanship is like all human instincts in the respect that when the occasion offers, the agent moved by its impulse not only runs through a sequence of actions suitable to the instinctive end, but he is also given to dwelling, more or less sentimentally, on the objects and activities about which his attention is engaged by the promptings of this instinctive propensity. In so far as he is moved by the instinct of workmanship man contemplates the objects with which he comes in contact from the point of view of their relevancy to ulterior results, their aptitude for taking effect in a consequential outcome. Habitual occupation with workmanlike conceptions,—and in the lower cultures all men and women are habitually so occupied, since there is no considerable class or season not engaged in the quest of a livelihood,—this occupation with workmanlike interests, leaving the attention alert in the direction towards workmanlike phenomena, carries with it habitual thinking in the terms in which the logic of workmanship runs. The facts of observation are conceived as facts of workmanship, and the logic of workmanship becomes the logic of events. Their apprehension in these terms is easy, since it draws into action the faculties of apperception and reflection that are already alert and facile through habitual use, and it assimilates the facts in an apperceptive system of relationships that is likewise ready and satisfactory, convincing through habitual service and by native proclivity to this line of systematisation. By instinct and habit observed phenomena are apprehended from this (teleological) point of view, and they are construed, by way of sytematisation, in terms of such an instinctive pursuit of some workmanlike end. In latterday psychological jargon, human knowledge is of a "pragmatic" character.

As all men habitually act under the guidance of instincts, and therefore by force of sentiment instinctively look to some end in all activity, so the objects with which the primitive workman has to do are also conceived as acting under impulse of an instinctive kind; and a bent, a teleological or pragmatic nature, is in some degree imputed to them and comes as a matter of course to be accepted as a constituent element in their apprehended make-up. A putative pragmatic bent innate in external things comes in this way to pass current as observed matter of fact. By force of the sense of workmanship external objects are in great part apperceived in respect of what they will do; and their most substantial characteristic therefore, their intimate individual nature, in so far as they are conceived as individual entities, is that they will do things.

In the workmanlike apprehension of them the nature of things is twofold: (*a*) what can be done with them as raw material for use under the creative hand of the workman who makes things, and (*b*) what they will do as entities acting in their own right and working out their own ends. The former is matter of fact, the latter matter of imputation; but both alike, and in the naïve apprehension of uncritical men both equally, are facts of observation and elements of objective knowledge. The two are, of course, of very unequal value for the purposes of workmanship. It should seem, at least on first contact with the distinction, that the former category alone can have effectually conduced or contributed to workmanlike efficiency, and so it should be the only substantial factor in the growth of technological insight and proficiency: while the latter category of knowledge should presumably have always been an unmitigated hindrance to effective work and to technological advance. But such does not appear on closer scrutiny to have been the case in the past: whether such sheer discrimination against the technological serviceability of all these putative facts would hold good in latter-day civilisation is a question which may perhaps best be left to the parties in interest in "pragmatic" and theological controversy.

These two categories of knowledge, or of *cognoscenda*, are incongruous, of course, and they seem incompatible when applied to the same phenomena, the same external objects. But such incongruity does not disturb anyone who is at all content to take facts at their face value,—

for both ways of apprehending the facts are equally given in the face value of the facts apprehended. And on the known lower levels of culture it appears that in the workman's apprehension of the facts with which he has to do there is no evident strain due to this twofold nature and twofold interpretation of the objects of knowledge. So, the Pueblo potter (woman) may (putatively) be aware of certain inherent, quasi-spiritual, pragmatic qualities, claims and proclivities personal to the clay beds from which her raw material is drawn: different clay beds have, no doubt, a somewhat different quasi-personality, which has, among other things, to do with the goodness of the raw material they afford. Even the clay in hand will have its pragmatic peculiarities and idiosyncracies which are duly to be respected; and, notably, the finished pot is an entity with a life-history of its own and with temperament, fortunes and fatalities that make up the substance of good and evil in its world.[1] But all that does not perceptibly affect the technology of the Pueblo potter's art, beyond carrying a sequence of ceremonial observance that may run along by the side of the technological process; nor does it manifestly affect the workmanlike use of the pot during its lifetime, except that the pragmatic nature of the given pot will decide, on grounds of ceremonial competency, to what use it may be put.[2]

[1] Cf., e. g., F. H. Cushing, "A Study of Pueblo Pottery as illustrative of Zuñi Culture Growth," *Report, Bureau of Ethnology*, 1882–1883 (vol. iv); J. W. Fewkes, "Archeological Expedition to Arizona in 1895," sections on "Pottery" and "Paleography of the Pottery," *ibid*, 1896–1897 (vol. xviii); W. H. Holmes, "The Ancient Art of Chiriqui," *ibid*, 1884–1885 (vol. vi).

[2] The restrictions in this respect are mainly those which devote the

Matter of fact and matter of imputation run along side by side in inextricable contact but with slight apparent mutual interference across the line. The potter digs her clay as best she has learned how, and it is a matter of workmanlike efficiency, in which empirical knowledge of the mechanical qualities of the material is very efficiently combined with the potter's trained proficiency in the discretionary use of her tools; the tools, of course, also have their (putative) temperamental idiosyncracies, but they are employed in her hands in uncritical conformity with such matter-of-fact laws of physics as she has learned. The clay is washed, kneaded and tempered with the same circumspect regard to the opaque facts known about clay through long handling of it. What and how much tempering material may best be used, and how it is to be worked in, may all have a recondite explanation in the subtler imputed traits of the clay; a certain clay may have a putative quasi-spiritual affinity for certain tempering material; but the work of selection and mixing is carried out with a watchful regard to the mechanical character of the materials and without doubt that the given materials will respond in definite, empirically ascertained ways to the pressure brought on them by the potter's hands, and without questioning the matter of fact that such and so much of manipulation will mix such and so much of tempering material with the given lot of clay. The clay is "as wax in her hands;" what comes of it is the product of her insight and proficiency. Still the pragmatic nature of all these materials viewed as distinct entities is never to be denied, and in those

"sacred" vessels, distinguished by peculiar shapes and decorations, to particular ceremonial uses.

respects in which she does not creatively design, manipulate and construct the work of her hands, its putative self-sufficiency of existence, meaning and propensity goes on its own recognisances unshorn and inalienable.

Technological efficiency rests on matter-of-fact knowledge, as contrasted with knowledge of the traits imputed to external objects in making acquaintance with them. Therefore every substantial advance in technological mastery necessarily adds something to this body of opaque fact, and with every such advance proportionably less of the behaviour of inanimate things will come to be construed in terms of an imputed workmanlike or teleological bent. At the same time the imputation of a teleological meaning or workmanlike bent to the external facts that are made use of is likely to take a more circumspect, ingenious and idealised form. Under the circumstances that condition an increasing technological mastery there is an evergrowing necessity to avoid conflict between the imputed traits of external objects and those facts of their behaviour that are constantly in evidence in their technological use. In so far, therefore, as a simple and immediate imputation of workmanlike self-direction is seen manifestly to traverse the facts of daily use its place will be supplied by more shadowy anthropomorphic agencies that are assumed to carry on their life and work in some degree of detachment from the material objects in question, and to these anthropomorphic agencies which so lie obscurely in the background of the observed facts will be assigned a larger and larger share of the required initiative and self-direction. For so alien to mankind, with its instinctive sense of workmanship, is the mutilation of brute creation into mere opaque matter-of-fact, and so indefeasibly does the "consciousness of kind" assert itself, that each successive renunciation of such an imputed bias of workmanship in concrete objects is sought to be redeemed by pushing the imputation farther into the background of observed phenomena and running their putative workmanlike bias in more consummately anthropomorphic terms. So an animistic conception [1] of things comes presently to supplement, and in part supplant, the more naïve and immediate imputation of workmanship, leading up to farther and more elaborate myth-making; until in the course of elaboration and refinement there may emerge a monotheistic and providential Creator seated in an infinitely remote but ubiquitous space of four dimensions.

This imputation of bias and initiative has doubtless lost ground among civilised communities, as contrasted with the matter-of-fact apprehension of things, so that where it once was the main body of knowledge it now is believed to live and move only within that margin of things not yet overtaken by matter-of-fact information,—at least so it is held in the vainglorious scepticism of the Western culture. Meantime it is to be noted that the proclivity to impute a workmanlike bias to external facts has not been lost, nor has it become inoperative even among the adepts of Occidental scepticism. On the one hand it still enables the modern scientist to generalise his observations in terms of causation,[2] and on the other hand it has preserved the life of God the Father unto this day. It is as the creative workman, the

[1] Cf. E. B. Tylor, *Primitive Culture*, especially ch. xvii.

[2] Cf. "The Evolution of the Scientific Point of View," *University of California Chronicle*, Oct., 1908.

Great Artificer, that he has taken his last stand against the powers of spiritual twilight.

Out of the simpler workday familiarity with the raw materials and processes employed in industry, in the lower cultures, there emerges no system of knowledge avowed as such; although in all known instances of such lower cultures the industrial arts have taken on a systematic character, such as often to give rise to definite, extensive and elaborate technological processes as well as to manual and other technological training; both of which will necessarily involve something like an elementary theory of mechanics systematised on grounds of matter-of-fact, as well as a practical routine of empirical ways and means. In the lower cultures the growth of this body of opaque facts and of its systematic coherence is simply the habitual growth of technological procedure. Considered as a knowledge of things it is prosy and unattractive; it does not greatly appeal to men's curiosity, being scarcely interesting in itself, but only for the use to be made of it. Its facts are not lighted up with that spiritual fire of pragmatic initiative and propensity which animates the same phenomena when seen in the light of an imputed workmanlike behaviour and so construed in terms of conduct. On the other hand, when the phenomena are interpreted anthropomorphically they are indued with a "human interest," such as will draw the attention of all men in all ages, as witness the worldwide penchant for myth-making.

Such animistic imputation of end and endeavour to the facts of observation will in no case cover the whole of men's apprehension of the facts. It is a matter of imputation, not of direct observation; and there is always a fringe of opaque matter-of-fact bound up with even the most animistically conceived object. Such is unavoidably the case. The animistic conception imputes to its subject a workmanlike propensity to do things, and such an imputation necessarily implies that, as agent, the object in question engages in something like a technological process, a workmanlike manipulation wherein he has his will with the raw materials upon which his workmanlike force and proficiency spends itself. Workmanship involves raw material, and in the respect in which this raw material is passively shaped to his purposes by the workman's manipulation it is not conceived to be actively seeking its own ends on its own initiative. So that by force of the logic of workmanship the imputation of a workmanlike (animistic) propensity to brute facts, itself involves the assumption of crude inanimate matter as a correlate of the putative workmanlike agent. The anthropomorphic fancy of the primitive workman, therefore, can never carry the teleological interpretation of phenomena to such a finality but that there will always in his apprehension be an inert residue of matter-of-fact left over. The material facts never cease to be, within reasonable limits, raw material; though the limits may be somewhat vague and shifting. And this residue of crude matter-of-fact grows and gathers consistency with experience and always remains ready to the hand of the workman for what it is worth, unmagnified and unbeautified by anthropomorphic interpretation.

The animistic, or better the anthropomorphic, elements so comprised by imputation in the common-sense apprehension of things will pass in the main for facts of observation. With the current of time and experience this may under favourable conditions grow into a developed animistic system and come to the dignity of myth, and ultimately of theology. But as it plays its part in the cruder uses of technology its common and most obstructive form is the inchoate animism or anthropomorphic bias spoken of above. In its bearing on technological efficiency, it commonly vitiates the available facts in a greater or less degree. Matter-of-fact knowledge alone will serve the uses of workmanship, since workmanship is effective only in so far as its outcome is matter-of-fact work. Any higher and more subtle potencies found in or imputed to the facts about which the artificer is engaged can only serve to divert and defeat his efforts, in that they lead him into methods and expedients that have only a putative effect.

This obstructive force of the anthropomorphic interpretation of phenomena is by no means the same in all lines of activity. The difficulty, at least in the earlier days, seems to be greatest along those lines of craft where the workman has to do with the mechanical, inanimate forces—the simplest in point of brute concreteness and the least amenable to a consistent interpretation in animistic terms. While man is conventionally distinguished from brute creation as a "tool-using animal," his early progress in the devising and use of efficient tools, taking the word in its native sense, seems to have gone forward very slowly, both absolutely and as contrasted with those lines of workmanship in which he could carry his point by manual dexterity unaided by cunningly devised implements and mechanical contrivances; [1] and

[1] So, e. g., the proficiency of Bushmen, Veddas, Australians, American

still more striking is the contrast between the incredibly slow and blindfold advance of the savage culture shown in the sequence of those typical stone implements which serve conventionally as land-marks of the early technology, on the one hand, and the concomitant achievements of the same stone-age peoples in the domestication and use of plants and animals on the other hand.

No man can offer a confident conjecture as to how long a time and what a volume of experience was taken up in the growth of technological insight and proficiency up to the point when the neolithic period begins in European prehistory. In point of duration it has been found convenient to count it up roughly in units of geologic time, where a thousand years are as a day. Attempts to reduce it to such units as centuries or millennia have hitherto not come to anything appreciable. In the present state of information on this head it is doubtless a safe conjecture that the interval between the beginning of the human era and the close of palæolithic time, say in Europe or within the cultural sequence in which Europe belongs, is to be taken as some multiple of the interval that has elapsed from the beginning of the neolithic culture in Europe to the present; [1] and the neolithic period itself was in its turn no doubt of longer duration than the history of Europe since the bronze first came in.[2]

Indians, and other peoples of a low technological plane, in tracking game has been remarked on with great admiration by all observers; and the efficiency of these and others of their like is no less admirable as regards swimming, boating, riding, climbing, stalking, etc.

[1] Cf. G. and A. de Mortillet, *Le Préhistorique*, especially the chapter "Données chronologiques," pp. 662–664; W. G. Sollas, *Ancient Hunters*, ch. i and xiv.

[2] Cf. Sophus Müller, *L'Europe Préhistorique.*

The series of stone implements recovered from palæolithic deposits show the utmost reach of palæolithic technology on its mechanical side, in the way of workmanlike mastery of brute matter simply; for these implements are the tools of the tool-makers of that technological era. They indicate the ultimate terms of the technological situation on the mechanical side, for the craftsman working in more perishable materials could go no farther than these primary elements of the technological equipment would carry him.

The strict limitation imposed on the technology of any culture, on its mechanical side, by the "state of the industrial arts" in respect of the primary tools and materials available, whether availability is a question of knowledge or of material environment, is illustrated, for instance, by the case of the Eskimo, the North-west Coast Indians, or some of the islands of the South Sea. In each of these cultures, perhaps especially in that of the Eskimo, technological mastery had been carried as far as the circumstances of the case would permit, and in each case the decisive circumstances that limit the scope and range of workmanship are the character of the primary tools of the tool-maker and the limits of his knowledge of the mechanical properties of the materials at his disposal for such use. The Eskimo culture, for instance, is complete after its kind, worked out to the last degree of workmanlike mastery possible with the Eskimo's knowledge of those materials on which he depended for his primary tools and on which he was able to draw for the raw materials of his industry. At the same time the Eskimo shows how considerable a superstructure of the secondary mechanic arts may be erected on a scant groundwork of the primary mechanical resources.[1]

In the light of such a familiar instance as the Eskimo or the Polynesian culture it is evident that very much must be allowed, in the case, *e. g.*, of the European stone age, for work in perishable materials that have disappeared; but after all allowance of this kind, the showing for palæolithic man is not remarkable, considering the ample time allowed him, and considering also that, in Europe at least, he was by native gift nowise inferior to some of the racial elements that still survive in the existing population and that are not notoriously ill furnished either in the physical or the intellectual respect. And what is true of palæolithic times as regards the native character of this population is true in a more pronounced degree for later prehistoric times.[2]

The very moderate pace of the technological advance in early times in the mechanic arts stands out more strikingly when it is contrasted with what was accom-

[1] Cf., e. g., *Report of Bureau of American Ethnology*, 1884–1885, Franz Boas, "The Central Eskimo;" *ibid*, 1887–1888, John Murdoch, "The Point Barrow Eskimo."

[2] What is assumed here is what is commonly held, viz. that the racial stocks that made up the late palæolithic population of Europe are still represented in a moderate way in the racial mixture that fills Europe today, and that these older racial types not only recur sporadically in the European population at large but are also present locally in sufficient force to give a particular character to the population of given localities. (See G. de Mortillet, *Formation de la nation française*, 4me partie, and Conclusions, pp. 275–329.) Great changes took place in the racial complexion of Europe in the beginning and early phases of the neolithic period, but since then no intrusion of new stocks has seriously disturbed the mixture of races, except in isolated areas, of secondary consequence to the cultural situation at large.

See also W. G. Sollas, *Ancient Hunters and their Modern Representatives*.

plished in those arts, or rather in those occupations, that have to do immediately with living matter. Some of the crop plants, for instance, and presently some of the domestic animals, make their appearance in Denmark late in the period of the kitchen middens; which falls in the early stone age of the Danish chronology, that is to say in the early part of the neolithic period as counted in terms of the European chronology at large. These, then, are improved breeds of plants and animals, very appreciably different from their wild ancestors, arguing not only a shrewd insight and consistent management in the breeding of these domesticated races but also a long continued and intelligent use of these items of technological equipment, during which the nature and uses of the plants and animals taken into domestication must have been sufficiently understood and taken advantage of, at the same time that a workmanlike selection and propagation of favourable variations was carried out. Some slight reflection on what is implied in the successful maintenance, use and improvement of several races of crop plants and domestic animals will throw that side of the material achievements of the kitchen-midden peoples into sufficiently high contrast with their chipped flint implements and the degree of mechanical insight and proficiency which these implements indicate.

To this Danish illustrative case it may of course be objected, and with some apparent reason, that these plants and animals which begin to come in evidence in a state of domestication in the kitchen middens, and which presently afforded the chief means of life to the later stone-age population, were introduced in a domestic state from outside; and that this technological gain was the product of another and higher culture than that into which they were thus intruded. The objection will have what force it may; the facts are no doubt substantially as set forth. However, the domestication and use of these races of plants and animals embodied no less considerable a workmanlike mastery of its technological problem wherever it was worked out, whether in Denmark—as is at least highly improbable—or in Turkestan, as may well have been the case. And the successful introduction of tillage and cattle-breeding among the kitchen-midden peoples from a higher culture, without the concomitant introduction of a corresponding gain in the mechanic arts from the same source, leaves the force of the argument about as it would be in the absence of this objection. The comparative difficulty of acquiring the mechanic arts, as compared with the arts of husbandry, would appear in much the same light whether it were shown in the relatively slow acquirement of these arts through a home growth of technological mastery or in the relatively tardy and inept borrowing of them from outside. So far as bears on the present question, much the same habits of mind take effect in the acquirement of such a technological gain whether it takes place by home growth or by borrowing from without. In either case the point is that the peoples of the kitchen-middens appear to have been less able to learn the use of serviceable mechanical expedients than to acquire the technology of tillage and cattle-breeding. The appearance of tillage and cattle-breeding ("mixed farming") at this period of Danish prehistory, without the concomitant appearance of anything like a similar technological gain in the mechanic arts, argues either (*a*) that in the culture from which husbandry was ultimately borrowed and in which the domestication was achieved there was no similarly substantial gain made in the mechanic arts at the same time, so that this culture from which the crop plants and animals originally came into the North of Europe had no corresponding mechanical gain to offer along with husbandry; or (*b*) that the kitchen-midden peoples, and the other peoples through whose hands the arts of husbandry passed on their way to the North, were unable to profit in a like degree by what was offered them in the primary mechanic arts. The known evidence seems to say that the visible retardation in the mechanic arts, as compared with husbandry, in prehistoric Denmark was due partly to the one, partly to the other of these difficulties.

To avoid confusion and misconception it may be pertinent to recall that, taken absolutely, the rate and magnitude of advance in the primary mechanic arts in Denmark at this time was very considerable; so much so indeed that the visible absolute gain in this respect has so profoundly touched the imagination of the students of that culture as to let them overlook the disparity, in point of the rate of gain, between the mechanic arts and husbandry. In the same connection it is also to be remarked that the entire neolithic culture of the kitchen-middens, as well as their husbandry, was introduced from outside of Europe, having been worked out in its early rudiments before the kitchen-midden peoples reached the Baltic seaboard. At the same time the raw materials for the mechanic arts of the neolithic culture were available to the kitchen-midden technologist in abundant quantity and unsurpassed quality; while the raw material of husbandry, the crop plants and domestic animals, were exotics. Further, in point of race, and therefore presumably in point of native endowment, the peoples of the Baltic seaboard at that time were substantially the same mixture of stocks that has in modern times carried the technology of the mechanic arts in western Europe and its colonies to a pitch of mastery never approached before or elsewhere. And the retardation in the mechanic arts as contrasted with husbandry is no greater, probably less, in neolithic Denmark than in any other culture on the same general level of efficiency.

Wherever the move may have been made, in one or in several places, and whatever may have been the particular circumstances attending the domestication and early use of crop plants and animals, the case sums up to about the same result. Through long ages of work and play men (perhaps primarily women) learned the difficult and delicate crafts of husbandry and carried their mastery of these pursuits to such a degree of proficiency, and followed out the lead given by these callings with such effect, that by the (geologic) date of early neolithic times in Europe virtually all the species of domesticable animals in three continents had been brought in and had been bred into improved races.[1] At the same time the leading crop plants of the old world, those on whose yield the life of the Western peoples depends today, had

[1] These improved races are commonly, if not always, a product of hybridisation, though it is conceivable that such a race might arise as a "sport," a Mendelian mutant. To establish such a race or "composite pure line" of hybrids and to propagate and improve it in the course of further breeding demands a degree of patient attention and consistent aim.

been brought under cultivation, improved and specialised with such effect that all the advance that has been made in these respects since the early neolithic period is greatly less than what had been accomplished up to that time. By early neolithic times as counted in West Europe, or by the early bronze age as counted in western Asia, the leading domestic animals had been distributed, in domesticated and improved breeds, throughout central and western Asia and the inhabited regions of Europe and North Africa. The like is true for the main crop plants that now feed the occidental peoples, except that these, in domesticated and specialised breeds, were distributed through this entire cultural region at an appreciably earlier date,—earlier by some thousands of years.[1] In

[1] The late neolithic, or "æneolithic," culture brought to light by Pumpelly at Anau in Transcaspia shows the synchronism of advance between the technology of the mechanic arts on the one hand and of tillage and cattle-breeding on the other hand in a remarkably lucid way. The site is held to date back to some 8000 B. C. or earlier and shows continuous occupation through a period of several thousand years. The settlers at Anau brought cereals (barley and wheat) when the settlement was made; so that the cultivation of these grains must date back some considerable distance farther into the stone age of Asia. In succeeding ages the people of Anau made some further advance in the use of crop plants; whether by improvement and innovation at home or by borrowing has not been determined. Presently, in the course of the next few thousand years, they brought into domestication and adapted to domestic use by selective breeding the greater number of those species of animals that have since made up the complement of live stock in the Western culture. In the mechanic arts the visible advance is slight as compared with the work in cattle-breeding, though it cannot be called insignificant taken by itself. The more notable improvements in this direction are believed to be due to borrowing. Perhaps the most characteristic trait of the mechanic technology at Anau is the total absence of weapons in the lower half of the deposits.—Raphael Pumpelly, *Explorations in Turkestan: Prehistoric Civilizations of Anau.* (Carnegie Publication No. 73.) Washington, 1908.

late modern times there have been added to the civilised world's complement of crop plants a very large and important contingent whose domestication and development was worked out in America and the regions of the Pacific; though most of these belong in the low latitudes and are on that account less available to the Western culture than what has come down from the prehistoric cultures of the old world. These are also the work of the stone age, in large part no doubt dating back to palæolithic times.

America, with the Polynesian and Indonesian cultural regions, shows the correlation and the systematic discrepancy in time between the rate, range and magnitude of the advance in tillage on the one hand and of the primary mechanic arts on the other hand. When this culture was interrupted it had, in the mechanical respect, reached an advanced neolithic phase at its best; but its achievements in the crop plants are perhaps to be rated as unsurpassed by all that has been done elsewhere in all time.[1] In the primary mechanic arts this cultural region had in the same time reached a stage of perfection comparable at its best with pre-dynastic Egypt, or neolithic Denmark, or pre-Minoan Crete. The really great advance achieved was in the selection, improvement, use and cultivation of the crop plants; and not in any appreciable degree even in the mechanical appliances employed in the cultivation and consumption of these crops; though something considerable is to be noted in this latter respect in such inventions as the man-

[1] Cf. O. F. Cook, "Food Plants of Ancient America." *Report of Smithsonian Institution*, 1903. E. J. Payne, *History of the New World Called America*, vol. i, (1892), pp. 336–427.

dioca squeezer and the metate; and great things were done in the way of irrigation and road building.[1] But the contrast, for instance, between the metate and the contrivances for making paper bread on the one side, and the technologically consummate corn-plant (maize) on the other, should be decisive for the point here in question. The mechanic appliances of corn cultivation had not advanced beyond the digging stick, a rude hoe and a rudimentary spade, though here as well as in other similar connections the local use of well-devised irrigation works, terraced fields,[2] and graneries is not to be overlooked; but the corn itself had been brought from its grass-like ancestral form to the maize of the present corn crop. Like most of the American crop plants the maize under selective cultivation had been carried so far from its wild form as no longer to stand a chance of survival in the wild state, and indeed so far that it is still a matter of controversy what its wild ancestor may have been.

Perhaps the races of this American-Polynesian region are gifted with some special degree of spiritual (instinctive) fitness for plant-breeding. They seem to be endowed with a particular proclivity for sympathetically identifying themselves with and patiently waiting upon the course of natural phenomena, perhaps especially the phenomena of animate nature, which never seem alien or incomprehensible to the Indian. Such at least is the consistent suggestion carried by their myths, legends and symbolism. The typical American cosmogony is a tissue of legends of fecundity and growth, even more than appears to hold true of primitive cosmogonies

[1] Cf. E. J. Payne, as above.

[2] Cf., e. g., Lumholtz, *Unknown Mexico*, vol. i, ch. vi.

elsewhere.[1] And yet some caution in accepting such a generalisation is necessary in view, for instance, of the mythological output along similar lines on the Mediterranean seaboard in early times. By native gift the Indian is a "nature-faker," given to unlimited anthropomorphism. Mechanical, matter-of-fact appreciation of external and material phenomena seems to be in a peculiar degree difficult, irrelevant and incongruous with the genius of the race.

But even if it should seem that this race, or group of races, is peculiarly given to such sympathetic interpretation of natural phenomena in terms of human instinct, the difference between them and the typical racial stocks of the old world in this respect is after all a difference in degree, not in kind. The like proclivity is in good evidence throughout, wherever any race of men have endeavoured to put their acquaintance with natural phenomena into systematic form. The bond of combination in the making of systems, whether cosmologic, mythic, philosophic or scientific, has been some putative human trait or traits. It may be that in their appreciation of facts and their making of systems the American races have by some peculiar native gift been inclined to an interpretation in terms of fertility, growth, nurture and life-cycles.

Any predisposition freely to accept and use the deliverances of sensible perception on their own recognisances simply, in the terms in which they come, and

[1] Cf., e. g., J. W. Powell, "Mythology of the North American Indians," Report, *Bureau of Eth.*, 1879–1880 (vol. i); F. H. Cushing, "Outlines of Zuñi Creation Myths," *ibid*, 1891–1892; J. O. Dorsey, "A Study of Siouan Cults," *ibid*, 1889–1890.

to connect them up in a system of knowledge in their own terms, without imputation of a spiritual (anthropomorphic) substratum,—for the purposes of workmanship such a predisposition should be of the first importance for effective work in the mechanic arts; and a strong instinctive bias to the contrary should be correspondingly pernicious. Any instinctive bias to colour, distort and derange the facts by imputing elements of human nature will unavoidably act to hinder and deflect the agent from an effectual pursuit of mechanical design. But the like is not true in the same degree as regards men's dealings with animate nature. Anthropomorphic interpretation is more at home and less disserviceable here. With less serious derangement in the objective results, plants and animals may be construed to have a conscious purpose in life and to pursue their ends somewhat after the human fashion; witness the facility with which the story-tellers recount plausible episodes (feigned or real) from the life of animals and plants, and the readiness with which such tales get a hearing. Readers and hearers find no great difficulty, if any, in giving make-believe credence to the tales so long as they recount only such adventures as are physically possible to the animals of which (whom?) they are told; the hearers are always ready to go with the story-teller down this highway of make-believe into the subhuman fairy land. Mechanical phenomena, happenings in the mechanic arts, characteristics of the existence of inanimate objects and the changes which they undergo, lend themselves with much less happy effect to the anthropomorphic story-teller's make-believe. Episodes from the feigned life-history of tools, machines and raw materials are not drawn on with anything like the same frequency, nor do the tales that recount them meet with the same untiring attention. There is always an unreality about them which even the most robust make-believe can overcome only for a short and doubtful interval. Witness the relative barrenness of primitive folk-tales on this inanimate side, as compared with the exuberance of the myths and legends that interpret the life of plants and animals; and where inanimate phenomena are drawn into the net of personation it happens almost unavoidably that a feigned person is thrown into the foreground of the tale plausibly to take the part of bearer, controller or intrigant in the episodes related.[1]

Even more to the same purpose, as showing the same insidious facility of anthropomorphic interpretation, are the bona-fide constructions of scientists and pseudo-scientists running on the imputation of purpose and deliberation to explain the behaviour of animals. Indeed, at the worst, and still in good faith, it may go so far as to impute some sort of quasi-conscious striving on the part of plants.[2] As good and temperate an instance as may be had of such anthropomorphic imputation of workmanlike gifts is afforded, for instance, by the work of Romanes on the behaviour of animals.[3] It goes to show how very plausibly some of the lower animals may be credited with these spiritual aptitudes and how far and well the imputation may be made to serve the scien-

[1] Witness, again, the tales collected under the caption of *The Day's Work*, where the anthropomorphic romance of mechanics is made the most of by the same master who told the tales of the *Jungle Book* and of "The Cat that Walked."

[2] Cf. Presidential Address by Francis Darwin at the Dublin meeting of the British Association for the Advancement of Science; cf. also H. Bergson, *Évolution créatrice*, and particularly passages that deal with the *élan de la vie*.

[3] Cf. G. J. Romanes, *Animal Intelligence*, especially the Introduction.

tist's end. So plausible, indeed, is this anthropomorphism as to disarm even the scepticism of the trained sceptic. It will also appear in the later course of this inquiry that anthropomorphism, and especially the imputation of workmanship, has borne a much greater part in the work of the scientists than the members of that craft would like to avow; so that the scientific use of the anthropomorphic fancy is by no means a unique distinction of Romanes and the large group or school of biologists of which his work is typical; nor does the presence of this bias in their work by any means strip it of scientific value. In point of fact, it seems to touch the substance of their objective results much less seriously than might be apprehended.

The modern scientist's watchward is scepticism and caution; and what he may be led to do concessively, in spite of himself, by too broad a consciousness of kind, the savage does joyously and with conviction. His measure of what he sees about him is himself, and his apprehension of what takes place is a comprehension of how such things would be done in the course of human conduct if they were physically possible to man. The man (more often perhaps the woman) who busies himself with the beginnings of plant and animal-breeding will sympathetically put himself in touch with their inclinations and aptitudes with a degree of intimacy and assurance never approached by the followers of Romanes. It is for him to use common sense and fall in with the drift and idiosyncracies of these others who are, mysteriously, denied the gift of speech. By the unambiguous leading of the anthropomorphic fancy he puts himself in the place of his ward, his animal or vegetable friend and cousin, and can so learn something of what is going on in the putative vegetable or animal mind, through patient observation of what comes to light in response to his attentions in the course of his joint life with them. The plant or animal manifestly does things, and the question follows, Why do these speechless others do those things which they are seen to do?—things which often do not lie within the range of things desirable to be accomplished, humanly speaking. Manifestly these non-human others seek other ends and seek them in other ways than man. Some of the objective results which it lies in their nature to accomplish in so working out their scheme of life are useful to their human cousins; and it stands to reason that when they are dealt kindly with, when man takes pains to further their ends in life, they will take thought and respond somewhat in kind. To turn the proposition about, those things which men find, by trial and error, to bring a good and kindly return from the speechless others are manifestly well received by them and must obviously be of a kind to fall in with their bent and minister to their inclinations; and prudence and fellow-feeling combine to lead men farther along the way so indicated at each move in the propitious direction.

To the unsophisticated—and even to the sophisticated sceptic—it is manifest that animate objects do things. What they aim to do, as well as the logic of their conduct in carrying out their designs, are not precisely the same as in the case of man. But by staying by and learning what they are bent on doing, and observing how they go about it, any peculiarity in the nature of their needs, spiritual and physical, and in their manner of approaching their ends, may be learned and assimilated; and their life-work can be furthered and amplified by judiciously ministering to their ascertained needs and making the way smooth for them in what they undertake, so long as their undertakings are such as man is interested in bringing to a successful issue. Of course they work toward ends that are good in their sight, though not always such as men would seek; but that is their affair and is not to be pried into beyond the bounds of a decent neighbourly interest. And they work by methods in some degree other, often wiser, than those of men, and these it is man's place to learn if he would profit by their companionship.

Much of the scheme of life of these speechless others is a scheme of fecundity, growth and nurture, and all these matters are natural to women rather than to men; and so in the early stages of culture the consciousness of kind and congruity has made it plain to all the parties in interest that the care of crops and animals belongs in the fitness of things to women. Indeed there is such a spiritual (magical) community between women and the fecundity of animate things that any intrusion of the men in the affairs of growth and fertility may by force of contrast come to be viewed with the liveliest apprehension. Since the life of plants and animals is primarily of a spiritual nature, since the initiative and trend of vegetable and animal life is of this character, it follows that some sort of propitious spiritual contact and communion should be maintained between mankind and that world of fertility and growth in which these animate things live and move. So a line of communication, of a spiritual kind, is kept open with the realm of the speechless ones by means of a sign-language systematised into ritual, and by a symbolism of amity reënforced with gifts and professions of good-will. Hence a growth of occult meanings and ceremonial procedure, to which the argument will have to return presently.[1]

By this indirect, animistic and magical, line of approach the matter-of-fact requirements of tillage and cattle-breeding can be determined and fulfilled in a very passable fashion, given only the necessary time and tranquillity. Time is by common consent allowed the stone-age culture in abundant measure; and common consent is coming, through one consideration and another, to admit that the requisite conditions of peace and quiet industry are also a characteristic feature of that early time. The fact, broad and profound, that the known crop plants and animals were for the most part domesticated in that time is perhaps in itself the most persuasive argument for the prevalence of peaceful conditions among those peoples, whoever they may have been, to whose efforts, or rather to whose routine of genial superstition, this domestication is to be credited. This domestication and use of plants and animals was of course not a mere blindfold diversion. Here as ever the instinct of workmanship was present with its prompting to make the most of what comes to hand; and the technology of husbandry, like the technology of any other industrial enterprise, has been the outcome of men's abiding penchant for making things useful.

The peculiar advantage of tillage and cattle-breeding

[1] Cf. Jane E. Harrison, *Prolegomena to the Study of Greek Religion*, especially ch. iv; The same, *Themis*, especially ch. i, ii, iii and ix; with which compare the Pueblo cults referred to above.

over the primary mechanic arts, that by which the former arts gained and kept their lead, seems to have been the simple circumstance that the propensity of workmanlike men to impute a workmanlike (teleological) nature to phenomena does not leave the resulting knowledge of these phenomena so wide of the mark in the case of animate nature as in that of brute matter. It will probably not do to say that the anthropomorphic imputation has been directly serviceable to the technological end in the case of tillage and cattle-breeding; it is rather that the disadvantage or disserviceability of such an interpretation of facts has been greater in the mechanic arts in early times. The instinct of workmanship, through the sentimental propensity to impute workmanlike qualities and conduct to external facts, has defeated itself more effectually in the mechanic arts. And as in the course of time, under favourable local conditions, the habitual imputation of teleological capacities has in some measure fallen into disuse, the mechanic arts have gained; and every such gain has in its turn, as conditions permitted, acted cumulatively toward the discredit and disuse of the teleological method of knowledge, and therefore toward an acceleration of technological gain in this field.

The inanimate factors which early man has to turn to account as a condition precedent to any appreciable advance in the industrial arts, outside of husbandry and of the use of fruits and fibres associated with it, do not lend themselves to an effectual approximation from the anthropomorphic side. Flint and similar minerals are refractory, they have no spiritual nature and no scheme or cycle of life that can be interpreted in some passable fashion as the outcome of instinctive propensities and workmanlike management. Anthropomorphic insight does not penetrate into the secret ways of brute matter, for all the reasonable concession to idiosyncracies, to recondite conceits, occult means and devious methods, with which unsophisticated man stands ready to meet them. He can see as far into a millstone as anyone along that line; but that is not far enough to be of any use, and he is debarred by his workmanlike common sense from systematically looking into the matter along any other line. It is only the blindfold, unsystematic accretions of opaque fact coming in, disjointed and unsympathetic, from the inhuman side of his technological experience that can help him out here. And experience of that kind can come upon him only inadvertently, for he has no basis on which to systematise these facts as they come, and so he has no means of intelligently seeking them. His intelligent endeavours to get at the nature of things will perforce go on the mass of knowledge which his intelligence has already comprehended, which is a knowledge of human conduct. Anthropomorphism is almost wholly obstructive in this field of brute matter, and in early times, before much in the way of accumulated matter-of-fact knowledge had forced itself upon men, the propensity to a teleological interpretation seems to have been nearly decisive against technological progress in the primary and indispensable mechanic arts. And in later phases of culture, where anthropomorphic interpretations of workmanship have been worked out into a rounded system of magic and religion, they have at times brought the technological advance to a full stop, particularly on the mechanical side, and have even led to the cancelment of gains that should have seemed secure.

It is likewise a notable fact that, as already intimated above, myth and legend have found this brute matter as refractory in their service as the instinct of workmanship has found it in the genesis of technology; and for the good reason that the same human penchant for teleological insight and elaboration has ruled in the one as in the other. Inanimate matter and the phenomena in which inanimate matter manifests its nature and force have, of course, taken a large place in folk-lore; but the folk-lore, whether myth, legend or magic, in which inanimate matter is conceived as speaking in its own right and working out its own spiritual content is relatively very scant. In magic it commonly plays a part as an instrumentality only, and indeed as an instrument which owes its magical efficacy to some efficacious circumstance external to it. It has most frequently an induced rather than intrinsic efficacy, being the vehicle whereby the worker of magic materialises and conveys his design to its execution. It is susceptible of magical use, rather than creative of magical effects.[1] No doubt this characterisation of the magical offices of inert matter applies to early and primitive times and situations rather than to the high-wrought later systems of occult science and alchemical lore that are built on some appreciable knowledge of metallurgy and chemical reactions. So likewise early myth and legend have had to take recourse to the intervention of personal, or at least animate agents, to make headway in the domain of brute matter, which

[1] Cf., e. g., Skeat, *Malay Magic*, perhaps especially ch. v, section on the cultivation of rice.

figures commonly as means in the hands of manlike agents of some sort, rather than as a self-directing agent with initiative and a natural bent of its own. The phenomena of inanimate nature are likely to be thrown into the hands of such putative agents, who are then conceived to control them and turn them to account for ulterior ends not given in the native character of the inanimate objects themselves.[1] Even so exceptionally available a range of phenomena as those of fire have not escaped this inglorious eventuality. In the mythical legends of fire it will be found that the fire and all its works come into the plot of the story only as secondary elements, and the interest centres about the fortunes of some manlike agency to whose initiative and exploits all the phenomena of fire are referred as their cause or occasion.[2] The legends of fire have commonly become legends of a fire-bringer, etc.,[3] and have come to turn about the plots and counterplots of anthropomorphic beasts and divinities who are conceived to have wrestled for, with and about the use of fire.

[1] Hence animism, which applies its conceptions to inanimate rather than animate objects.

[2] The like applies in the case of the seasonal and meteorological myths; where it happens rarely if at all that the phenomena of the seasons or the forces that come in evidence in meteorological changes are personified directly or unambiguously. It is always some god or dæmon that controls or uses the wind and the weather, some indwelling sprite or manlike giant that inhabits and watches over the hill or spring or river, and it is always the interests of the indwelling personality rather than that of the tangible objects in the case that are to be safeguarded by the superstitious practices with which the myth surrounds men's intercourse with these features of the landscape.

[3] As in the legends of Prometheus; compare legends and ritual of fire from various cultures in L. Frobenius, *The Childhood of Man*, ch. xxv–xxvii.

So, on the other hand, as an illustration from the side of technology, to show how matters stood in this connection through the best days of anthropomorphism, fire had been in daily and indispensable use through an indefinite series of millennia before men, in the early modern times of Occidental civilisation, learned the use of a chimney. And all that hindered the discovery of this simple mechanical expedient seems to have been the fatal propensity of men to impute a teleological nature and workmanlike design to this phenomenon with which no truce or working arrangement can be negotiated in spiritual terms.[1]

A doubt may plausibly suggest itself as to the competency of such an explanation of these phenomena. It would seem scarcely to lie in the nature of an instinct of workmanship to enlist the workman in the acquisition of knowledge which he cannot use, and guide him in elaborating it into a system which will defeat his own ends; to build up obstructions to its own working, and yet in the long run to overcome them. In part this discrepancy in the outcome arises from the fact that the sense of workmanship affords a norm of systematisation for the facts that come into knowledge. This leads to something like a dramatisation of the facts, whereby they fall into some sort of a sequence of conduct among them-

[1] For an interesting illustration of this point see a paper by Duncan Mackenzie on "Cretan Palaces" in the *Annual of the British School at Athens* for 1907–1908, where the whole discussion hangs on the fact, unquestioned by any one of the disputants in a wide and warm controversy, that during some centuries of unwholesome nuisance from smoky fires in draughty rooms the great civilisation of the Mediterranean seaboard never hit on the ready solution of the difficulty by putting in a chimney.

selves, become personalised, are conceived as gifted with discrimination, inclinations, preferences and initiative; and in so far as the facts are conceived to be involved in immaterial or hyperphysical relations of this character they cannot effectually be made use of for the purposes of technology. All conceptions that exceed the scope of material fact are useless for technology, and in so far as such conceptions are intruded into the body of information drawn on by the workman they become obstructive.

But in good part the discrepancies of the outcome are due to complications with an instinctive curiosity, the presence of which has tacitly been assumed throughout the argument,—an "idle" curiosity by force of which men, more or less insistently, want to know things, when graver interests do not engross their attention. Comparatively little has been made of this instinctive propensity by the students of culture, though the fact of its presence in human nature is broadly recognised by psychologists,[1] and the like penchant comes in evidence among the lower animals, as appears in many investigations of animal behaviour.[2] Indeed, it has been taken somewhat lightly, in a general way, as being a genial infirmity of human nature rather than a creative factor in civilisation. And the reason of its being dealt with in so slight a manner is probably to be found in the nature of the instinct itself. With the instinct of workmanship it shares that character of pliancy and tractability common in some degree to the whole range of instincts, and especially characteristic of those instinctive predisposi-

[1] Cf., e. g., W. James, *Principles of Psychology*, ch. xxiv; McDougall, *Social Psychology*, ch. iii.

[2] Cf., e. g., M. F. Washburn, *The Animal Mind*, ch. xii, xiii.

tions that distinguish human nature from the simpler and more refractory spiritual endowment of the lower animals.

Like the other instinctive propensities, it is to be presumed, the idle curiosity takes effect only within the bounds of that metabolic margin of surplus energy that comes in evidence in all animal life, but that appears in larger proportions in the "higher" animals and in a peculiarly obtrusive manner in the life of man. It seems to be only after the demands of the simpler, more immediately organic functions, such as nutrition, growth and reproduction, have been met in some passably sufficient measure that this vaguer range of instincts which constitutes the spiritual predispositions of man can effectually draw on the energies of the organism and so can go into effect in what is recognised as human conduct. The wider the margin of disposable energy, therefore, the more freely should the characteristically human predispositions assert their sway, and the more nearly this metabolic margin is drained by the elemental needs of the organism the less chance should there be that conduct will be guided by what may properly be called the spiritual needs of man. It is accordingly characteristic of this whole range of vaguer and less automatically determinate predispositions that they transiently yield somewhat easily to the pressure of circumstances.

This is eminently true of the idle curiosity, as it is also true in a somewhat comparable degree of the sense of workmanship. But these instincts at the same time, and perhaps by the same fact, have also the other concomitant and characteristically human trait of a ubiquitous resiliency whenever and in so far as there is nothing to hinder.

Their staying power is, in a way, very great, though their driving force is neither massive nor intractable. So that even though the idle curiosity, like the sense of workmanship, may be momentarily thrust aside by more urgent interests, yet its long-term effects in human culture are very considerable. Men will commonly make easy terms with their curiosity when there is a call to action under the spur of a more elemental need, and even when circumstances appear to be favourable to its untroubled functioning a sustained and consistent response to its incitement is by no means an assured consequence. The common man does not eagerly pursue the quest of the idle curiosity, and neither its guidance nor its award of fact is mandatory on him.[1] Sporadic individuals who are endowed with this supererogatory gift largely in excess of the common run, or who yield to its enticements with very exceptional abandon, are accounted dreamers, or in extreme cases their more sensible neighbours may even rate them as of unsound mind. But the long-term consequences of the common run of curiosity, helped out by such sporadic individuals in whom the idle curiosity runs at a higher tension, counts up finally, because cumulatively, into the most substantial achievement of the race,—its systematised knowledge and quasi-knowledge of things.

This instinctive curiosity, then, comes in now and again serviceably to accelerate the gain in technological insight by bringing in material information that may be turned to account, as well as by persistently disturbing the habitual body of knowledge on which workmanship

[1] For illustrations see Dudley Kidd, *The Essential Kafir*, especially ch. ii, on "Native Beliefs."

draws. Human curiosity is doubtless an "idle" propensity, in the sense that no utilitarian aim enters in its habitual exercise; but the material information which is by this means drawn into the agent's available knowledge may none the less come to serve the ends of workmanship. A good share of the facts taken cognisance of under the spur of curiosity is of no effect for workmanship or for technological insight, and that any of it should be found serviceable is substantially a fortuitous circumstance. This character of "idleness," the absence of a utilitarian aim or utilitarian sentiment in the impulse of curiosity, is doubtless a great part of the reason for its having received such scant and rather slighting treatment at the hands of the psychologists and of the students of civilisation alike.

Of the material so offered as knowledge, or fact, workmanship makes use of whatever is available. In ways already indicated this utilisation of ascertained "facts" is both furthered and hindered by the fact that the information which comes to hand through the restless curiosity of man is reduced to systematic shape, for the most part or wholly, under canons of workmanship. For the large generality of human knowledge this will mean that the raw material of observed fact is selectively worked over, connected up and accumulated on lines of a putative teleological order of things, cast in something like a dramatic form. From which it follows that the knowledge so gained is held and carried over from generation to generation in a form which lends itself with facility to a workmanlike manipulation; it is already digested for assimilation in a scheme of teleology that instinctively commends itself to the workmanlike sense of fitness. But it also follows that in so far as the personalised, teleological, or dramatic order so imputed to the facts does not, by chance, faithfully reflect the causal relations subsisting among these facts, the utilisation of them as technological elements will amount to a borrowing of trouble. So that the concurrence of curiosity and workmanship in the assimilation of facts in this way may, and in early culture must, result in a retardation of the technological advance, as contrasted with what might conceivably have been the outcome of this work of the idle curiosity if it had not been congenitally contaminated with the sense of workmanship and thereby lent itself to conceptions of magical efficacy rather than to mechanical efficiency.[1]

The further bearing of the parental bent on the early growth of technology also merits attention in this connection. This instinct and the sentiments that arise out of its promptings will have had wide and free play in early times, when the common good of the group was still perforce the chief economic interest in the habitual view of all its members. It will have had an immediate effect on the routine of life and work, presumably far beyond what is to be looked for at any later stage. In the time when pecuniary competition had not yet become an institution, grounded in the ownership of goods in severalty and on their competitive consumption, the promptings of this instinct will have been more insistent and will have met with a more unguarded response than

[1] Cf. "The Place of Science in Modern Civilisation," *Journal of Sociology*, March, 1906, pp. 585–609; "The Evolution of the Scientific Point of View," *University of California Chronicle*, vol. x, pp. 396–415.

later on, after these institutional changes have taken effect. A manifest and inveterate distaste of waste, in great part traceable on analysis to this instinct, still persistently comes in evidence in all communities, although it is greatly disguised and distorted by the principles of conspicuous waste [1] among all those peoples that have adopted private ownership of goods; and serviceability to the common good likewise never ceases to command at least a genial, speculative approval from the common run of men, though this, too, may often take some grotesque or nugatory form due to preconceptions of a pecuniary kind. This bias for serviceability and against waste falls in directly with the promptings of the instinct of workmanship, so that these two instinctive predispositions will reënforce one another in conducing to an impersonally economical use of materials and resources as well as to the full use of workmanlike capacities, and to an endless taking of pains.

Some reference has also been made already to the technological value of those kindly, "humane" sentiments that are bound up with the parental bent,—if they may not rather be said substantially to constitute the parental bent. It is of course in the non-mechanical arts of plant and animal breeding that these humane extensions of the parental instinct have their chief if not their only industrial value, both in furthering the day's work and in contributing to the advance of technology. In the primary mechanic arts, *e. g.*, an affectionate disposition of this kind toward the inanimate appliances with which their work is occupied does no doubt still, as ever, to some extent animate the workmen as well

[1] Cf. *Theory of the Leisure Class*, ch. iv, v.

as those who may have the remoter oversight of the work. But the part played by such humane sentiments is after all relatively slight in men's dealings with brute matter, nor do they invariably conduce to expeditious work or to a hard-headed insight into the mechanics of those things with which this work has to do. In fact such tender emotions so placed may somewhat easily become a source of mischief, in a manner similar to the mischievous technological consequences of anthropomorphism already spoken of.

It is otherwise with the bearing of the parental bent on the arts of tillage and cattle-breeding. Here its promptings are almost wholly serviceable to technological gain as well as to assiduous workmanship. The kindly sentiments intrinsic to the parental bent are admirably in place in the care of plants and animals, and their good effects in so giving a propitious turn to the technology of early tillage and cattle-breeding are only re-enforced by the parental and workmanlike inclination to husband resources and make the most of what comes to hand. The particular turn given to the anthropomorphic bias by this line of preconceptions also is rather favourable than otherwise to a working insight into the requirements of the art. And it has had certain specific consequences for the early technology of husbandry, as well as for the early culture in which husbandry was the chief material factor, such as to call for a more circumstantial account.

Under the canons of workmanship a teleological animus—an instinctive or "spiritual" nature—is imputed to the plants and animals brought into domestication. The art of husbandry proceeds on the apprehended needs and proclivities so imputed, and the technology of the craft therefore takes the form of a "tendance" designed to further these quasi-animistically conceived beings in whatever ends they have at heart by virtue of their natural bent, and to so direct this tendance upon them as will conduce to shaping their scheme of life in ways advantageous to man. Like other sentient beings, as is known to shrewd and unsophisticated man, they have spiritual needs as well as material needs, and they are putatively to be influenced by the attitude of their human cousins towards them and their conduct, interests, and adventures. Further, their life and comfort are manifestly conditioned by the run of the seasons and of the weather; various inclemencies are discouraging and discomforting to them, as to mankind, and other vicissitudes of rain and shine and tempest are of the gravest consequence to them for good or ill. Under these delicate circumstances it is incumbent on the keepers of crops and flocks to walk circumspectly and cultivate the good-will not only of their crops and flocks but also of the natural phenomena that count for so much in the life of the crops and flocks. These natural phenomena are of course also conceived anthropomorphically, in the sense that they too are seen to follow their natural bent and do what they will,—or perhaps more commonly what the personal agents will, in whose keeping these natural phenomena are conceived to lie; for unsophisticated man has no other available terms in which to conceive them and their behaviour than the terms of initiative, design and endeavour immediately given in his own conscious action.

Now, as has already been said, the scheme of life of the

crops and flocks is, at least in the main, and particularly in so far as it vitally and always interests their keepers, a scheme of fecundity, fertility and growth. But these matters, visibly and by conscious sentiment, pertain in a peculiarly intimate sense to the women. They are matters in which the sympathetic insight and fellow-feeling of womankind should in the nature of things come very felicitously to further the propitious course of things. Besides which the life of the women falls in these same lines of fecundity, nurture and growth, so that their association and attendance on the flocks and crops should further the propitious course of things also by the subtler means of sympathetic suggestion. There is a magical congruity of great force as between womankind and the propagation of growing things. And these subtler ways of influencing events are especially to the point in all contact with these non-human sentient beings, since they are speechless and must therefore in the main be led by living example rather than by precept and expostulation. And, again, being sentient, somewhat after the fashion of mankind, it is not to be believed that they have not the gift visibly common to mankind and many animals, of following their leader by force of sympathetic imitation. It may not be easy to say how far this instinctive impulse of imitation, necessarily credited to all phenomena to which anthropomorphic traits are imputed, is to be accounted the ground of all sympathetic magic; but it is at least to be accepted as sufficient to account for much of what is done to induce fertility in flocks and crops.

So that on many accounts it is evident that in the nature of things, the care of flocks and crops is the women's affair, and it follows that all intercourse with the flocks and crops in the early days had best be conducted by the women, who alone may be presumed intuitively to apprehend what is timely, due and permissible in these premises. It is all the more evident that communion with these wordless others should fall to the women, since the like wordless communion with their own young is perhaps the most notable and engaging trait of their own motherhood. The parental bent also throws a stress of sentiment on this simple and obvious phase of motherhood, such as has made it in all men's apprehension the type of all kindly and unselfish tendance; at the same time this ubiquitous parental instinct tends constantly to place motherhood in the foreground in all that concerns the common good, in as much as all that is worth while, humanly speaking, has its beginning here. In that early phase of culture in which the beginnings of tillage and cattle-breeding were made and in which the common good of the group was still the chief daily interest about which men's solicitude and forethought are habitually engaged, motherhood will always have been the central fact in the scheme of human things. So that in this cultural phase the parental bent and the sense of workmanship will have worked together to bring the women into the chief place in the technological scheme; and the sense of imitative propriety, as well as the recognised constraining force exercised by example and mimetic representation through the impulse of imitation, will have guided workmanship shrewdly to play up womankind and motherhood in an ever-growing scheme of magical observances designed to further the natural increase of flocks and crops. Where anthropomorphic imputation runs free and with conviction, such observances, designed to act sympathetically on the natural course of phenomena, unavoidably become an integral feature of the technological scheme, no less indispensable and putatively no less efficacious to this end than the mechanical operations with which these observances are associated. There is no practicable line of division to be drawn between sympathetic magic and anthropomorphic technology; and in the known cultures of this early type it is for the most part an open question whether the magical observances are to be accounted an adjunct to what we would recognise as the technological routine of the art, or conversely. The two are not commonly held apart as distinct categories, and both are efficacious and indispensable; and in both the felt efficacy runs on much the same grounds of imputed anthropomorphic traits.[1]

On grounds of magical-technological expediency, then, as well as by force of the sense of intrinsic propriety, women come to take the leading rôle in the industrial community of the early time, and the community's material interests come to centre about them and their relation to the natural products of the fields; and since this interest bears immediately on the fecundity of the flocks and crops, it is particularly in their character of motherhood that the women come most vitally into the case. The natural produce on which the life of the group depends, therefore, will appertain to the women, in some

[1] This technological blend of manual labour with magical practice is well seen, for instance, in the Malay ritual of rice culture.—W. W. Skeat, *Malay Magic*, various passages dealing with the ceremonial of the planting, growth and harvesting of the rice-crop.

intimate sense of congruity, so that in the fitness of things this produce will properly come to the good of the community through their hands and will logically be dispensed somewhat at their discretion. So great is the reach of this logic of congruity that in the known cultures which show much reminiscence of this early technological phase it is commonly possible to detect some remnant of such discretionary control of the natural produce by the women. And modern students, imbued with modern preconceptions of ownership and predaceous mastery, have even found themselves constrained by this evidence to discover a system of matriarchy and maternal ownership in these usages that antedate the institution of ownership. Conceivably, the usages growing out of this preferential position of women in the technology and ritual of early husbandry will, now and again, by the uniform drift of habituation have attained such a degree of consistency, been wrought into so rigid a form of institutions, as to have been carried over into a later phase of culture in which the ownership of goods is of the essence of the scheme; and in such case these usages may then have come to be reconstrued in terms of ownership, to the effect that the ownership of agricultural products vests of right in the woman, the mother of the household.

But if the magical-technological fitness and efficacy of women has led to the growth of institutions vesting the disposal of the produce in the women, in a more or less discretionary way, the like effect has been even more pronounced, comprehensive and lasting as regards the immaterial developments of the case. With great uniformity the evidence from the earlier peaceable agricultural civilisations runs to the effect that the primitive ritual of husbandry, chiefly of a magical character, is in the hands of the women and is made up of observances presumed to be particularly consonant with the phenomena of motherhood.[1] And presently, when the more elaborate phases of these magical rites of husbandry come, by further superinduction of anthropomorphism, to grow into religious observances and mythological tenets, the greater *daimones* and divinities that emerge in the shuffle are women, and again it is the motherhood of women that is in evidence. The deities, great and small, are prevailingly females; and the great ones among them seem invariably to have set out with being mothers.

In the creation of female and maternal divinities the parental instinct has doubtless greatly re-enforced the drift of the instinct of workmanship in the same direction. The female deities have two main attributes or characteristics because of which they came to hold their high place; they are goddesses of fertility in one way or another, and they are mothers of the people. It is perhaps unnecessary to hold these two concomitant attributions apart, as many if not most of the great deities claim precedence on both grounds. But the lower orders of female divinities in the matriarchal scheme of things divine will much more commonly specialise in fertility of crops than in maternity of the people. The number of divinities that have mainly or solely to do with fertility is greater than that of those which figure as mothers of the people, either locally or generally. And perhaps in the majority of cases there is some suggestive evidence

[1] Cf. J. E. Harrison, *Prolegomena to the Study of Greek Religion*, especially ch. iv; J. G. Frazer, *Adonis, Attis, Osiris*, bk. i, ch. iii.

that the great female deities have primarily been goddesses of fertility having to do with the growth of crops—and, usually in the second place, of animals—rather than primarily mothers of the tribe;[1] which would suggest that their genesis and character is due to the canons of the sense of workmanship more than to the parental bent, although the latter seems to have had its part in shaping many of them if not all.

The female divinities belong characteristically to the early or simpler agricultural civilisation, and what has been said goes to argue that they stand on technological grounds in the main; indeed, in their genesis and early growth, they are in good part of the nature of technological expedients. They are at home with the female technology of early tillage especially, and perhaps only in the second place do they serve the magical and religious needs of peoples given mainly to breeding flocks and herds; although it is to be noted that most of the greater known goddesses of the ancient Western world, as well as many of the minor ones, are also found to be closely related to various of the domestic animals. In America and the Far East, of course, any connection

[1] Such seems to be the evidence, for instance, for Cybele, Astarte (Aphrodite, Ishtar), Mylitta, Isis, Demeter (Ceres), Artemis, and for such doubtfully late characters as Hera (Juno),—see Harrison, *Prolegomena to the Study of Greek Religion;* Frazer, *Adonis, Attis, Osiris,* and *The Golden Bough.* Quanon may be a doubtful case, as possibly also Amaterazu. The evidence from such American instances as the great mother goddesses of the Pueblos and other Indian tribes runs perhaps the other way, or at the best it may leave the point in doubt. See, for instance, Matilda C. Stevenson, "The Zuñi Indians," *Report Bureau of American Ethnology,* 1901–1902, section on "Mythology;" The same, *ibid,* 1889–1890, "The Sia;" Frank H. Cushing, *ibid,* 1891–1892, "Zuñi Creation Myths."

with the domestication of animals would appear improbable.

With a change of base, from this early husbandry to a civilisation in which the main habitual interest is of another kind, and in which the habitual outlook of men is less closely limited by the same anthropomorphic conceptions of nurture and growth, the goddesses begin to lose their preferential claim on men's regard and fall into place as adjuncts or consorts of male divinities designed on other lines and built out of different materials and serving new ends.[1] But the hegemony of the mother goddesses has unquestionably been very wide-reaching and very enduring, as it should be to answer to the extent in time and space of the civilisation of tillage as well as to its paramount importance in the life of mankind, and as it is shown to have been by the archæological and ethnological evidence.

A further concomitant variation in the cultural scheme, associated with and presumably traceable to the same technological ground, is maternal descent, the counting of relationship primarily or solely in the female line. In the present state of the evidence on this head it would probably be too broad a proposition to say that the counting of relationship by the mother's side is due wholly to preconceptions arising out of the technology of fertility and growth and that it so is remotely a creature of the instinct of workmanship; but it is at least equally probable that that ancient conceit must be abandoned according to which the system of maternal descent arises out of an habitual doubt of paternity. The mere

[1] Cf., e. g., Frazer, *Adonis, Attis, Osiris*, bk. ii, ch. iii, bk. iii, ch. vi and xi.

obvious congruity of the cognatic system as contrasted with the agnatic, has presumably had as much to do with the matter as anything, and under the rule of the primitive technology of tillage and cattle-breeding this obvious congruity of the cognate relationship will have been very materially re-enforced by the current preconceptions regarding the preferential importance of the female line for the welfare of the household and the community. And so long as that technological era lasted, and until the more strenuous culture of predation and coercion came on and threw the male element in the community into the place of first consequence, maternal descent as well as the mother goddess appear to have held their own.

It will have been noticed that through all this argument runs the presumption that the culture which included the beginnings and early growth of tillage and cattle-breeding was substantially a peaceable culture. This presumption is somewhat at variance with the traditional view, particularly with the position taken as a matter of course by earlier students of ethnology in the nineteenth century. Still it is probably not subject to very serious question today. As the evidence has accumulated it has grown increasingly manifest that the ancient assumption of a primitive state of nature after the school of Hobbes cannot be accepted. The evidence from contemporary sources, as to the state of things in this respect among savages and many of the lower barbarians, points rather to peace than to war as the habitual situation, although this evidence is by no means unequivocal; besides which, the evidence from these contemporary lower cultures bears only equivocally on the point of first interest here,—viz., the antecedents of the Western civilisation. What is more to the point, though harder to get at in any definitive way, is the prehistory of this civilisation. Here the inquiry will perforce go on survivals and reminiscences and on the implications of known facts of antiquity as well as of certain features still extant in the current cultural scheme.

It seems antecedently improbable that the domestication of the crop plants and animals could have been effected at all except among peoples leading a passably peaceable, and presently a sedentary life. And the length of time required for what was achieved in remote antiquity in this respect speaks for the prevalence of (passably) peaceable conditions over intervals of time and space that overpass all convenient bounds of chronology and localisation. Evidence of maternal descent, maternal religious practices and maternal discretion in the disposal of goods meet the inquiry in ever increasing force as soon as it begins to penetrate back of the conventionally accepted dawn of history; and survivals and reminiscences of such institutions appear here and there within the historical period with increasing frequency the more painstaking the inquiry becomes. And that institutions of this character require a peaceable situation for their genesis as well as for their survival is not only antecedently probable on grounds of congruity, but it is evidenced by the way in which they incontinently decay and presently disappear wherever the cultural situation takes on a predatory character or develops a large-scale civilisation, with a coercive government, differentiation of classes—especially in the pecuniary respect—warlike ideals and ambitions, and a considerable accumulation of wealth.

Some further discussion of this early peaceable situation will necessarily come up in connection with the technological grounds of its disappearance at the transition to that predatory culture which has displaced it in all cases where an appreciably advanced phase of civilisation has been reached.

CHAPTER III

The Savage State of the Industrial Arts

Technological knowledge is of the nature of a common stock, held and carried forward collectively by the community, which is in this relation to be conceived as a going concern. The state of the industrial arts is a fact of group life, not of individual or private initiative or innovation. It is an affair of the collectivity, not a creative achievement of individuals working self-sufficiently in severalty or in isolation. In the main, the state of the industrial arts is always a heritage out of the past; it is always in process of change, perhaps, but the substantial body of it is knowledge that has come down from earlier generations. New elements of insight and proficiency are continually being added and worked into this common stock by the experience and initiative of the current generation, but such novel elements are always and everywhere slight and inconsequential in comparison with the body of technology that has been carried over from the past.

Each successive move in advance, every new wrinkle of novelty, improvement, invention, adaptation, every further detail of workmanlike innovation, is of course made by individuals and comes out of individual experience and initiative, since the generations of mankind live only in individuals. But each move so made is necessarily made by individuals immersed in the community and exposed to the discipline of group life as it runs in the community, since all life is necessarily group life. The phenomena of human life occur only in this form. It is only as an outcome of this discipline that comes with the routine of group life, and by help of the commonplace knowledge diffused through the community, that any of its members are enabled to make any new move that may in this way be traceable to their individual initiative. Any new technological departure necessarily takes its rise in the workmanlike endeavours of given individuals, but it can do so only by force of their familiarity with the body of knowledge which the group already has in hand. A new departure is always and necessarily an improvement on or alteration in that state of the industrial arts that is already in the keeping of the group at large; and every expedient or innovation, great or small, that so is hit upon goes into effect by going into the common stock of technological resources carried by the group. It can take effect only in this way. Such group solidarity is a necessity of the case, both for the acquirement and use of this immaterial equipment that is spoken of as the state of the industrial arts and for its custody and transmission from generation to generation.

Within this common stock of technology some special branch or line of proficiency, bearing on some special craft or trade, may be held in a degree of isolation by some caste-like group within the community, limited by consanguinity, initiation, and the like, and so it may be held somewhat out of the common stock and transmitted in some degree of segregation. In the lower cultures the elements of technology that are so engrossed by a fraction of the community and held out of the common stock are most commonly of a magical or ceremonial nature, rather than effective elements of workmanship; since any such matters of ritual observance lend themselves with greater facility to exclusive use and transmission within lines of class limitation than do the matter-of-fact devices of actual workmanship. In the lower cultures the exclusive training and information so held and transmitted in segregation by various secret organisations appear in the main to be of this magical or ceremonial character;[1] although there is no reason to doubt that this technological make-believe is taken quite seriously and counts as a substantial asset in the apprehension of its possessors. In a more advanced state of the industrial arts, where ownership and the specialisation of industry have had their effect, trade secrets, patent and copyrights are often of substantial value, and these are held in segregation from the common stock of technology. But it is evident without argument that facts of this class are after all of no grave or enduring consequence in comparison with the great commonplace body of knowledge and skill current in the community. At the same time, any such segregated line of technological gain and transmission, if it has any appreciable significance for the state of the industrial arts and is not wholly made up of ritual observances, leans so greatly on the technological equipment at large that its isolation is at the most partial and one-sided; it takes effect only by the free use of the general body of

[1] Cf., e. g., Hutton Webster, *Primitive Secret Societies*, especially ch. iii, iv, v; Spencer and Gillen, *Native Tribes of Central Australia*, ch. vii, viii, ix, xvi.

knowledge which is not so engrossed, and it has also in all cases been acquired and elaborated only by the free use of that commonplace knowledge that is held in no man's exclusive possession. Such is more particularly the case in all but those latest phases of the industrial development in which the volume of the technology and the consequent specialisation of occupations have been carried very far.

In the earlier, or rather in all but the late phases of culture and technology, this immaterial equipment at large is accessible to all members of the community as a matter of course through the unavoidable discipline that comes with the workday routine of getting along. Few, if any, can avoid acquiring the essential elements of the industrial scheme by use of which the community lives, although they need not each gain any degree of proficiency in all the manual operations or industrial processes in which this technological scheme goes into effect, and few can avoid being so trained into the logic of the current scheme that their habitual thinking will in all these bearings run within the bounds of experience embodied in this general scheme.

All have free access to this common stock of immaterial equipment, but in all known cultures there is also found some degree of special training and some appreciable specialisation of knowledge and occupations; which is carried forward by expert workmen whose peculiar and exceptional proficiency is confined to some one or a few distinct lines of craft. And in all, or at least in all but the lowest known cultures, the available evidence goes to say that this joint stock of technological mastery can be maintained and carried forward only by way of some such specialisation of training and differentiation of employments. No one is competent to acquire such mastery of all the lines of industry included in the general scheme as would enable him (or her) to transmit the state of the industrial arts to succeeding generations unimpaired at all points.

Some degree of specialisation there always is, even where there appears to be no urgent technological need of it. The circumstances of their life differ sufficiently for different individuals, so that a certain individuation in workmanship will result from commonplace experience, even apart from any deliberate specialisation of occupations. And with any considerable increase in the size of the group a more or less deliberate specialisation of occupations will also set in. Individuals who are in this way occupied wholly or mainly with some one particular line of work will carry proficiency in this line to a higher pitch than the generality of workmen and will bring out details of technological procedure that may never fully become the common possession of the group at large, that may not in all details become part of the commonplace technological information current in the community. There seems, in fact, never to have been a time when the industrial scheme was so slight and narrow that all members of the community could master it in the greatest feasible degree of proficiency at every point. But at the same time it holds true for all the more archaic phases of the development that all members of the community appear always to have had a comprehensive and passably exhaustive acquaintance with the technique of all industries practised in their time.

This necessary specialisation and detail training has

large consequences for the growth of technology as well as for its custody and transmission. It follows that a large and widely diversified industrial scheme is impossible except in a community of some size,—large enough to support a number and variety of special occupations. In effect, substantial gains in industrial insight and proficiency can apparently be worked out only through such close and sustained attention to a given line of work as can be given only within the lines of a specialised occupation. At the same time the industrial community must comprise a full complement of such specialised occupations, and must also be bound together in a system of communication sufficiently close and facile to allow the technological contents of all these occupations to be readily assimilated into a systematic whole. The industrial system so worked out need not be of the same extent as any one local group of the people who get their living by its use; but it seems to be required that if several local groups are effectively to be comprised in a single industrial system conditions of peace must prevail among them. Community of language seems also to be nearly necessary to the maintenance of such a system. Where the various local groups are on hostile terms, each will tend to have an industrial system of its own, with a technological character somewhat distinct from its neighbours.[1] If the degree of isolation is pronounced, so that traffic and communication do not run freely between groups, the size of the local group will limit the state of the industrial arts somewhat rigidly; and on the other hand a marked advance in the industrial arts, such

[1] Cf. for instance, Codrington, *The Melanesians;* Seligmann, *The Melanesians of British New Guinea.*

as the domestication of crop plants or animals or the introduction of metals, is likely to bring about such a redistribution of population and industry as to increase the effective size of the community.[1]

Among the peoples on the lower levels of culture there prevails commonly a considerable degree of isolation, or even of estrangement. In a great degree each community is thrown on its own resources, and under these circumstances the size of the community may become a matter of decisive importance for the industrial arts. Where a serious decline in the numbers of any of these savage or barbarous peoples is recorded it is also commonly noted that they have suffered a concomitant decay

[1] These considerations may of course imply nothing, directly, as to the size of the political organisation or of the national territory or population; though national boundaries are likely both to affect and to be affected by such changes in the industrial system. A community may be small, relatively to the industrial system in and by which it lives, and may yet, if conditions of peace permit it, stand in such a relation of complement or supplement to a larger complex of industrial groups as to make it in effect an integral part of a larger community, so far as regards its technology. So, for instance, Switzerland and Denmark are an integral part of the cultural and industrial community of the Western civilisation as effectually as they might be with an area and population equal to those of the United Kingdom or the German Empire, and they are doubtless each a more essential part in this community than Russia. At the same time, as things go within this Western culture, national boundaries have a very considerable obstructive effect in industrial affairs and in the growth of technology. It will probably be conceded on the one hand that any appreciable decline in the aggregate population of Christendom would result in some curtailment or retardation of the technological advance in which these peoples are jointly and severally engaged; and it is likewise to be conceded on the other hand that the like effect would follow on any marked degree of success from the efforts of those patriotic and dynastic statesmen who are endeavouring to set these peoples asunder in an armed estrangement and neutrality.

in their technological knowledge and workmanship.[1] In view of these considerations it is probably safe to say that under settled conditions any community is, commonly, no larger than is required to keep up and carry forward the state of the industrial arts as it runs. The known evidence appears to warrant the generalisation that the state of the industrial arts is limited by the size of the industrial community, and that whenever a given community is broken up or suffers a serious diminution of numbers its technological heritage will deteriorate and dwindle even though it may apparently have been meagre enough before.

The considerations recited above are matters of commonplace observation and might fairly be taken for granted without argument. But so much of current and recent theoretical speculation proceeds on tacit assumptions at variance with these commonplaces that it seems pertinent to recall them, particularly since they will come in as premises in later passages of the inquiry.

Given the material environment, the rate and character of the technological gains made in any community will depend on the initiative and application of its members, in so far as the growth of institutions has not seriously diverted the genius of the race from its natural bent; it will depend immediately and obviously on individual talent for workmanship—on the workmanlike

[1] Cf., as an extreme case, Matilda C. Stevenson, "The Sia," *Report Bur. Eth.*, xi (1889–1890).

The like decline is known to have occurred in many parts of Europe consequent on the decline of population due to the Black Death and the Plague.

bent and capacity of the individual members of the community. Therefore any difference of native endowment in this respect between the several races will show itself in the character of their technological achievements as well as in the rate of gain. Races differ among themselves in this matter, both as to the kind and as to the degree of technological proficiency of which they are capable.[1] It is perhaps as needless to insist on this spiritual difference between the various racial stocks as it would be difficult to determine the specific differences that are known to exist, or to exhibit them convincingly in detail. To some such ground much of the distinctive character of different peoples is no doubt to be assigned, though much also may as well be traceable to local peculiarities of environment and of institutional circumstances. Something of the kind, a specific difference in the genius of the people, is by common consent assigned, for instance, in explanation of the pervasive difference in technology and workmanship between the Western culture and the Far East. The like difference in "genius" is still more convincingly shown where different races have long been living near one another under settled cultural conditions.[2]

It should be noted in the same connection that hybrid peoples, such as those of Europe or of Japan, where somewhat widely distinct racial stocks are mingled, should afford a great variety and wide individual varia-

[1] On such native differences between the leading races of Europe, cf., e. g., G. V. de Lapouge, *Les Sélections Sociales;* and *l'Aryen;* O. Ammon, *Die Gesellschaftsordnung;* G. Sergi, *Arii e Italici.*

[2] For instance, the Japanese and the Ainu, the Polynesians and the Melanesians, the Cinghalese and the Veddas. On the last named, cf. Seligmann, *The Veddas.*

tion of native gifts, in workmanship as in other respects. Hybrid stocks, indeed, have a wider range of usual variability than the combined extreme limits of the racial types that enter into the composition of the hybrid. So that a great variety, even aberration and eccentricity, of native gifts is to be looked for in such cases, and this wide range of variation in workmanlike initiative should show itself in the technology of any such peoples. Yet there may still prevail a strikingly determinate difference between any two such hybrid populations, both in the characteristic features of their technology and in their routine workmanship; as is illustrated in the contrast between Japan and the Western nations. These racial differences in point of endowment may be slight in the first instance, but as they work cumulatively their ulterior effect may still be very marked; and they may result in marked differences not only in respect of the character of the technological situation at a given point of time but also in the rate of advance and the direction taken by the technological advance. So in the case of the Far East, as contrasted with the Occidental peoples, the genius of the races engaged has prevailingly taken the direction of proficiency in handicraft, rather than that somewhat crude but efficient recourse to mechanical expedients which chiefly distinguishes the technology of the West.

The stability of racial types makes it possible to study the innate characters of the existing population under less complex and confusing circumstances than those of the cultural situation in which this population is now found. By going back into the earlier phases of the Western culture the scrutiny of the living population of Europe and its colonies can, in effect, be pushed back in a fragmentary way over an interval of some thousands of years. Such acquaintance as may in this way be gained with the spiritual makeup of the peoples of the Western culture at any point in its past history and prehistory should bear immediately and without serious abatement on the native character of the generation in whose hands the fortunes of that culture now rest; provided only that the inquiry assures itself of the racial continuity, racial identity, of these peoples through this period of time. This question of race identity is no longer a matter of serious debate so far as concerns the peoples of northern and western Europe, within the effective bounds of the Occidental civilisation and as far back as the beginning of the neolithic period. Assuredly there is debate and uncertainty as to local details of racial mixture in nearly all parts of this cultural area at some point in past time, but these uncertainties of detail are not of such a nature or such magnitude as to vitiate the data for an inquiry into the general characteristics of the races concerned. By and large, the mixture of races in north Europe has apparently not varied greatly since early neolithic times, and the changes that have taken place are known with some confidence, in the main. Much the same holds true for the Mediterranean seaboard, although the changes in that region appear to have been more considerable and are perhaps less readily traceable. For northern and western Europe taken together, in spite of considerable local fluctuations, the variations in the general racial composition of the peoples has, on the whole, not been extensive or extremely serious since the latter part of the stone age. The three great racial stocks[1] of Western civilisation have apparently shared their joint dominance in this culture among themselves since about the time when the use of bronze first came into Europe, which should be before the close of the stone age. And these three stocks are not greatly alien to one another; two of them, the Mediterranean and the blond, being apparently somewhat closely related in point of descent and therefore presumably in point of spiritual makeup.

It is with less confidence that any student of these modern cultures can test his case by evidence drawn from existing or historical communities living on the savage or lower barbarian plane and not closely related, racially, to the peoples of Western Europe. The discrepancies in such a case are of two kinds: (*a*) The racial type, and therefore the spiritual (instinctive) make-up of these alien savages or barbarians, is not the same as that of the modern Europeans; hence the culture worked out under the control of their somewhat different endowment of instincts should come to a different result, particularly since any such racial discrepancy in the matter of instincts should be expected to work cumulatively to a different cultural outcome. These alien communities of the lower cultures can therefore not be accepted off-hand as representing an earlier phase of Occidental civilisation. This infirmity attaches to any recourse to an existing savage or barbarian community

[1] Cf. W. Z. Ripley, *The Races of Europe;* G. Sergi, *The Mediterranean Race;* V. de Lapouge, *L'Aryen;* cf. also, J. Deniker, *Les races européennes*, and "Les six races composant la population de l'Europe," *Journal Anthropological Institute*, vol. 34.

for object-lessons to illustrate the working of European human nature in similarly primitive circumstances, in the degree in which the community in question may be remote from the Europeans in point of racial type; which reduces itself to a difficult question as to the point in the family-tree of the races of man from which the two contrasted races have diverged, and of the number, character, and magnitude of the racial mutations that may have intervened between the presumed point of divergence and the existing racial types so contrasted. (*b*) It is commonly said, and it is presumably true enough, that all known communities on the lower levels of culture are far from a state of primitive savagery; that they are not to be taken as genuinely archaic, but are the result either of a comparatively late reversion, under special circumstances, from a past higher stage, or they are peoples which have undergone so protracted an experience in savagery that their present state is one of extreme sophistification in all "the beastly devices of the heathen," rather than substantially an early or archaic type of culture, such as would have marked a transient stage in the development of those peoples that have attained civilised life.

No doubt there is some substance to these objections, but they contain rather a modicum of truth than an inclusive presentation of the facts relevant to the case. As to (*a*), the races of man are, after all, more alike than unlike, and the evidence drawn from the experience of any one racial stock or mixture is not to be disregarded as having no significance for the probable course of things experienced by any other racial stock during a corresponding interval in its life-history. Yet there is doubtless a wide and debatable margin of error to be allowed for in the use of all evidence of this class. As to (*b*), by virtue of the stability of racial types the populations of existing communities of the lower cultures should be today what they were at the outset, in respect of the most substantial factor in their present situation, their spiritual (instinctive) make-up; and this unaltered complement of instincts should, under similar circumstances and with a moderate allowance of time, work out substantially the same general run of cultural results whether the resulting phase of culture were reached by approach from a near and untroubled beginning or by regression from a "higher plane." So that the existing communities of savages or lower barbarians should present a passably competent object lesson in archaic savagery and barbarism whether their past has been higher, lower, or simply more of the same.

All this, of course, assumes the stability of racial types. But since, tacitly, that assumption is habitually made by ethnologists, all that calls for apology or explanation here is the avowal of it. The greater proportion of ethnological generalisations on this range of questions would be quite impotent without that assumption as their major premise. What has not commonly been assumed or admitted, except by subconscious implication, is the necessary corollary that these stable types with which ethnologists and anthropologists busy themselves must have arisen by mutation from previously existing types, rather than by a long continued and divergent accumulation of insensible variations. A result of avowing such a view of the genesis of races will be that the various races cannot be regarded as being all of the same date and racial maturity, or of the same significance for any discussion bearing on the higher cultures. The races engaged in the Western culture will presumably be found to be of relatively late date, as having arisen out of relatively late mutational departures, as rated in terms of the aggregate life-history of mankind. Presumably also many of the other races will be found to be somewhat widely out of touch with the members of this Occidental aggregation of racial stocks; some more, others less remotely related to them, according as their mutational pedigree may be found to indicate.

An advantage derivable from such an avowal of the stability of types, as against its covert assumption and overt disavowal, is that it enables the student to look for the beginning, in time and space, of any given racial stock with which his inquiry is concerned, and to handle it as a unit throughout its life-history.

In all probability each of the leading racial stocks of Europe began its life-history on what would currently be accounted a low level of savagery. And yet this phase of savagery, whatever it may have been like, will have been removed from the first beginnings of human culture by a long series of thousands of years. That such was the case, for instance, with the European blond is scarcely to be questioned;[1] and it is at least highly

[1] The available evidence indicates that the dolicho-blond race of northern Europe probably originated in a mutation (from the Mediterranean as its parent stock?) during the early neolithic period, that is to say about at the beginning of the neolithic in western Europe. There is less secure ground for conjecture as to the date and circumstances under which any one of the other European races originated, but the date and place of their origin seems to lie outside of Europe and earlier than the

probable that the other stocks now associated with the blond, though probably older, must also have come into being relatively late in the life-history of the species.

Vague as this dating may be, it signifies that the initial phase in the life-history of at least one, and presumably of all, of the leading races of Europe falls in a savage culture of a relatively advanced kind as compared with the rudest human beginnings. Therefore when these stocks began life, and so were required to make good their survival, the selective conditions imposed on them, and to which they were required to conform on pain of extinction, were the conditions of a savage culture which had already made some appreciable advance in the arts of life. They had not to meet brute nature in the helpless nakedness of those remote ancestors in whom humanity first began. Mutationally speaking, the stock was born to the use of tools and to the facile mastery of a relatively advanced technology. And conversely it is a fair inference that these stocks that have peopled Europe would have been unfit to survive if they had come into the world before some appreciable advance in technology had been made. That is to say, these stocks could not by native gift have been fit for a wild life, in the unqualified sense of the term; nor have they ever lived a life of nature in any such sense. They came into the savage world after the race had lived through many thousand years of technological experience and (presumably) many successive mutational alterations of racial type,

European neolithic period. Unfortunately there has been little direct or succinct discussion of this matter among anthropologists hitherto.—Cf. "The Mutation Theory and the Blond Race," *Journal of Race Development*, April, 1913.

and they were fitted to the exigencies of the savage world into which they came rather than those of any earlier phase of savagery. The youngest of them, the latest mutant, emerged in early neolithic times, and since he eminently made good his fitness to survive under those conditions he presumably emerged with such an endowment of traits, physical and spiritual, as those conditions called for; and also presumably with no appreciable burden of aptitudes, propensities, instincts, capacities that would be disserviceable, or perhaps even that would be wholly unserviceable, in the circumstances in which he was placed. And since the other racial elements of the European population, at least the two main ones, do not differ at all radically from the blond in their native capacities, it is likewise to be presumed that they also emerged from a mutation under circumstances of culture, and especially of technology, not radically different in degree from those that first surrounded the blond.

The difference between these three racial stocks is much more evident in their physical traits than in their instinctive gifts or their intellectual capacity; and yet the similarity of the three is so great and distinctive even on the physical side that anthropologists are inclined to class the three together as all and several distinctively typical of a "white" or "caucasic" race, to which they are held collectively to belong. Something to the like effect seems to hold true for the distinctive groups of racial stocks that have made the characteristic civilisations of the Far East on the one hand and of southern Asia on the other hand; and something similar might, again, be said for the group of stocks that were concerned in the ancient civilisations of America.

It may be pertinent to add that, except for a long antecedent growth of technology, that is to say a long continued cumulative experience in workmanship, with the resultant accumulated knowledge of the ways and means of life, none of the characteristic races of Europe could have survived. In the absence of these antecedent technological gains, together with the associated growth of institutions, such mutants, with their characteristic gifts and limitations, must have perished.

On that level of savagery on which these European stocks began, and to which the several European racial types with their typical endowment of instincts are presumably adapted, men appear to have lived a fairly peaceable, though by no means an indolent life; in relatively small groups or communities; without any of the more useful domestic animals, though probably with some domestic plants; and busied with getting their living by daily work. Since they survived under the conditions offered them it is to be presumed that these men and women, say of the early neolithic time, took instinctively and kindly to those activities and mutual relations that would further the life of the group; and that, on the whole, they took less kindly and instinctively to such activities as would bring damage and discomfort on their neighbours and themselves.[1] Any racial type of

[1] The Melanesians may be contrasted with the Baltic peoples in this respect, though the comparison is perhaps rather suggestive than convincing. The Melanesians are apparently endowed with a very respectable capacity for workmanship, as regards both insight and application, and with a relatively high sense of economic expediency. They are also possessed of an alert and enduring group solidarity. But they apparently lack that reasonable degree of "humanity" and congenital tolerance that

which this had not been true, under the conditions known then to have prevailed in their habitat, must have presently disappeared from the face of the land, and the later advance of the Western culture would not have known their breed. Some other racial type, temperamentally so constituted as better to meet these requirements of survival under neolithic conditions, would have taken their place and would have left their own offspring to populate the region.[1]

What is known of the conditions of life in early neolithic times[2] indicates that the first requisite of competitive survival was a more or less close attention to the

has on the whole kept the peoples of the Baltic region from fatal extravagances of cruelty and sustained hatred between groups. Not that any excess of humanity has marked the course of culture in North Europe. But it seems at least admissible to say that mutual hatred, distrust and disparagement falls more readily into abeyance among these peoples than among the Melanesians; particularly when and in so far as the material interest of the several groups visibly suffers from a continued free run of extravagant animosity. The difference in point of native propensity may not be very marked, but such degree of it as there is has apparently thrown the balance in such a way that the Baltic peoples have, technologically, had the advantage of a wide and relatively easy contact and communication; whereas the Melanesians have during an equally protracted experience spent themselves largely on interstitial animosities.—Cf. Codrington, *The Melanesians;* Seligmann, *The Melanesians of British New Guinea.*

[1] These considerations apparently apply with peculiar force to the blond race, in that the evidence of early times goes to argue that this stock never lived in isolation from other, rival stocks. It began presumably as a small minority in a community made up chiefly of a different racial type, its parent stock, and in an environment at large in which at least one rival stock was present in force from near the outset; so that race competition, that is to say competition in terms of births and deaths, was instant and unremitting. And this competition the given conditions enforced in terms of group subsistence.

[2] Cf., e. g., Sophus Müller, *Vor Oldtid,* "Stenalderen."

business in hand, the providing of subsistence for the group and the rearing of offspring—a closer attention, for instance, than was given to this business by those other rival stocks whom the successful ones displaced; all of which throws into the foreground as indispensable native traits of the successful race the parental bent and the sense of workmanship, rather than those instinctive traits that make for disturbance of the peace.[1]

But through it all the suggestion insinuates itself that the latest, or youngest, of the three main European stocks, the blond, has more rather than less of the pugnacious and predatory temper than the other two, and that this stock made its way to the front in spite of, if not by force of these traits. The advantage of the blond as a fighter seems to have been due in part to an adventurous and pugnacious temper, but also in part to a superior physique,—superior for the purpose of fighting hand to hand or with the implements chiefly used in warfare and piracy down to a date within the nineteenth century. The same physical traits of mass, stature and katabolism will likewise have been of great advantage in the quest of a livelihood under the conditions that prevailed in the North-sea region, the habitat of the dolicho-blond, in the stone age. Something to the same effect is true of the spiritual traits which are said to characterise the blond,—a certain canny temerity and unrest.[2] So that

[1] It has not commonly been noted, though it will scarcely be questioned, that fighting capacity and the propensity to fight have rarely, if ever, been successful in the struggle between races and peoples when brought into competition with a diligent growing of crops and children, if success be counted in terms of race survival.

[2] It is apparently an open question whether these spiritual traits are properly to be ascribed to the dolicho-blond as traits of that type taken

the point is left somewhat in doubt; the traits which presently made the northern blond the most formidable disturber of the peace of Europe and kept him so for many centuries may at the outset have been chiefly conducive to the survival of the type by their serviceability for industrial purposes under the peculiar circumstances of climate and topography in which the race first came up and made good its survival.

In modern speculations on the origins of culture and the early history of mankind it has until recently been usual to assume, uncritically, that human communities have from the outset of the race been entangled in an inextricable web of mutual hostilities and beset with an all-pervading sentiment of fear; that the "state of nature" was a state of blood and wounds, expressing itself in universal malevolence and suspicion. Latterly, students of primitive culture, and more especially those engaged at first hand in field work, who come in contact with peoples of the lower culture, have been coming to realise that the facts do not greatly support such a presumption, and that a community which has to make its own living by the help of a rudimentary technological equipment can not afford to be habitually occupied with annoying its neighbours, particularly so long as its neighbours have not accumulated a store of portable wealth which will make raiding worth while. No doubt, many savage and barbarian peoples live in a state of conven-

by itself, rather than traits characteristic of the hybrid offspring of the blond stock crossed on one or other of the racial stocks associated with it in the populations of Europe. The evidence at large seems rather to bear out the view that any hybrid population is likely to be endowed with an exceptional degree of that restlessness and discontent that go to make up what is spoken of as a "spirit of enterprise" in the race,

tional feud or habitual, even if intermittent, war and predation, without substantial inducement in the way of booty. But such communities commonly are either so placed that an easy livelihood affords them a material basis for following after these higher things out of mere fancy;[1] or they are peoples living precariously hand-to-mouth and fighting for their lives, in great part from a fancied impossibility of coming to terms with their alien and unnaturally cruel neighbours.[2] Communities of the latter class are often living in a state of squalor and discomfort, with a population far short of what their environment would best support even with their inefficient industrial organisation and equipment, and their technology is usually ill-suited to a settled life and unpromising for any possible advance to a higher culture. There is no urgent reason for assuming that the races which have made their way to a greater technological efficiency, with settled life and a large population, must have come up from this particular phase of civilisation as their starting point, or that such a culture should have been favourable to the survival and increase of the leading racial stocks of Europe, since it does not appear to be especially favourable to the success of the communities known to be now living after that fashion.[3]

The preconception that early culture must have been warlike has not yet disappeared even among students of these phenomena, though it is losing their respect; but a derivative of it still has much currency, to the effect

[1] As, e. g., the inhabitants of many Polynesian islands at the time of their discovery. See, also, Codrington, *The Melanesians*.

[2] Not an unusual state of things among the Melanesians and Micronesians, and in a degree among the Australians.

[3] See note, p. 120.

that all savage peoples, as also the peoples of the lower barbarism, live in a state of universal and unremitting fear, particularly fear of the unknown. This chronic fear is presumed to show itself chiefly in religion and other superstitious practices, where it is held to explain many things that are otherwise obscure. There is not a little evidence from extant savage communities looking in this direction, and more from the lower barbarian cultures that are characteristically warlike.[1] Wherever this animus is found its effect is to waste effort and divert it to religious and magical practices and so to hinder the free unfolding of workmanship by enjoining a cumbersome routine of ritual and by warning the technologist off forbidden ground. But it is doubtless a hasty generalisation to carry all this over uncritically and make it apply to all peoples of the lower culture, past and present. It is known not to be true of many existing communities,[2] and the evidence of it in some ancient cultures is very dubious. Such a characterisation of the neolithic culture of Europe, whether north-European or Ægean, finds no appreciable support in the archæological evidence. These two regions are the most significant for the neolithic period in Europe, and the material from both is relatively very poor in weapons, as contrasted with tools, on the one hand, and there is at the same time little or nothing to indicate the prevalence of superstitious practices based on fear. Indeed, the material is surprisingly poor in elements of any kind that can safely be set down to the account of religion or magic, whether as inspired by fear or by more genial sentiments. It is one

[1] E. g., some Australian natives and some of the lower Malay cultures.
[2] E. g., the Pueblo and the Eskimo.

of the puzzles that beset any student who insists on finding everywhere a certain normal course of cultural sequence, which should in the early times include, among other things, a fearsome religion, a wide fabric of magical practices, and an irrepressible craving for manslaughter. And when, presently, something of a symbolism and apparatus of superstition comes into view, in the late neolithic and bronze ages, the common run of it is by no means suggestive of superstitious fear and religious atrocities. The most common and characteristic objects of this class are certain figurines and certain symbolical elements suggestive of fecundity, such as might be looked for in a peaceable, sedentary, agricultural culture on a small scale.[1] A culture virtually without weapons, whose gods are mothers and whose religious observances are a ritual of fecundity, can scarcely be a culture of dread and of derring-do. With the fighting barbarians, on the other hand, male deities commonly take the first rank, and their ritual symbolises the mastery of the god and the servitude of the worshipper.

It is true, of course, that both of weapons and of cult objects far the greater number that were once in use will have disappeared, since most of the implements and utensils of stone-age cultures are, notoriously, made of wood or similar perishable materials.[2] So that the finds

[1] Indeed, such as very suggestively to recall the ritual objects and observances of the Pueblo Indians.

[2] For an extreme case of this among living communities, see Skeat and Blagden, *Pagan Races of the Malay Peninsula*, vol. i, pp. 242–250, where the generalisation is set down (p. 248) that "the rudimentary stage of culture through which these tribes have passed, and in some cases are still passing, may perhaps be more accurately described as a wood and bone age than as an age of stone," in as much as the evidence goes to show that

give no complete series of the appliances in use in their time; whole series of objects that were of first-rate importance in that culture having probably disappeared without leaving a trace. But what is true in this respect of weapons and cult objects should be equally true of tools, or nearly so. So that the inference to be drawn from the available material would be that the early neolithic culture of north Europe, the Ægean, and other explored localities presumed to belong in the same racial and cultural complex, must have been of a prevailingly peaceable complexion. With the advance in technology and in the elaboration and abundance of objects that comes into sight progressively through the later neolithic period, down to its close, this disproportion between tools and weapons (and cult objects) grows more impressive and more surprising. Hitherto this disproportion has been more in evidence in the Scandinavian finds than in the other related fields of stone-age culture, unless an exception should be made in favour of the late neolithic sites explored at Anau.[1] But this archæological outcome, setting off the Baltic stone age as peculiarly scant of weapons and peculiarly rich in tools, may be provisional only, and may be due to the more exhaustive exploration of the Scandinavian countries and the uncommonly abundant material from that region. In the later (mainly Scandinavian) neolithic material, where

before they began to get metals from the Malays their only implements of a more durable material were "the anvil and hammer (unwrought) . . ., the whetstone, chips or flakes used as knives, and cooking stones." From the different character of their environment this recourse to wood and bone could scarcely have been carried to such an extreme by the savages of the Baltic region.

[1] Cf. Pumpelly, *Explorations in Turkestan*.

the weapons are to be counted by dozens the tools are to be counted by hundreds, according to a scheme of classification in which everything that can be construed as a weapon is so classed, and there are many more hundreds of the one class than there are dozens of the other.[1] As near as can be made out, cult objects are similarly infrequent among these materials even after some appreciable work in pottery comes in evidence.

What has just been said is after all of a negative character. It says that nothing like a warlike, predatory, or fearsome origin can be proven from the archæological material for the neolithic culture of those racial stocks that have counted for most in the early periods of Europe. The presumption raised by this evidence, however, is fairly strong. And considerations of the material circumstances in which this early culture was placed, as well as of the spiritual traits characteristically required by these circumstances and shown by the races in question, point to a similar conclusion. The proclivity to unreasoning fear that is visible in the superstitious practices of so many savage communities and counts for so much in the routine of their daily life,[2] is to all appearance not so considerable an element in the make-up of the chief European stocks. Perhaps it enters in a less degree in the spiritual nature of the European blond

[1] A casual visit to the Scandinavian museums will scarcely convey this impression. To meet the prepossessions of the public, and perhaps of the experts, the weapons are made much of in the showcases, as is to be expected; but they are relatively scarce in the store-rooms, where the tools on the other hand are rather to be estimated by the cubic yard than counted by the piece.

[2] Seen, e. g., in the observance and sanction of tabu in many of the lower cultures.

than in that of any other race; that race—or its hybrid offspring—has at any rate proved less amenable to religious control than any other, and has also shown less hesitation in the face of unknown contingencies. And the circumstances of the presumed initial phase of the life-history of this race would appear not to have favoured a spiritual (instinctive) type largely biassed by an alert and powerful sentiment of unreasoning fear. So also an aggressive humanitarian sentiment is as well at home in the habits of thought of the north-European peoples as in any other, such as sorts ill with a native predatory animus. If it be assumed, as seems probable, that the situation which selectively tested the fitness of this stock to survive was that of the early post-glacial time, when its habitat in Europe was slowly being cleared of the ice-sheet, it would appear antecedently probable that the new (mutant) type, which made good its survival in following up the retreating fringe of the ice-sheet and populating the land so made available, will not have been a people peculiarly given to fear or to predation. A great facility of this kind, with its concomitants of caution, conservatism, suspicion and cruelty, would not be serviceable for a race so placed.[1]

Even if it were a possible undertaking it would not be much to the present purpose to trace out in detail the

[1] The Eskimo are placed in circumstances that are in some respects similar to those presumed to have conditioned the life of the blond race and its hybrids during the early phases of its life-history, and among the traits that have made for the survival of the Eskimo is undoubtedly to be counted the somewhat genial good-fellowship of that race, coupled as it is with a notable disinclination to hostilities. So also the Indians of the North-West Coast, whose situation perhaps parallels that of the

many slow and fumbling moves by which any given race or people, in Europe or elsewhere, have worked out the technological particulars that have led from the beginnings down through the primitive and later growth of culture. Such a work belongs to the ethnologists and archæologists; and it is summed up in the proposition that men have applied common sense, more or less hesitatingly and with more or less refractory limitations, to the facts with which they have had to deal; that they have accumulated a knowledge of technological expedients and processes from generation to generation, always going on what had already been achieved in ways and means, and gradually discarding or losing such elements of the growing technological scheme as seemed no longer to be worth while,[1] and carrying along a good many

neolithic Baltic culture more closely even than the Eskimo, are not among the notably warlike peoples of the earth, although they undoubtedly show more of a predatory animus than their northern neighbours. In this case it is probably safe to say that their technological achievements have in no degree been furthered by such warlike enterprise as they have shown, and that their comfort and success as a race would have been even more marked if they had been gifted with less of the warlike spirit and had kept the peace more consistently throughout their habitat than they have done.—Cf. Franz Boas, "The Central Eskimo," *Bureau of American Ethnology*, Report, 1884–1885; The same, "The Secret Societies and Social Organisation of the Kwakiutl Indians," *Report, National Museum*, 1895; A. P. Niblack, "Coast Indians of Southern Alaska and Northern British Columbia," *ibid*, 1888.

[1] Such loss by neglect of technological elements that have been superseded may have serious consequences in case a people of somewhat advanced attainments suffers a material set-back either in its industrial circumstances or in its cultural situation more at large,—as happened, e. g., in the Dark Ages of Europe. In such case it is likely to result that the community will be unable to fall back on a state of the industrial arts suited to the reduced circumstances into which it finds itself thrown, having lost the use of many of the technological elements familiar to

elements that were of no material effect but were imposed by the logic of the scheme or of its underlying principles (habits of thought).

Of the early technological development in Europe, so far as it is genetically connected with the later Western civilisation, the culture of the Baltic region affords as good and illustrative an object lesson as may be had; its course is relatively well known, simple and unbroken. Palæolithic times do not count in this development, as the neolithic culture begins with a new break in Europe.

It is known, then, that by early neolithic times on the narrow Scandinavian waters men had learned to make and use certain rude stone and bone implements found in the kitchen-middens (refuse heaps, shell-mounds of Denmark), that they had ways and appliances (the nature of which is not known) for collecting certain shell-fish and for catching such game and fish as their habitat afforded, and that they presently, if not from the outset, had acquired the use of certain crop plants and had learned to make pottery of a crude kind. From this as a point of departure in the period of the kitchen-middens the stone implements were presently improved and multiplied, the methods of working the material (flint) and of using the products of the flint industry were gradually improved and extended, until in the long course of time

earlier generations that lived under similar circumstances, and so the industrial community finds itself in many respects driven to make a virtually new beginning, from a more rudimentary starting point than the situation might otherwise call for. This in turn acts to throw the people back to a more archaic phase of technology and of institutions than the initial cultural loss sustained by the community would of itself appear to warrant.

the utmost that has anywhere been achieved in that class of industry was reached. Domestic animals began to be added to the equipment relatively early,[1] though at a long interval from the neolithic beginnings as counted in absolute time. Improvement and extension in all lines of stone-working and wood-working industry went forward: except that stone-dressing and masonry are typically absent, owing, no doubt, to the extensive use of woodwork instead.[2] Along with this advance in the mechanic arts goes a growing density of population and a wide extension of tillage; until, at the coming of bronze, the evidence shows that these communities were populous, prosperous, and highly skilled in those industrial arts that lay within their technological range.

Apart from the pottery, which may have some merit as an art product, there is very little left to show what may have been their proficiency in the decorative arts, or what was their social organisation or their religious life. The evidences of warlike enterprise and religious practices are surprisingly scanty, being chiefly the doubtful evidence of many and somewhat elaborate tombs. From the tombs (mounds and barrows) and their distribution something may be inferred as to the social organisation; and the evidence on this head seems to indicate a widespread agricultural population, living (probably) in small communities, without much centralised or authoritative control, but with some appre-

[1] Sophus Müller, *Vor Oldtid*, "Stenalderen," sec. iii, "Tidsforhold i den ældre Stenalder;" O. Montelius, *Les temps préhistoriques en Suède*, ch. i, p. 20.

[2] Compare the case of the Indians of the North-West Coast, who have occupied a region comparable to the neolithic Baltic area in the distribution of land and water as well as in the abundance of good timber.

ciable class differences in the distribution of wealth in the later phases of the period.

With interruptions, more or less serious, from time to time, and with increasing evidence of a penchant for warlike or predatory enterprise on the one hand and of class distinctions on the other hand, much the same story runs on through the ages of bronze and early iron. Evidences of borrowing from outside, mainly the borrowing of decorative technique and technological elements, are scattered through the course of this development from very early times, showing that there was always some intercourse, perhaps constant intercourse, with other peoples more or less distant. So that in time, by the beginning of the bronze age, there is evidence of settled trade relations with peoples as remote as the Mediterranean seaboard.

In many of its details this prehistoric culture shows something of the same facility in the use of mechanical expedients as has come so notably forward again in the late development of the industrial arts of western Europe. It is in its mechanical efficiency that the technology of the latterday Western culture stands out preëminent, and it is similarly its easy command of the mechanical factors with which it deals that chiefly distinguishes the prehistoric technology of North Europe. In other respects the prehistoric material from this region does not argue a high level of civilisation. There are no ornate or stupendous structures; what there is of the kind is mounds and barrows of moderately great size and using only undressed stone where any is used, but making a mechanically effective use of this. There is, indeed, nothing from the stone age in the way of edifices, fabrics or decorative work that is to be classed, in point of excellence in design or execution, with the polished-flint woodworking axe or chisel of that time. From the bronze age at its best there is much excellent bronze work of great merit both in workmanship and in decorative effect; but the artistic merit of this work (from the middle and early half of the bronze age) lies almost wholly in its workmanlike execution and in the freedom and adequacy with which very simple mechanical elements of decoration are employed. It is an art which appeals to the sense of beauty chiefly through the sense of workmanship, shown both in the choice of materials and decorative elements and in the use made of them. When this art aspires to more ambitious decorative effects or to representation of life forms, or indeed to any representation that has not been conventionalised almost past recognition, as it does in the later periods of of the bronze age, the result is that it can be commended for its workmanship alone, and so far as regards artistic effect it is mainly misspent workmanship.[1]

The same workmanlike insight and facility comes in evidence in the matter of borrowing, already spoken of. Borrowing goes on throughout this prehistoric culture, and the borrowed elements are assimilated with such despatch and effect as to make them seem home-bred almost from the start. It is a borrowing of technological elements, which are rarely employed except in full and competent adaptation to the uses to which they are turned; so much so that the archæologists find it exceptionally difficult to trace the borrowed elements to specific

[1] Sophus Müller, *Vor Oldtid*, "Bronzealderen," secs. xiii, xiv; Montelius, *Les temps préhistoriques en Suède*, ch. ii.

sources, in spite of the great volume and frequency of this borrowing.

There is a further and obscurer aspect to this facile borrowing. In the cultures where the technological and decorative elements are first invented, or acquired at first-hand by slow habituation, there will in the nature of the case come in with them into the scheme of technology or of art more or less, but presumably a good deal, of extraneous or extrinsic by-products of their acquirement, in the way of magical or symbolic efficacy imputed and adhering to them in the habits of thought of their makers and users. Something of this kind has already been set out in some detail as regards the domestication and early use of the crop plants and animals; and the like is currently held to be true, perhaps in a higher degree, for the beginnings of art, both representative and decorative, by the latterday students of that subject; the beginnings of art being held to have been magical and symbolic in the main, so far as regards the prime motives to its inception and its initial principles.[1]

In the origination and indigenous working-out of any given technological factor, e. g., such as the use of the crop plants or the domestic animals, elements of imputed anthropomorphism are likely to be comprised in the habitual apprehension of the nature of these factors, and so find lodgment in the technological routine that has to do with them; the result being, chiefly, a limitation on their uses and on the ways and means by which they are utilised, together with a margin of lost motion in the way of magical and religious observances presumed to

[1] Cf., e. g., C. A. Haddon, *Evolution in Art*, section on "Magic and Religion."

be intrinsic to the due working of such factors. The ritual connected with tillage and cattle-breeding shows this magical side of a home-bred technology perhaps as felicitously as anything; but similar phenomena are by no means infrequent in the mechanic arts, and in the fine arts these principles of symbolism and the like are commonly present in such force as to afford ground for distinguishing one school or epoch of art from another.

Now, when any given technological or decorative element crosses the frontier between one culture and another, in the course of borrowing, it is likely to happen that it will come into the new culture stripped of most or all of its anthropomorphic or spiritual virtues and limitations, more particularly, of course, if the cultural frontier in question is at the same time a linguistic frontier; since the borrowing is likely to be made from motives of workmanlike expediency, and the putative spiritual attributes of the facts involved are not obvious to men who have not been trained to impute them. The chief exception to such a rule would be any borrowing that takes effect on religious grounds, in which case, of course, the magical or symbolic efficacy of the borrowed elements are the substance that is sought in the borrowing. Herein, presumably, lies much of the distinctive character of the north-European prehistoric culture, which was in an eminent degree built up out of borrowed elements, so far as concerns both its technology and its art. And to this free and voluminous borrowing may likewise be due the apparent poverty of this early culture in religious or magical elements.

A further effect follows. The borrowing being (relatively) unencumbered with ritual restrictions and magical exactions attached to their employment, they would fall into the scheme of things as mere matter-of-fact, to be handled with the same freedom and unhindered sagacity with which a workman makes use of his own hands, and could, without reservation, be turned to any use for which they were mechanically suited. Something of symbolism and superstition might, of course, be carried over in the borrowing, and something more would unavoidably be bred into the borrowed elements in the course of their use; but the free start would always count for something in the outcome, both as regards the rate of progress made in the exploitation of the expedients acquired by borrowing and in the character of the technological system at large into which they had been introduced. Both the relative freedom from magical restraint and the growth of home-made anthropomorphic imputations may easily be detected in the course of this northern culture and in its outcome in modern times. Cattle, for instance, are a borrowed technological fact in the Baltic and North-Sea region, but superstitious practices seem never to have attached to cattle-breeding in that region in such volume and rigorous exaction as may be found nearer the original home of the domesticated species; and yet the volume of folk-lore, mostly of a genial and relatively unobstructive character, that has in later times grown up about the care of cattle in the Scandinavian countries is by no means inconsiderable.

CHAPTER IV

The Technology of the Predatory Culture

The scheme of technological insight and proficiency current in any given culture is manifestly a product of group life and is held as a common stock, and as manifestly the individual workman is helpless without access to it. It is none too broad to say that he is a workman only because and so far as he effectually shares in this common stock of technological equipment. He may be gifted in a special degree with workmanlike aptitudes, may by nature be stout or dextrous or keen-sighted or quick-witted or sagacious or industrious beyond his fellows; but with all these gifts, so long as he has assimilated none of this common stock of workmanlike knowledge he remains simply an admirable parcel of human raw material; he is of no effect in industry. With such special gifts or with special training based on this common stock an individual may stand out among his fellows as a workman of exceptional merit and value, and without the common run of workmanlike aptitudes he may come to nothing worth while as a workman even with the largest opportunities and most sedulous training. It is the two together that make the working force of the community; and in both respects, both in his inherited and in his acquired traits, the individual is a product of group life.

Using the term in a sufficiently free sense, pedigree is

no less and no more requisite to the workman's effectual equipment than the common stock of technological mastery which the community offers him. But his pedigree is a group pedigree, just as his technology is a group technology. As is sometimes said to the same effect, the individual is a creature of heredity and circumstances. And heredity is always group heredity,[1] perhaps peculiarly so in the human species.

The promptings of invidious self-respect commonly lead men to evade or deny something of the breadth of their inheritance in respect of human nature. "I am not as the publican yonder," whether I have the grace to thank God for this invidious distinction or more simply charge it to the account of my reputable ancestors in the male line. With a change of venue by which the cause is taken out of the jurisdiction of interested parties, its complexion changes. So evident is the fact of group heredity in the lower animals, for instance, that biologists have no inclination to deny its pervading force, apart from any conceivably parthenogenetic lines of descent,—and, to the inconvenience of the eugenic pharisee, parthenogenetic descent never runs in the male line, besides being of extremely rare occurrence in the human species. As a matter of course the Darwinian biologists have the habit of appealing to group heredity as the main factor in the stability of species, and they are very curious about the special circumstances of any given case in which it may appear not to be fully operative: and they have, on the other hand, even looked hopefully to fortuitous isolation of particular lines of descent as a possible factor in the differentiation and fixation of

[1] Except for species that habitually breed by parthenogenesis.

specific types, being at a loss to account for such differentiation or fixation so long as no insuperable mechanical obstacle stands in the way of persistent crossing. The like force of group heredity is visible in the characteristic differences of race. The heredity of any given race of mankind is always sufficiently homogeneous to allow all its individuals to be classed under the race. And when an individual comes to light in a fairly pure-bred community who shows physical traits that vary obviously from the common racial type of the community, the question which suggests itself to the anthropologists is not, How does this individual differ from others of the same breed? but, What is the alien strain, and how has it come in? And what is true of the physical characters of the race in this respect is only less obviously true of its spiritual traits.

In a culture where all individuals are hybrids, in point of pedigree, as is the case with all the leading peoples of Christendom, the ways of this group heredity are particularly devious, and the fortunes of the individual in this respect are in a peculiar degree exposed to the caprice of Mendelian contingencies; so that his make-up, physical and spiritual, is, humanly speaking, in the main a chapter of accidents. Where each individual draws for his hereditary traits on a wide ancestry of unstable hybrids, as all civilised men do, his chances are always those of the common lot, with some slight antecedent probability of his resembling the nearer ones among his variegated ancestry. But he has also and everywhere in this hybrid panmixis an excellent chance of being allotted something more accentuated, for good or ill, in the way of hereditary traits than anything shown by his varied assortment of ancestors. It commonly happens in such a hybrid community that in the new crossing of hybrids that takes place at every marriage, some new idiosyncracy, slight or considerable, comes to light in the offspring, beyond anything visible in the parents or the remoter pedigree; for in the crossing of what may be called multiple-hybrid parents, complementary characters that may have been dormant or recessive in the parents will come in from both sides, combine, re-enforce one another, and cumulatively give an unlooked-for result. So that in a hybrid community the fortunes of all individuals are somewhat precarious in respect of heredity.

Such are the conditions which have prevailed among the peoples of Europe since the first beginnings of that culture that has led up to the Western civilisation as known to history. In these circumstances any individual, therefore, owes to the group not only his share of that certain typical complement of traits that characterise the common run, but usually something more than is coming to him in the way of individual qualities and infirmities if he is in any way distinguishable from the common run, as well as a blind chance of transmitting almost any traits that he is not possessed of.[1]

In the lower cultures, where the division of labour is slight and the diversity of occupations is mainly such as marks the changes of the seasons, the common stock of technological knowledge and proficiency is not so extensive or so recondite but that the common man may

[1] The caution is perhaps unnecessary that it is not hereby intended to suggest a doubt of Mr. Galton's researches or to question the proposals of the Eugenicals, whose labours are no doubt to be taken for all they are worth.

compass it in some fashion, and in its essentials it is accessible to all members of the community by common notoriety, and the training required by the state of the industrial arts comes to everyone as a matter of course in the routine of daily life. The necessary material equipment of tools and appliances is slight and the acquisition of it is a simple matter that also arranges itself as an incident in the routine of daily life. Given the common run of aptitude for the industrial pursuits incumbent on the members of such a community, the material equipment needful to find a livelihood or to put forth the ordinary productive effort and turn out the ordinary industrial output can be compassed without strain by any individual in the course of his work as he goes along. The material equipment, the tools, implements, contrivances necessary and conducive to productive industry, is incidental to the day's work; in much the same way but in a more unqualified degree than the like is true as to the technological knowledge and skill required to make use of this equipment.[1]

As determined by the state of the industrial arts in such a culture, the members of the community co-operate in much of their work, to the common gain and to no one's detriment, since there is substantially no individual, or private, gain to be sought. There is substantially no bartering or hiring, though there is a recognised obligation in all members to lend a hand; and there is of course no price, as there is no property and no ownership, for the sufficient reason that the habits of life under these

[1] See, e. g., Skeat and Blagden, *Pagan Races of the Malay Peninsula*, vol. ii, part ii; *Report, Bureau of American Ethnology*, 1884–1885, F. Boas, "The Central Eskimo."

circumstances do not provoke such a habit of thought. Doubtless, it is a matter of course that articles of use and adornment pertain to their makers or users in an intimate and personal way; which will come to be construed into ownership when in the experience of the community an occasion for such a concept as ownership arises and persists in sufficient force to shape the current habits of thought to that effect. There is also more or less of reciprocal service and assistance, with a sufficient sense of mutuality to establish a customary scheme of claims and obligations in that respect. So also it is true that such a community holds certain lands and customary usufructs and that any trespass on these customary holdings is resented. But it would be a vicious misapprehension to read ideas and rights of ownership into these practices, although where civilised men have come to deal with instances of the kind they have commonly been unable to put any other construction on the customs governing the case; for the reason that civilised men's relations with these peoples of the lower culture have been of a pecuniary kind and for a pecuniary purpose, and they have brought no other than pecuniary conceptions from home.[1] There being little in hand worth owning and little purpose to be served by its ownership, the habits of thought which go to make the institution of ownership and property rights have not taken shape. The slight facts which would lend themselves to ownership are not of sufficient magnitude or urgency to call the institution into effect and are better handled under customs which do not yet take cognisance of property

[1] Cf. Basil Thomson, *The Diversions of a Prime Minister*, and *The Figians*.

rights. Naturally, in such a cultural situation there is no appreciable accumulation of wealth and no inducement to it; the nearest approach being an accumulation of trinkets and personal belongings, among which should, at least in some cases, be included certain weapons and perhaps tools.[1] These things belong to their owner or bearer in much the same sense as his name, which was not held on tenure of ownership or as a pecuniary asset before the use of trade-marks and merchantable good-will.

The workman—more typically perhaps the work-woman—in such a culture, as indeed in any other, is a "productive agent" in the manner and degree determined by the state of the industrial arts. What is obvious in this respect here holds only less visibly for any other, more complicated and technologically full-charged cultural situation, such as has come on with the growth of population and wealth among the more advanced peoples. He or she, or rather they—for there is substantially no industry carried on in strict severalty in these communities—are productive factors or industrial agents, in the sense that they will on occasion turn out a surplus above their necessary current consumption, only because and so far as the state of the industrial arts enables them to do so. As workman, labourer, producer, breadwinner, the individual is a creature of the technological scheme; which in turn is a creation of the group life of the community. Apart from the common stock

[1] The extent of this "quasi-personal fringe" of objects of intimate use varies considerably from one culture to another. It may often be inferred from the range of articles buried or destroyed with the dead among peoples on this level of culture.

of knowledge and training the individual members of the community have no industrial effect. Indeed, except by grace of this common technological equipment no individual and no family group in any of the known communities of mankind could support their own life; for in the long course of mankind's life-history, since the human plane was first reached, the early mutants which were fit to survive in a ferine state without tools and without technology have selectively disappeared, as being unfit to survive under the conditions of domesticity imposed by so highly developed a state of the industrial arts as any of the savage cultures now extant.[1] The *Homo Javensis* and his like are gone, because there is technologically no place for them between the anthropoids to the one side and the extant types of man on the other. And never since the brave days when *Homo Javensis* took up the "white man's burden" for the better regulation of his anthropoid neighbours has the technological scheme admitted of any individual's carrying on his life in severalty. So that industrial efficiency, whether of an individual workman or of the community at large, is a function of the state of the industrial arts.[2]

[1] A doubt may suggest itself in this connection touching such cultures and peoples as the pagan races of the Malay peninsula, the Mincopies of the Andaman Islands, or (possibly) the Negritos of Luzon, but these conceivable exceptions to the rule evidently do not lessen its force.

[2] It may be pertinent to take note of the bearing of these considerations on certain dogmatic concepts that have played a part in the theoretical and controversial speculations of the last century. Much importance has been given by economists of one school and another to the "productivity of labour," particularly as affording a basis for a just and equitable distribution of the product; one school of controversialists having gone so far against the current of received economic doctrine as to allege that labour is the sole productive factor in industry and that the Labourer is on

The simple and obvious industrial system of this archaic plan leaves the individuals, or rather the domestic groups, that make up the community, economically independent of one another and of the community at large, except that they depend on the common technological stock for the immaterial equipment by means of which to get their living. This is of course not felt by them as a relation of dependence; though there seems commonly to be some sense of indebtedness on part of the young, and of responsibility on part of the older generation, for the proper transmission of the recognised elements of technological proficiency. It is impossible to say just at what point in the growth and complication of technology this simple industrial scheme will begin to give way to new exigencies and give occasion to a new scheme of institutions governing the economic relations of men; such that the men's powers and functions in the industrial community come to be decided on other grounds than workmanlike aptitude and special training. In the nature of things there can be no hard and fast limit to this phase of industrial organisation. Its dis-

this ground entitled, in equity, to "the full product of his labor." It is of course not conceived that the considerations here set forth will dispose of these doctrinal contentions; but they make it at least appear that the productivity of labor, or of any other conceivable factor in industry, is an imputed productivity—imputed on grounds of convention afforded by institutions that have grown up in the course of technological development and that have consequently only such validity as attaches to habits of thought induced by any given phase of collective life. These habits of thought (institutions and principles) are themselves the indirect product of the technological scheme. The controversy as to the productivity of labor should accordingly shift its ground from "the nature of things" to the exigencies of ingrained preconceptions, principles and expediencies as seen in the light of current technological requirements and the current drift of habituation.

appearance or supersession in any culture appears always to have been brought on by the growth of property, but the institution of property need by no means come in abruptly at any determinate juncture in the sequence of technological development. So that this archaic phase of culture in which industry is organised on the ground of workmanship alone may come very extensively to overlap and blend with the succeeding phase in which property relations chiefly decide the details of the industrial organisation,—as is shown in varying detail by the known lower cultures.

The forces which may bring about such a transition are often complex and recondite, and they are seldom just the same in any given two instances. Neither the material situation nor the human raw material involved are precisely the same in all or several instances, and there is no coercively normal course of things that will constrain the growth of institutions to take a particular typical form or to follow a particular typical sequence in all cases. Yet, in a general way such a supersession of free workmanship by a pecuniary control of industry appears to have been necessarily involved in any considerable growth of culture. Indeed, at least in the economic respect, it appears to have been the most universal and most radical mutation which human culture has undergone in its advance from savagery to civilisation; and the causes of it should be of a similarly universal and intrinsic character.

It may be taken as a generalisation grounded in the instinctive endowment of mankind that the human sense of workmanship will unavoidably go on turning to account what there is in hand of technological knowledge, and so will in the course of time, by insensible gains perhaps, gradually change the technological scheme, and therefore also the scheme of customary canons of conduct answering to it; and in the absence of overmastering circumstances this sequence of change must, in a general way, set in the direction of great technological mastery. Something in the way of an "advance" in workmanlike mastery is to be looked for, in the absence of inexorable limitations of environment. The limitations may be set by the material circumstances or by circumstances of the institutional situation, but on the lower levels of culture the insurmountable obstacles to such an advance appear to have been those imposed by the material circumstances; although institutional factors have doubtless greatly retarded the advance in most cases, and may well have defeated it in many. In some of the known lower cultures such an impassable conjuncture in the affairs of technology has apparently been reached now and again, resulting in a "stationary state" of the industrial arts and of social arrangements, economic and otherwise. Such an instance of "arrested development" is afforded by the Eskimo, who have to all appearance reached the bounds of technological mastery possible in the material circumstances in which they have been placed and with the technological antecedents which they have had to go on. At the other extreme of the American continent the Fuegians and Patagonians may similarly have reached at least a provisional limit of the same nature; though such a statement is less secure in their case, owing to the scant and fragmentary character of the available evidence. So also the Bushmen, the Ainu, various representative communities of the Negrito and perhaps of the Dravidian stocks, appear to have reached a provisional limit—barring intervention from without. In these latter instances the decisive obstacles, if they are to be accepted as such, seem to lie in the human-nature of the case rather than in the material circumstances. In these latter instances the sense of workmanship, though visibly alert and active, appears to have been inadequate to carry out the technological scheme into further new ramifications for want of the requisite intellectual aptitudes,—a failure of aptitudes not in degree but in kind.

The manner in which increasing technological mastery has led over from the savage plan of free workmanship to the barbarian system of industry under pecuniary control is perhaps a hazardous topic of speculation; but the known facts of primitive culture appear to admit at least a few general propositions of a broad and provisional character. It seems reasonably safe to say that the archaic savage plan of free workmanship will commonly have persisted through the palæolithic period of technology, and indeed somewhat beyond the transition to the neolithic. This is fairly borne out by the contemporary evidence from savage cultures. In the prehistory of the north-European culture there is also reason to assume that the beginnings of a pecuniary control fall in the early half of the neolithic period.[1] There seems to be no sharply definable point in the technological advance that can be said of itself to bring on this revolutionary change in the institutions governing economic life. It appears to be loosely correlated with techno-

[1] See Sophus Müller, *Vor Oldtid*, "Stenalderen," and *Aarböger for nordisk Oldkyndighed*, 1906.

logical improvement, so that it sets in when a sufficient ground for it is afforded by the state of the industrial arts, but what constitutes a sufficient ground can apparently not be stated in terms of the industrial arts alone. Among the early consequences of an advance in technology beyond the state of the industrial arts sche matically indicated above, and coinciding roughly with the palæolithic stage, is on the one hand an appreciable resort to "indirect methods of production", involving a systematic cultivation of the soil, domestication of plants and animals; or an appreciable equipment of industrial appliances, such as will in either case require a deliberate expenditure of labour and will give the holders of the equipment something more than a momentary advantage in the quest of a livelihood. On the other hand it leads also to an accumulation of wealth beyond the current necessaries of subsistence and beyond that slight parcel of personal effects that have no value to anyone but their savage bearer.

Hereby the technological basis for a pecuniary control of industry is given, in that the "roundabout process of production" yields an income above the subsistence of the workmen engaged in it, and the material equipment of appliances (crops, fruit-trees, live stock, mechanical contrivances) binds this roundabout process of industry to a more or less determinate place and routine, such as to make surveillance and control possible. So far as the workman under the new phase of technology is dependent for his living on the apparatus and the orderly sequence of the "roundabout process" his work may be controlled and the surplus yielded by his industry may be turned to account; it becomes worth while to own the material means of industry, and ownership of the material means in such a situation carries with it the usufruct of the community's immaterial equipment of technological proficiency.

The substantial fact upon which the strategy of ownership converges is this usufruct of the industrial arts, and the tangible items of property to which the claims of ownership come to attach will accordingly vary from time to time, according as the state of the industrial arts will best afford an effectual exploitation of this usufruct through the tenure of one or another of the material items requisite to the pursuit of industry. The chief subject of ownership may accordingly be the cultivated trees, as in some of the South Sea islands; or the tillable land, as happens in many of the agricultural communities; or fish weirs and their location, as on some of the salmon streams of the American north-west coast; or domestic animals, as is typical of the pastoral culture; or it may be the persons of the workmen, as happens under divers circumstances both in pastoral and in agricultural communities; or, with an advance in technology of such a nature as to place the mechanical appliances of industry in a peculiarly advantageous position for engrossing the roundabout processes of production, as in the latterday machine industry, these mechanical appliances may become the typical category of industrial wealth and so come to be accounted "productive goods" in some eminent sense.

The institutional change by which a pecuniary regulation of industry comes into effect may take one form or another, but its outcome has commonly been some form of ownership of tangible goods. Particularly has that been the outcome in the course of development that has led on to those great pecuniary cultures of which Occidental civilisation is the most perfect example. But just in what form the move will be made, if at all, from free workmanship to pecuniary industry and ownership, is in good part a question of what the material situation of the community will permit. In some instances the circumstances have apparently not permitted the move to be made at all. The Eskimo culture is perhaps an extreme case of this kind. The state of the industrial arts among them has apparently gone appreciably beyond the technological juncture indicated above as critical in this respect. It involves a considerable specialisation and accumulation of appliances, such as boats, sleds, dogs, harness, various special forms of nets harpoons and spears, and an elaborate line of minor apparatus necessary to the day's work and embodying a minutely standardised technique. At the same time these articles of use, together with their household and personal effects, represent something appreciable in the way of portable wealth. Yet in their economic (pecuniary and industrial), domestic, social, or religious institutions the Eskimo have substantially not gone beyond the point of customary regulation commonly associated with the simpler, hand-to-mouth state of the industrial arts typical of the palæolithic savage culture. And this archaic Eskimo culture, with its highly elaborated technology, is apparently of untold antiquity; it is even believed by competent students of antiquity to have stood over without serious advance or decline since European palæolithic times—a period of not less than ten thousand years.[1] The causes conditioning this "backward" type of culture among the Eskimo, coupled with a relatively advanced and extremely complete technological system, are presumed to lie in their material surroundings; which on the one hand do not permit a congestion of people within a small area or enable the organisation and control of a compact community of any considerable size; while on the other hand they exact a large degree of co-operation and common interest, on pain of extreme hardship if not of extinction.

More perplexing at first sight is the case of such sedentary agricultural communities as the Pueblo Indians, who have also not advanced very materially beyond the simpler cultural scheme of savage life, and have not taken seriously to a system of property and a pecuniary control of industry, in spite of their having achieved a very considerable advance in the industrial arts, particularly in agriculture, such as would appear to entitle them to something "higher" than that state of peaceable, non-coercive social organisation, in which they were found on their first contact with civilised men, with maternal descent and mother-goddesses, and without much property rights, accumulated wealth or pecuniary distinction of classes. Again an explanation is probably to be sought in special circumstances of environment, perhaps re-enforced by peculiarities of the racial endowment; though the latter point seems doubtful, since both linguistically and anthropometrically the Pueblos are found to belong to two or three distinct stocks, at the same time that their culture is notably uniform throughout the Pueblo region, both on the technological and on

[1] Cf. W. G. Sollas, *Ancient Hunters.*

the institutional side. The peculiar material circumstances that appear to have conditioned the Pueblo culture are (*a*) a habitat which favours agricultural settlement only at isolated and widely separated spots, (*b*) sites for habitation (on detached mesas or on other difficult hills or in isolated valleys or canyons) easily secured against aggression from without and not affording notable differential advantages or admitting segregation of the population within the pueblo, (*c*) the absence of beasts of burden, such as have enabled the inhabitants of analogous regions of the old world effectually to cover long distances and make raiding a lucrative, or at least an attractive enterprise.

These, and other peculiar instances of what may perhaps be called cultural retardation, indicate by way of exception what may have been the ruling causes that have governed in the advance to a higher culture under more ordinary circumstances,—by "ordinary" being intended such circumstances as have apparently led to a different and, it would be held, a more normal result in the old world, and particularly in the region of the Western civilisation.

In the ordinary course, it should seem, such an advance in the industrial arts as will result in an accumulation of wealth, a considerable and efficient industrial equipment, or in a systematic and permanent cultivation of the soil or an extensive breeding of herds or flocks, will also bring on ownership and property rights bearing on these valuable goods, or on the workmen, or on the land employed in their production. What has seemed the most natural and obvious beginnings of property rights, in the view of those economists who have taken an interest in the matter, is the storing up of valuables by such of the ancient workmen as were enabled, by efficiency, diligence or fortuitous gains, to produce somewhat more than their current consumption. There are difficulties, though perhaps not insuperable, in the way of such a genesis of property rights and pecuniary differentiation within any given community. The temper of the people bred in the ways of the simpler plan of hand-to-mouth and common interest does not readily bend itself to such an institutional innovation, even though the self-regarding impulses of particular members of the community may set in such a direction as would give the alleged result.[1]

There are other and more natural ways of reaching the same results, ways more consonant with that archaic scheme of usages on which the new institution of property is to be grafted. (*a*) In the known cultures of this simpler plan there are usually, or at least frequently, present a class of magicians (shamans, medicine men, angekut), an inchoate priestly class, who get their living in part "by their wits," half parasitically, by some sort of tithe levied on their fellow members for supernatural ministrations and exploits of faith that are worth as much as they will bring.[2] As the industrial efficiency of the community increases with the technological gain, and an increasing disposable output is at hand, it should

[1] See, e. g., Basil Thomson, *The Figians*, especially ch. iv, xiv, xxviii, xxxi.

[2] The Pueblos offer a curious exception to this common rule of a parasitic priesthood. While they are much given to religious observances and have an extensive priestly organisation, comprising divers orders and sub-orders, this priesthood appears commonly to derive no income, or even appreciable perquisites, from their office.

naturally follow, human nature being what it is, that the services of the priests or magicians should suffer an advance in value and so enable the priests to lay something by, to acquire a special claim to certain parcels of land or cultivated trees or crops or first-fruits or labour to be performed by their parishioners. There is no limit to the value of such ministrations except the limit of tolerance, "what the traffic will bear." And much may be done in this way, which is in close touch with the accustomed ways of life among known savages and lower barbarians. To the extent to which such a move is successful it will alter the economic situation of the community by making the lay members, in so far, subject to the priestly class, and will gather wealth and power in the hands of the priests; so introducing a relation of master and servant, together with class differences in wealth, the practice of exclusive ownership, and pecuniary obligations. (*b*) With an accumulation of wealth, whether in portable form or in the form of plantations and tillage, there comes the inducement to aggression, predation, by whatever name it may be known. Such aggression is an easy matter in the common run of lower cultures, since relations are habitually strained between these savage and barbarian communities. There is commonly a state of estrangement between them amounting to constructive feud, though the feud is apt to lie dormant under a *modus vivendi* so long as there is no adequate inducement to open hostilities, in the way of booty. Given a sufficiently wealthy enemy who is sufficiently ill prepared for hostilities to afford a fighting chance of taking over this wealth by way of booty or tribute, with no obvious chance of due reprisals, and the opening of hostilities will commonly arrange itself. The communities mutually concerned so pass from the more or less precarious peaceful customs and animus common to the indigent lower cultures, to a more or less habitual attitude of predatory exploit. With the advent of warfare comes the war chief, into whose hands authority and pecuniary emoluments gather somewhat in proportion as warlike exploits and ideals become habitual in the community.[1] More or less of loot falls into the hands of the victors in any raid. The loot may be goods, cattle if any, or men, women and children; any or all of which may become (private) property and be accumulated in sufficient mass to make a difference between rich and poor. Captives may fall into some form of servitude, and in an agricultural community may easily become the chief item of wealth. At the same time an entire community may be reduced to servitude, so falling into the possession of an absentee owner (master), or under resident masters coming in from the victorious enemy.

In any or all of these ways the institution of ownership is likely to arise so soon as there is provocation for it, and in all cases it is a consequence of an appreciable advance in the industrial arts. Yet in a number of recorded cases a sufficient advance in technology does not appear to have been followed by so prompt an introduction of ownership, at least not in the fully developed

[1] The difference in importance and powers between the war chief of the peaceable Pueblos on the one hand and of the predatory Aztecs on the other hand shows how such an official's status may change *de facto* without a notable change *de jure*.—Cf. also Basil Thomson, *The Figians*, ch. iv, xxxi, on "Constitution of Society," and "The Tenure of Land," where the growth of custom is shown to throw pecuniary prerogative and control into the hands of the successful war chief.

form, as the surface facts would seem to have called for. Custom in the lower cultures is extremely tenacious, and what might seem an excessive allowance of time appears to be needed for so radical an innovation in the habitual scheme of things as is involved in the installation of rights of ownership. There are cases of a fairly advanced barbarian culture, with sufficiently coercive government control, an authoritative priesthood, and well-marked class distinctions which hold good both in economic and social relations, and yet where the line of demarkation between ownership and mastery is not drawn in any unambiguous fashion—where it is perhaps as accurate a statement as the case permits, to say that this distinction has not yet been made, and so would, if applied, mark a difference that does not yet exist.[1]

So long as overt predatory conditions continue to rule the case,—e. g., so long as the community in question continues, in a sense, under martial law, "in a state of seige," where the holders of the economic advantage hold it on a tenure of prowess or by way of delegated power and prerogative from a superior of warlike antecedents and dynastic right,—so long the rights of ownership are not likely to be well differentiated from those of mastery. Much the same characterisation of such a

[1] For instance, somewhat generally in the island states of Polynesia. Something suggestively reminiscent of such a condition of things is visible in early feudal Europe, where feudal holdings changed hands with a change in the status of their holders in a way that suggests that ownership was in great measure a corollary following from the tenure of certain civil powers. So, also, in ecclesiastical holdings of the same period and later. And, again, in the doubtful and changing status of the servile classes of feudal Europe, where the distinction between mastery and ownership often seems something of a legal fiction or a distinction without a difference. Feudal Japan affords evidence to much the same effect.

state of things is conveyed in the current phrase that "the rights of person and property are not secure." The very wide prevalence in the barbarian cultures of some such state of things argues that the genesis of property rights is likely to have been something of this kind in the common run, though it does not in other cases preclude a different and more peaceable development out of workmanlike or priestly economies.

But even if it should be found, when the matter has been sifted, that the genesis of ownership is of the latter kind, it would also in all probability be found that among the peoples whose institutional growth has a serious genetic bearing on the Western culture the holding of property has, late or early, passed through a phase of predatory tenure in which the distinction between ownership and mastery has so far fallen into abeyance as to have had but a slight effect on the further development. Where, as appears frequently to have been the case both in Europe and elsewhere, the kingship and temporal power has arisen out of the priestly office and spiritual power—or perhaps better where the inchoate kingship was in its origins chiefly of a priestly complexion, with a gradual shifting of kingly power and prerogative to a temporal basis,[1]—there the transition from a creation of property and mastery rights by priestly economies (fraud?) to a tenure of wealth and authority by royal prerogative (force?) will have so blended the two methods

[1] Cf. J. G. Frazer, *Lectures on the Early History of the Kingship*. The drift of evidence for the North-European cultures of pagan antiquity appears to set strongly in this direction, though the term "priestly," as applied to these pagan kings, is likely to convey too broad an implication of solemnity and vicariously divine power.

of genesis as to leave the attempt at a hard fast discrimination between them somewhat idle.

But whatever may be conceived to have been the genesis of ownership, the institution is commonly found, in the barbarian culture, to be tempered with a large infusion of predatory concepts, of status, prerogative, differential respect of persons and economic classes, and a corresponding differential respect of occupations. Whether property provokes to predation or predation initiates ownership, the situation that results in early phases of the pecuniary culture is much the same; and the causal relation in which this situation stands to the advance in workmanship is also much the same. This relation between workmanship and the pecuniary culture brought on with the advent of ownership is a twofold one, or, perhaps better, it is a relation of mutual give and take. The increase in industrial efficiency due to a sufficient advance in the industrial arts gives rise to the ownership of property and to pecuniary appreciations of men and things, occupations and products, habits, customs, usages, observances, services and goods. At the same time, since predation and warlike exploit are intimately associated with the facts of ownership through its early history (perhaps throughout its history), there results a marked accentuation of the self-regarding sentiments; with the economically important consequence that self-interest displaces the common good in men's ideals and aspirations. The animus entailed by predatory exploit is one of self-interest, a seeking of one's own advantage at the cost of the enemy, which frequently, in the poetically ideal case, takes such an extreme form as to prefer the enemy's loss to one's own gain. And in the emulation which the predatory life and its distinctions of wealth introduce into the community, the end of endeavour is likely to become the differential advantage of the individual as against his neighbours rather than the undifferentiated advantage of the group as a whole, in contrast with alien or hostile groups. The members of the community come to work each for his own interest in severalty, rather than for an undivided interest in the common lot. Such sentiment of group solidarity as there may remain falls also into the invidious and emulative form; whereby the fighting patriot becomes the type and exemplar of the public spirited citizen, whose ideal then is to follow his leader and humble the pride of those whom the chances of contention have thrown in with the other side of the game. The sentiment of common interest, itself in good part a diffuse working-out of the parental instinct, comes at the best to converge on the glory of the flag instead of the fulness of life of the community at large, or more commonly it comes to be centred in loyalty, that is to say in subservience, to the common war-chief and his dynastic successors.

In the shifting of activities, ideals and aims so brought in with the advent of wealth and ownership, the part of the priests and their divinities is not to be overlooked, for herein lies one of the greater cultural gains brought on by the technological advance at this juncture. The margin of service and produce available for consumption in the cult increases, and by easy consequence the spiritual prestige and the temporal power and prerogatives of the priesthood grow greater. The jurisdiction of the gods of the victors is extended, through the vicarious power of the priests, over the subject peoples, and as the temporal dominion is enlarged and an increasing measure of coercion is employed in controlling these dominions, so also in the affairs of the gods and their priests there is an accession of power and dignity. It commonly happens where predatory enterprise comes to be habitual and successful that the temporal power tends to centre in an autocratic and arbitrary ruler; and in this as in so much else, spiritual affairs are likely to take their complexion from the temporal, resulting in a strong drift toward an autocratic monotheism, which in the finished case comes to a climax in an omnipotent, omniscient deity of very exalted dignity and very exacting temper. For the habits of thought enforced in the affairs of daily life are carried over into men's sense of what is right and good in the life of the gods as well. If there is any choice among the gods under whose auspices a people has successfully entered on a career of predation, so that some of the gods have more of a reputation for rapacity and inhumanity than others, the most atrocious among them is likely, other things being equal, to become the war-god of the conquering host, and so eventually to be exalted to the suzerainty among the gods, and even in time to become the one and only incumbent of the divine czardom.

Should it happen that a relatively humane, tolerant and tractable deity comes in for exaltation to the divine suzerainty, as well may be if such a one has already a good prior claim standing over from the more peaceable past, he will readily acquire the due princely arrogance and irresponsibility that vests the typical heavenly king. It may be added that as a matter of course no degree of imputed inhumanity in the most high God will stand in the way of a god-fearing and astute priesthood volubly ascribing to him all the good qualities that should grace an elderly patriarchal gentleman of the old school; so that even his most infamous atrocities become ineffably meritorious and are dispensed of his mercy.[1]

With the terrors of a jealous and almighty God behind them, and with faith in their own mission and sagacity in its administration, the priesthood are in a position to make the affairs of the heavenly king count for much in the affairs of men; more particularly since this spiritual power enters into working arrangements with the temporal power; so that in the outcome these institutions which in their origins have grown out of a precarious margin of product above subsistence come to possess themselves of the output at large and leave a precarious margin of subsistence to the community at large.[2]

These further matters of "natural law in the spiritual world" are not in themselves of direct interest to the present inquiry, and they are also matters of somewhat tedious commonplace. Yet this run of things has grave consequences in the further working-out of the technological situation as well as in the course of material welfare for the community on whom it is incumbent to turn the technological knowledge to account, to conserve or improve and transmit it, and for this reason it has

[1] Witness the alleged dealings of Jahve with his chosen people and the laudation bestowed on Him by His priests for "conduct unbecoming a gentleman."

[2] As witness Pharaonic Egypt, Ancient Peru, Babylon, Assyria, Israel under Solomon and his nearer successors.

seemed necessary summarily to recall those general features of the cultural scheme that are inherently associated with the earlier pecuniary culture, — the full-blown barbarian culture. And it seems pertinent also to add something further in the same connection before leaving this aspect of the case.

It is necessary to hark back to what was said in an earlier chapter, of the relations of tillage and cattle-breeding to the instinct of workmanship and the course of technological advance. Both the technological and the institutional bearing of cattle-breeding is particularly notable in this connection. As already spoken of in what has gone before, cattle-breeding has the technological peculiarity that it may be successfully entered on and carried forward with a larger admixture of anthropomorphic concepts than the mechanic arts, or even than the domestication and care of the crop plants. It is perhaps not to be admitted that the penchant of early man to take an anthropomorphic view of the lower animals and impute to them the common traits of human nature has directly conduced to their successful domestication, but it should be within the mark to say that this penchant may have been primarily responsible for the course of conduct that led to the domestication of animals,[1] and that it has apparently never been a serious drawback to any pastoral culture. Now, wealth in flocks and herds is peculiar not only in being eminently portable, even to the extent that in the usual course of this industry it is necessary for a pastoral community to migrate, or to go over an extended itinerary with the changing seasons, but it has also the peculiar quality of mul-

[1] See F. B. Jevons, *Introduction to the History of Religion*, ch. x.

tiplying spontaneously, given only a degree of surveillance and a sufficient range of pasture lands. It follows that cattle are easy and tempting to acquire by predation, will accumulate through natural increase without notable exertion on the part of their owners, and will multiply beyond the bearing capacity of any disposable range. Hence a pastoral people, or a people given in great part to pastoral pursuits, will somewhat readily take to a predatory life; will have to be organised for defence (and offence) against raids of encroachments from its neighbours engaged in the same pursuits; will find itself short of range lands throught the natural increase of its flocks or herds, and so will even involuntarily be brought into feud with neighbouring herdsmen through mutual trespass. Further, the work of herding, on the scale imposed by the open continental cattle and sheep ranges, is man's work, as is also the incidental fighting, raiding, and cattle-lifting.

The effects of these technological conditions on the general culture of a pastoral people are such as are set forth in their most favourable light in the early historical books of the Old Testament, or such conditions as may be found today on the great cattle ranges of west and north-central Asia. The community falls necessarily into a patriarchal regime; with considerable concentration of wealth in individual hands; great disparity in wealth and social standing, commonly involving both chattel slavery and serfdom; a fighting organisation under patriarchal-despotic leadership, which serves both for civil, political and religious purposes; domestic institutions of the same cast, involving a degree of subjection of women and children and commonly polygamy for the patriarchal upper or ruling class; a religious system of a monotheistic or monarchical complexion and drawn on lines of patriarchal despotism; with the priestly office vested in the patriarchal head of the community (the eldest male of the eldest male line) if the group is small enough to admit the administration of both the temporal and spiritual power at the hands of one man—as Israel at the time of the earlier sojourn in Canaan—or vested in a specialised priesthood if the group is of great size—as Israel on their return to Palestine.

Such a culture is manifestly fit to succeed both in avowedly predatory enterprise and in pecuniary enterprise of a more peaceable sort, so long as range lands are at its disposal or so long as it can find a sufficiently large and compact agricultural community to reduce to servitude, or so long as it can find ways and means of commercial enterprise while still occupying a position defensible against all comers. Its population is organised for offence and defence and trained in the habits of subordination necessary to any successful war, and the patriarchal authority and pecuniary ideals inbred in them give them facility in co-operation against aliens, as well as the due temper for successful bargaining. Such a culture has the elements of national strength and solidarity, given only some adequate means of subsistence while still retaining its militant patriarchal organisation. Not least among its elements of national strength is its religion, which fosters the national pride of a people chosen by the Most High, at the same time that it trains the population in habits of subordination and loyalty, as well as in patient submission to exactions. But it is essentially a parasitic culture, despotic, and, with due training, highly superstitious or religious. What a people of these antecedents is capable of is shown by the Assyrians, Babylonians, Medes, Persians, the Hindu invaders of India, the Hyksos invaders of Egypt, and in another line by Israel and the Phœnicians, and in a lesser degree by the Huns, Mongols, Tatars, Arabs and Turks.

It is from peoples of this culture that the great religions of the old world have come, near or remote, but it is not easy to find any substantial contribution to human culture drawn indubitably from this source apart from religious creed, cult and poetry. The domestication of animals, for instance, is not due to them; with the possible exception of the horse and the dog, that work had to be done in peaceable, sedentary communities, from whom the pastoral nomads will have taken over the stock and the industry and carried it out on a scale and with cultural consequences which do not follow from cattle-breeding under sedentary conditions. Their religion, on the other hand, seems in no case to have been carried up to the consummate stage of despotic monotheism during the nomadic-pastoral phase of their experience, but to have been worked out to a finished product presently after they had engaged on a career of conquest and had some protracted experience of warfare and despotism on a relatively large scale. The history of these great civilisations with pastoral antecedents appears to run somewhat uniformly to the effect that they collapsed as soon as they had eaten their host into a collapse. The incidents along the way between their beginning in conquest and their collapse in exhaustion are commonly no more edifying and of no more lasting significance to human culture than those which have similarly marked the course of the Turk. These great monarchies were organised by and for an intrusive dynasty and ruling class, of pastoral antecedents, and they drew their subsistence and their means of oppression from a subjugated agricultural population. In the course of this further elaboration of a predatory civilisation, the institutions proper to a large scale and to a powerful despotism and nobility resting on a servile people, were developed into a finished system; in which the final arbiter is always irresponsible force and in which the all-pervading social relation is personal subservience and personal authority. The mechanic arts make little if any progress under such a discipline of personalities, even the arts of war, and there is little if any evidence of sensible gain in any branch of husbandry. There were great palaces and cities built by slave labour and corvée, embodying untold misery in conspicuously wasteful and tasteless show, and great monarchs whose boast it was that they were each and several the best friend or nearest relative of some irresponsible and supreme god, and whose dearest claim to pre-eminence was that they "walked on the faces of the black-head race." Seen in perspective and rated in any terms that have a workmanlike significance, these stupendous dynastic fabrics are as insignificant as they are large, and none of them is worth the least of the fussy little communities that came in time to make up the Hellenic world and its petty squabbles.

In their general traits these various civilisations founded (in conquest) by the pastoral peoples are of the same character as is the pecuniary culture as found elsewhere, but they have certain special features which set them off somewhat in a class by themselves. They are predatory in a peculiarly overt and accentuated degree, so that their institutions foster the invidious sentiments, the self-regarding animus of servility and of arrogance, beyond what commonly happens in the pecuniary culture at large; and they carry a large content of peculiarly high-wrought religious superstitions and fear of the supernatural, which likewise works out from and into an animus of servility and arrogance. In these cultures it is true, even beyond the great significance which the proposition has in the barbarian culture elsewhere, that the fear of God is the beginning of wisdom. The discipline of life in such a culture, therefore, is consistently unfavourable to any technological gain; the instinct of workmanship is constantly dominated by prevalent habits of thought that are worse than useless for any technological purpose.

Much the same, of course, is true for any civilisation founded on personal government of the coercive kind, whatever may be the remoter antecedents of the dynastic and ruling classes; but these other cultures have not the same secure and ancient patriarchal foundation, ready to hand, and so they are constrained to build their institutions of coercion, domestic, civil, political and military, more slowly and with a more doubtful outcome; nor does their religious system so readily work out in a monarchical theology with an omnipotent sovereign and in all-pervading fear of God. A home-bred despotism in an agricultural community that has set out with maternal descent, a matriarchal clan system, and mother goddesses, is hampered both on the temporal and the spiritual side by ancient and inbred usage and preconceptions that can be effectually overcome only in the long course of time. The civilisations of Asia-Minor and the Ægean region, and even of Egypt and Rome, however much of pastoral and patriarchal elements may have been infused into them in the course of time, show their shortcomings in this respect to the last; perhaps in their religions more than in any other one cultural trait, since religion is after all an epigenetic feature and follows rather than leads in the unfolding of the cultural scheme.

But these great civilisations dominated by pastoral antecedents have no grave significance for the modern culture, except as drawbacks, and none at all for modern technology or for that matter-of-fact knowledge on which modern technology runs. The Western peoples, whose cultural past is of more immediate interest, have also had their warlike experience, late and early, but it seems never to have reached the consummate outcome to be seen in the East. Neither as regards the scale on which dynastic organisation has been carried out nor as regards the thoroughness with which their institutions have been permeated by predatory preconceptions have the Western peoples in their earlier history approached the standard of the oriental despotisms. Even now, it may be remarked, advocates of war and armaments commonly speak (doubtless disingenuously) for the predatory régime as being a necessity of defence rather than something to be desired on its own merits. Not that the predatory régime has not been a sufficiently grave fact in the history of occidental civilisation; to take such a view of history one would have to overlook the Roman

Empire, the barbarian invasions, the feudal system, the Catholic church, the Era of state-making, and the existing armed neutrality of the powers; but these have, all but the last, proved to be episodes on a grand scale rather than such an historical finality as any one of the successive monarchies in the Mesopotamian-Chaldæan country,—the test being that occidental civilisation has not died of any one of these maladies, though it has come through more than one critical period.

Western civilisation has gone through these eras of accentuated predation and has at all times shown an appreciable admixture of predatory conceptions in its scheme of institutions and ideals, in its domestic institutions and its public affairs, in its art and religion, but it is after all within the mark to say that, at least since the close of the Dark Ages, a distinctive characteristic that sets off this civilisation in contradistinction from any definitively predatory phase of the pecuniary culture, has been a pertinacious pursuit of the arts of peace, to which those peoples that have led in this civilisation have ever returned at every respite. For an appreciation of the relations subsisting between the sense of workmanship and the discipline of habituation in the modern culture, therefore, the phenomena of peaceful ownership are of greater, or at least of more vivid interest than those of the predatory phase of the pecuniary culture.

Modern civilisation, and indeed all history for that matter, lies within the pecuniary culture as a whole; but the Western culture of modern times belongs, perhaps somewhat precariously, to the secondary or peaceable phase of this pecuniary culture, rather than to that predatory phase with which the pecuniary scheme of life began somewhere in the lower barbarism, and that has repeatedly closed its life cycle in the collapse of one and another of the great dynastic empires of the old world.

As in the predatory phase, so also in the peaceable pecuniary culture, the dominant note is given by the self-regarding impulses; and the sense of workmanship is therefore characteristically hedged about and guided by the institutional exigencies and preconceptions incident to life under the circumstances imposed by ownership,—in a situation where the economic interest, the interest in those material means of life with which workmanship has to deal, converges on property rights. Ownership is self-regarding, of course, and the rights of ownership are of a personal, invidious, differential, emulative nature; although in the peaceable phase of the civilisation of ownership, force and fraud are, in theory, barred out of the game of acquisition,—wherein this differs from the predatory phase proper.

An obvious consequence following immediately on the emergence of ownership in any community is an increased application to work. This has been taken as a matter of course in theoretical speculations and is borne out by the observation of peoples among whom trade relations have been introduced in recent times. An immediate result is greater diligence, accompanied apparently in all cases, if the reports of observers are to be accepted, by an increase in contention, distrust and chicanery [1] and an increasingly wasteful consumption of goods. The diligence so fostered by emulative self-interest is directed to the acquisition of property, in

[1] Cf., e. g., Basil Thomson, *The Figians*, ch. iv.

great part to the acquisition of more than is possessed by those others with whom the invidious comparison in ownership is made; and under the spur of ownership simply, it is only secondarily, as a means to the emulative end of acquisition, that productive work, and therefore workmanship in its naïve sense, comes into the case at all. Ownership conduces to diligence in acquisition and therefore indirectly to diligence in work, if no more expeditious means of acquiring wealth can be devised. In its first incidence the incentive to diligence afforded by ownership is a proposition in business not in workmanship. Its effects on workmanship, industry and technology, therefore, are necessarily somewhat uncertain and uneven. Apparently from the start there is some appreciable resort to fraudulent thrift, to the production of spurious or inferior goods.[1] This of course very presently is corrected in the increased astuteness and vigilance exercised in men's dealings with one another, whereby an appreciable portion of energy goes to defeat these artifices of disingenuous worldly wisdom.

It should be added that the pecuniary incentive to work takes the direction of making the most of the means at hand, considered as means of pecuniary gain rather than as means of serviceability, and that it conduces therefore to the fullest (pecuniary) exploitation of the standard accepted ways and means of industry rather than to the improvement of these ways and means beyond the conjuncture at hand. Further, though this is also somewhat of a tedious commonplace, since the

[1] As shown, for instance, by the pottery and baskets made for trade by the American Indians where they come in trade contact with civilised men.

only authentic end of work under the pecuniary dispensation is the acquisition of wealth; since the possession of wealth in so far exempts its possessor from productive work; and since such exemption is a mark of wealth and therefore of superiority over those who have nothing and therefore must work; it follows that addiction to work becomes a mark of inferiority and is therefore discreditable. Whereby work becomes distasteful to all men instructed in the proprieties of the pecuniary culture; and it has even become so irksome to men trained in the punctilios of the servile, predatory, phase of this culture that it was once credibly proclaimed by a shrewd priesthood as the most calamitous curse laid on mankind by a vindictive God. Also, since wealth affords means for a free consumption of goods, the conspicuous consumption of goods becomes a mark of pecuniary excellence, and so it becomes an element of respectability in any pecuniary culture, and presently becomes a meritorious act and even a requirement of pecuniary decency. The outcome is conspicuous wastefulness of consumption, the limits of which, if any, have apparently not been approached hitherto.[1]

The bearings of this pecuniary culture on workmanship and technology are wide and diverse. Most immediate and perhaps most notable is the conventional disesteem of labour spoken of above, which seems to follow as a necessary consequence from the institution of ownership in all cases where distinctions of wealth are at all

[1] For a more detailed discussion of these secondary consequences of the institution of ownership, the irksomeness of labour and the conspicuous waste of goods, which cannot be pursued here, see *The Theory of the Leisure Class*, ch. ii–vi.

considerable or where property rights are associated with facts of mastery and prestige. The pecuniary disrepute of labour acts to discourage industry, but this may be offset, at least in part, by the incentive given to emulation by the good repute attaching to acquisition. The wasteful expenditure of goods and services enjoined by the pecuniary canons of conspicuous consumption gives an economically untoward direction to industry, at the same time that it greatly increases the hardships and curtails the amenities of life. So also, estrangement and distrust between persons, classes and nations necessarily pervades this cultural era, due to the incessant gnawing of incompatible pecuniary interests; and this state of affairs appreciably lowers the aggregate efficiency of human industry and sets up bootless obstacles to be overcome and irrelevant asperities to be put up with.

These and the like consequences of pecuniary emulation are simple, direct and obvious; but the discipline of the pecuniary culture bears on workmanship also in a more subtle way, indirect and less evident at first sight. The discipline of daily life imparts its own bent to the sense of workmanship through habituation of the workman to that scheme and logic of things that rules this pecuniary culture. The outcome as concerns industry is somewhat equivocal; the discipline of self-seeking at some points favours workmanship and at others not. At one period or phase of the pecuniary culture, generally speaking an early or crude phase, the bent so given to workmanship and technology seems necessarily to be conducive to inefficiency; at another (later or maturer) phase the contrary is likely to be true.

The pecuniary discipline of invidious emulation takes

effect on the state of the industrial arts chiefly and most pervasively through the bias which it gives to the knowledge on which workmanship proceeds. It may be called to mind that the body of knowledge (facts) turned to account in workmanship, the facts made use of in devising technological processes and appliances, are of the nature of habits of thought. This is particularly applicable to those (tactical) principles under whose control the information in hand is construed and connected up into a system of uses, agencies and instrumentalities. These habits of thought, elements of knowledge, items of information, accepted facts, principles of reality, in part represent the mechanical behaviour of objects, the brute nature of brute matter, and in part they stand for qualities, aptitudes and proclivities imputed to external objects and their behaviour and so infused into the facts and the generalisations based on them. The sense of workmanship has much to do with this imputation of traits to the phenomena of observation, perhaps more than any other of the proclivities native to man. The traits so imputed to the facts are in the main such as will be consonant with the sense of workmanship and will lend themselves to a concatenation in its terms. But this infusion of traits into the facts of observation, whether it takes effect at the instance of the sense of workmanship, or conceivably on impulse not to be identified with this instinct, is a logical process and is carried out by an intelligence whose logical processes have in all cases been profoundly biassed by habituation. So that the habits of life of the individual, and therefore of the community made up of such individuals, will pervasively and unremittingly bend this work of imputation with the set of their own current, and will accordingly involve incoming elements of knowledge in a putative system of relations consistent with these habits of life. This comprehensive scheme of habitual apprehensions and appreciations is what is called the "genius," spirit, or character of any given culture. In all this range of habitual preconceptions touching the nature of things there prevails a degree of solidarity, of mutual support and re-enforcement among the several lines of habitual activity comprised in the current scheme of life; so that a certain characteristic tone or bias runs through the whole,—in so far as the cultural situation has attained that degree of maturity or assimilation that will allow it to be spoken of as a distinctive whole, standing out as a determinate and coherent phase in the life-history of the race. To this bias of scope and method in the current scheme of life, intellectual and sentimental, any new element or item must be assimilated if it is not to be rejected as alien and unreal or to fall through by neglect.

All this bears on the scope and method of knowledge, and therefore on the facts made use of in the industrial arts, just as it bears on any other feature of human life that is of the nature of habit. And the immediate question is as to the bias or drift of the pecuniary culture as it affects the apprehension of facts serviceable for technological ends. This pecuniary bias or bent may be described as invidious, personal, emulative, looking to differential values in respect of personal force or competitive success, looking to gradations in respect of comparative potency, validity, authenticity, propriety, reputability, decency. The canons of pecuniary repute preclude the well-to-do, who have leisure for such things, from inquiring narrowly into the facts of technology, since these things are beneath their dignity, conventionally distasteful; familiarity with such matters can not with propriety be avowed, nor can they without offence and humiliation be canvassed at all intimately among the better class. At the same time pecuniary competition, when carried to its ideal pitch, works the lower industrial classes to exhaustion and allows them no appreciable leisure or energy for indulging any possible curiosity of this kind on their part. The habitual (ideal) frame of mind is that of invidious self-interest on the one hand, due to the imperative and ubiquitous need of gain in wealth or in rank, and on the other hand class discrimination due to the ubiquitous prevalence of distinctions in prerogatives and authentic standing. The discipline of the pecuniary religions, or of the religious tenets and observances proper to the pecuniary culture, runs to a similar effect; more decisively so in the earlier, or distinctively predatory, phases of this culture than in the peaceable or commercial phase. The vulgar facts of industry are beneath the dignity of a feudalistic deity or of his priesthood; at the same time that the overmastering need of standing well in the graces of an all-powerful, exacting and irresponsible God throws a deeper shadow of ignobility over the material side of life, and makes any workmanlike preoccupation with industrial efficiency presumptively sinful as well as indecorous.

The pecuniary culture is not singular in this matter. Always and everywhere the acquirement of knowledge is a matter of observation guided and filled out by the imputation of qualities, relations and aptitudes to the observed phenomena. Without this putative content of active presence and potency the phenomena would lack reality; they could not be assimilated in the scheme of things human. It is only a commonplace of the logic of apperception that the substantial traits of objective facts are a figment of the brain. Under the discipline of this pecuniary phase of culture the requisite imputation of character to facts runs, as ever, in anthropomorphic terms; but it is an anthropomorphism which by habit conforms to the predatory-pecuniary scheme of preconceptions, such as the routine of life has made ready and convincing to men living under the discipline of emulation, invidious distinctions and authentic pecuniary decorum. Under these circumstances it is not in the anthropomorphism of naïve workmanship that the putative reality of facts is to be sought, but in their conformity to the conventionally definitive preconceptions of invidious merit, authentic excellence, force of character, mastery, complaisance, congruity with the run of the established institutional values and the ordinances of the Most High. The canons of reality, under which sense impressions are reduced to objective fact and so become available for use, and under which, again, facts are put in practice and turned to technological account, are the same canons of invidious distinction that rule in the world of property and among men occupied with predatory and pecuniary precedence. In effect men and things come to be rated in terms of what they (putatively) are—their intrinsic character—rather than in terms of what they (empirically) will do.

Without pursuing the question farther at this point, it should be evident that the bias of the pecuniary culture must on the whole act with pervasive force so to bend men's knowledge of the things with which they have to do as to lessen its serviceability for technological ends. The result is a deflection from matter-of-fact to matter of imputation, and the imputation is of the personal character here spoken of. The dominant note appears to be a differential rating in respect of aggressive self-assertion, whether in human or non-human agents. Theological preconceptions are commonly strong in the pecuniary culture, and under their rule this differential rating developes into a scheme of graded powers and efficacies vested in the phenomena of external nature by delegation from an overruling personal authority. Such a bent is necessarily prejudicial to workmanship, and it may seem that the ubiquitous repressive force of this metaphysics of authority and authenticity should serve the same disserviceable end for workmanship as the more genial and diffuse anthropomorphism of the lower cultures, but with more decisive effect since it runs in a more competently organised, compact and prescriptive fashion.

Where the pecuniary culture has been carried through consistently on the predatory plan, without being diverted to that commercial phase current in the latterday Western civilisation, the conclusion of the matter has been decay of the industrial arts and effectual dissipation of that system of matter-of-fact knowledge on which technological efficiency rests. In the West, where the predatory phase proper has eventually given place to a commercial phase of the same pecuniary culture, the general run of events in this bearing has been a decline of knowledge, technology and workmanship, running on so long as the predatory (coercive) rule prevailed unbroken, but followed presently by a slow recovery and advance in technological efficiency and scientific insight; somewhat in proportion as the commercialisation of this culture has gained ground, and therefore correlated also in a general way with the decline of religious fear.

This run of events may tempt to the inference that while the predatory phase proper of this pecuniary civilisation is inimical to matter-of-fact knowledge and to technological insight, the rule of commercial ideas and ideals characteristic of its subsequent peaceable phase acts to propagate these material elements of culture. But what has already appeared in the course of the inquiry into that still earlier cultural phase that went before the coercive and invidious regime of predation suggests that the case is not so simple nor so flattering to our latterday self-complacency. The self-regarding sentiments of arrogance and abasement, out of whose free habitual exercise the pecuniary culture, with its institutions of prerogative and differential advantage, has been built up, are not the spiritual source from which such an outcome is to be looked for. These sentiments and the instinctive proclivities of which these sentiments are the emotional expression are presumed to have remained unchanged in force and character through that long course of cumulative habituation that has given them their ascendency in the institutions of the pecuniary culture, and of their own motion they will yield now results of the same kind as ever. But the like is true also for those other instincts out of whose working came the earlier gains made in knowledge and workmanship under the savage culture, before the self-regarding sentiments underlying the pecuniary culture took the upper hand.

The parental bent and the instincts of workmanship and of curiosity will have been overborne by cumulative habituation to the rule of the self-regarding proclivities that triumphed in the culture of predation, and whose dominion has subsequently suffered some impairment in the later substitution of property rights for tenure by prowess, but these instincts that make for workmanship remain as intrinsic to human nature as the others. What is to be said for the current commercial scheme of life, therefore, appears to be that it is only less inimical to the functioning of those instinctive propensities that serve the common interest. Hence, gradually, these instincts and the non-invidious interests which they engender have been coming effectually into bearing again as fast as the stern repression of them exercised by the full-charged predatory scheme of life has weakened into a less and less effectual inhibition, under the discipline of compromise and mitigated self-aggrandisement embodied in the rights of property.

That authentication of ownership out of which the sacred rights of property have apparently grown may well have arisen as a sort of mutual insurance among owners as against the disaffection of the dispossessed; which would presently give rise to a sentiment of solidarity within the class of owners, would acquire prescriptive force through habitual enforcement, become a matter of customary right to be consistently respected under the institutional forms of property, and eventuate in that highly moralised expression of self-aggrandisement which it is today. But with the putting-away of fancy-free predation, as being a conventionally disallowed means of self-aggrandisement, sentiments of equity and solidarity would presently come in—perhaps at the outset by way of disingenuous make-believe—and so the way would be made easier under the shelter of this range of conceptions for a rehabilitation of the primordial parental instinct and its penchant for the common good. And when ownership has once been institutionalised in this impersonal and quasi-dispassionate form it will lend but a decreasingly urgent bias to the cultural scheme in the direction of differential respect of persons and a differential rating of natural phenomena in respect of the occult potencies and efficacies imputed to them.

As the institutional ground has shifted from free-swung predation to a progressively more covert régime of self-aggrandisement and differential gain, the instinct of workmanship has progressively found freer range and readier access to its raw material. The differential good repute of wealth and rank has of course continued to be of much the same nature in the later (commercial) stages of the pecuniary culture as in the earlier (predatory) stages. An aristocratic (or servile) scheme of life must necessarily run in invidious terms, since that is the whole meaning of the phenomenon; and resting as any such scheme does on pecuniary distinctions, whether direct or through the intermediary term of predatory exploit, it will necessarily involve the corollary that wealth and exemption from work (*otium cum dignitate*) is honourable and that poverty and work is dishonourable. But with the progressive commercialisation of gain and ownership it also comes to pass that peaceable application to the business in hand may have much to do with the acquirement of a reputable standing; and so long as work is of a visibly pecuniary kind and is sagaciously and visibly directed to the acquisition of wealth, the disrepute intrinsically attaching to it is greatly offset by its meritorious purpose. So much so, indeed, that there has even grown up something of a class feeling, among the class who have come by their wealth through industry and shrewd dealing, to the effect that peaceable diligence and thrift are meritorious traits.

This is "middle-class" sentiment of course. The aristocratic contempt for the tradesman and all his works has not suffered serious mitigation through all this growth of new methods of reputability. The three conventionally recognised classes, upper, middle, and lower, are all and several pecuniary categories; the upper being typically that (aristocratic) class which is possessed of wealth without having worked or bargained for it; while the middle class have come by their holdings through some form of commercial (business) traffic; and the lower class gets what it has by workmanship. It is a gradation of (*a*) predation, (*b*) business, (*c*) industry; the former being disserviceable and gainful, the second gainful, and the third serviceable. And no modern civilised man is so innocent of the canons of reputability as not to recognise off-hand that the first category is meritorious and the last discreditable, whatever his individual prejudices may lead him to think of the second. Aristocracy without unearned wealth, or without predatory antecedents, is a misnomer. When an aristocratic class loses its pecuniary advantage it becomes questionable. A poverty-stricken aristocrat is a "decayed gentleman;" and "the nobility of labour" is a disingenuous figure of speech.

The transition from the original predatory phase of

the pecuniary culture to the succeeding commercial phase signifies the emergence of a middle class in such force as presently to recast the working arrangements of the cultural scheme and make peaceable business (gainful traffic) the ruling interest of the community. With the same movement emerges a situation which is progressively more favourable to the intellectual animus required for workmanship and an advance in technology. The state of the industrial arts advances, and with its advance the accumulation of wealth is accelerated, the gainfulness of business traffic increases, and the middle (business) class grows along with it. It is in the conscious interest of this class to further the gainfulness of industry, and as this end is correlated with the productiveness of industry it is also, though less directly, correlated with improvements in technology.

With the transition from a naïvely predatory scheme to a commercial one, the "competitive system" takes the place of the coercive methods previously employed, and pecuniary gain becomes the incentive to industry. At least superficially, or ephemerally, the workman's income under this pecuniary régime is in some proportion to his product. Hence there results a voluntary application to steady work and an inclination to find and to employ improvements in the methods and appliances of industry. At the same time commercial conceptions come progressively to supplant conceptions of status and personal consequence as the primary and most familiar among the habits of thought entailed by the routine of daily life. This will be true especially for the common man, as contrasted with the aristocratic classes, although it is not to be overlooked that the standards of propriety imposed on the community by the better classes will have a considerably corrective effect on the frame of mind of the common man in this respect as in others, and so will act to maintain an effective currency of predatory ideals and preconceptions after the economic situation at large has taken on a good deal of a commercial complexion. The accountancy of price and ownership throws personal prestige and consequence notably less into the foreground than does the rating in terms of prowess and gentle birth that characterises the predatory scheme of life. And in proportion as such pecuniary accountancy comes to pervade men's relations, correspondingly impersonal terms of rating and appreciation will make their way also throughout men's habitual apprehension of external facts, giving the whole an increasingly impersonal complexion. So far as this effect is had, the facts of observation will lend themselves with correspondingly increased facility and effect to the purposes of technology. So that the commercial phase of culture should be favourable to advance in the industrial arts, at least permissively and as regards the immediate incidence of its discipline.

CHAPTER V

Ownership and the Competitive System

I. Peaceable Ownership

The pecuniary system of social organisation that so results has grave and lasting consequences for the welfare of society. It brings class divergence of material interests, class prerogative and differential hardship, and an accentuated class disparity in the consumption of goods, involving a very extensive resort to the conspicuous waste of goods and services as an evidence of wealth. These consequences of the pecuniary economy may be interesting enough in themselves, even to the theoretician, but they need not be pursued here except in so far as they have an appreciable bearing on the community's workmanlike efficiency and the further development of technology.[1] But the more direct and immediate technological consequences of this move from a predatory to a peaceable or quasi-peaceable economic system are also sufficiently grave—partly favourable to workmanship and partly otherwise—and these it is necessary for the purposes of this inquiry to follow up in some detail.

The interest and attention of the two typical pecuniary

[1] For some further analysis of the relation between ownership, earnings and the material equipment see *Quarterly Journal of Economics*, August, 1908, "On the Nature of Capital;" as also a paper by H. J. Davenport in the same Journal for November, 1910, on "Social Productivity *versus* Private Acquisition."

classes between whom the affairs of industry now come to lie, presently part company and enter on a course of progressive differentiation along two divergent lines. The workmen, labourers, operatives, technologists,—whatever term may best designate that general category of human material through which the community's technological proficiency functions directly to an industrial effect,—these have to do with the work, whereby they get their livelihood, and their interest as well as the discipline of their workday life converges, in effect on a technologically competent apprehension of material facts. In this respect the free workmen under this peaceable régime of property are very differently placed from the servile workman of the predatory régime of mastery and servitude. The latter has little if any interest in the efficiency of the industrial processes in which he is engaged, less so the more widely his status differs from that of the free workman. His case is analogous to that of the tenant at will, who has nothing to gain from permanent improvement of the land which he cultivates. Whereas the free workman is, at least immediately and transiently, and particularly in his own current apprehension of the matter, quite intimately dependent on his own technological proficiency and vitally interested in any available technological expedient that promises to heighten his efficiency. Such is particularly the case during the earlier phases of the régime of peaceable ownership, so long as the free workman is in the typical case working at his own discretion and disposes of his own product in a limited market. And such continues to be the case, on the whole, under the wage system so long as the large-scale production and investment have not put an end to the employer's intimate supervision of his employés. Indeed, under the driving exigencies of the competitive wage system the workmen are somewhat strenuously held to such a workmanlike apprehension of things, even though they may no longer have the same intimate concern in their own current efficiency as in the earlier days of handicraft. The severe pressure of competitive wages and large organisation, it might well be thought, should logically offset the slighter attraction which work as such has for the hired workman as contrasted with the man occupied with his own work. The effect of this régime of free labour should logically be, as it apparently has in great part been, a close and progressively searching recourse to the logic of matter-of-fact in all the workmen's habitual thinking, and in all their outlook on matters of interest, whether in industry or in the other concerns of life that may conceivably be of more capital interest.

On the other hand the owners under this régime of peaceable ownership have to do with the pecuniary management, the gainful manipulation of property. In the transitional beginnings of this system of peaceable ownership and free workmen the owners are in the typical case owners of land or similar natural resources; but in due course of time there arises a class of owners holding property in the material equipment of industry and deriving their gains and livelihood from a businesslike management of this property, at the same time that the landlords also fall into more businesslike relations with their tenants on the one hand and with the industrial community that supplies their wants on the other hand. These owners, investors, masters, employers, undertakers, businessmen, have to do with the negotiation of advantageous bargains; it is by bargaining that their discretionary control of property takes effect, and in one way or another their attention centres on the quest of profits. The training afforded by these occupations and requisite to their effectual pursuit runs in terms of pecuniary management and insight, pecuniary gain, price, price-cost, price-profit and price-loss; and these men are held to an ever more exacting recourse to the logic of the price system, and so are trained to the apprehension of men and things in terms which count toward a gainful margin on investments and business undertakings; that is to say in terms of the self-regarding propensities and sentiments comprised in human nature, and perhaps especially in terms of human infirmity.

This last point in the characterisation may seem unwarranted, and may even strike unreflecting persons as derogatory. It is, of course, not so intended; and any degree of reflection will bring out its simple bearing on the facts of business. As is well and obviously known, the sole end of business as such is pecuniary gain, gain in terms of price. It need not be held, as has sometimes been argued, that one businessman's gain is necessarily another's loss; although that principle was once taken for granted, as the foundation of the Mercantilist policies of Europe, and is still acted on uncritically by the generality of statesmen. But it is at any rate true, because it is contained in the terms employed, that a successful business negotiation is more successful in proportion as the party of the second part is less competent to take care of his own pecuniary interest, whether through native or acquired incapacity for pecuniary discretion or from pecuniary inability to stand out for such terms as he otherwise might conceivably exact. A shrewd businessman can, notoriously, negotiate advantageous terms with an inexperienced minor or a necessitous customer or employé. Pecuniary gain is a differential gain and business is a negotiation of such differential gains; not necessarily a differential of one businessman as against or at the cost of another; but more commonly, and more typical of the competitive system, it is a differential as between the businessman's outlay and his returns,—that is to say, as between the businessman and the unbusinesslike generality of persons with whom directly or indirectly he deals as customers, employés, and the like. For the purposes of such a negotiation of differentials the weakness of one party (in the pecuniary respect) is as much to the point as the strength of the other,—the two being substantially the same fact. The discipline of the business occupations should accordingly run to the habitual rating of men, things and affairs in terms of emulative human nature and of precautionary wisdom in respect of pecuniary expediency. Instead of workmanlike or technological insight, this discipline conduces to worldly wisdom.[1]

But the disparity between the discipline of the business occupations and that of industry is by no means so sheer as this contrast in their main characteristics would imply, nor do the men engaged in these two divergent lines of work differ so widely in their habitual outlook on affairs or their insight into

[1] For a more detailed discussion of this disciplinary disparity between business and industrial occupations, cf. *The Theory of Business Enterprise*, ch. iv, viii and ix.

facts. Such is particularly the case in the earlier and simpler phases of the régime, before the specialisation of occupations had gone so far as to divide the working community in any consistent fashion into the two contrasted classes of businessmen on the one side and workmen on the other. As this modern régime of peaceable ownership and pecuniary organisation has advanced and its peculiar features of organisation and workmanship have reached a sharper definition, the division between the two contrasted kinds of endeavour—business and workmanship—has grown wider and the disparity in the distinctive range of habits engendered by each has grown more marked. So that something of a marked and pervading contrast should logically be found between the habitual attitude taken by members of the business community on the one hand and that of the body of workmen on the other hand; and this contrast should, logically, go on increasing with each successive move in advance along this line of specialisation of occupations and "division of labour." Some such result has apparently followed; but neither has the specialisation been complete and consistent, nor has the resulting differentiation in respect of their intellectual and spiritual attitude set the two contrasted classes of persons apart in so definitive a fashion as a first and elementary consideration of the causes at work might lead one to infer.

Businessmen have to do with industry; more or less remotely perhaps, but often at near hand, for it is out of industry that their business gains come; and they are also subject to the routine of living imposed by the use of the particular range of industrial appliances and processes available for that use. The workmen on the other hand have also to do with pecuniary matters, for they are forever in contact with the market in one way and another, and it is in pecuniary terms that the livelihood comes to them for which they are set to work. And both businessmen and workmen enter on their two divergent lines of training with much the same endowment of propensities and aptitudes. Yet it appears that the training in pecuniary wisdom that makes up the career of the typical businessman is after all of little avail in the way of technological insight or efficiency, as witness the ubiquitous mismanagement of industry at the hands of businessmen who are, presumably, doing their best to enhance the efficiency of the industries under their control with a view to the largest net gain from the output.[1] If the "efficiency engineers" are to be credited, it is probably within the mark to say that the net aggregate gains from industry fall short of what they might be by some fifty per cent, owing to the trained inability of the businessmen in control to appreciate and give effect to the visible technological requirements of the industries from which they draw their gains. To appreciate the kind and degree of this commonplace mismanagement of industry it is only necessary to contrast the facility, circumspection, shrewd strategy and close economy shown by these same businessmen in the organisation and management of their pecuniary, fiscal and monetary operations, as against the waste of time, labour and materials that abounds in the industries under their control. But for the workmen likewise, their daily

[1] Cf., e. g., Harrington Emerson, *Efficiency as a Basis for Operation and Wages*, ch. i, iv.

work and their insight into its requirements and possibilities are, by more than half, a "business proposition," a proposition in the pecuniary calculus of how to get the most in price for the least return in weight and tale.

These various considerations, taken crudely in their first incidence, would seem to preclude any technological advance under this quasi-peaceable régime of business. Business principles and pecuniary distinctions rule the familiar routine of life, and even the common welfare is conceived in terms of price, and so of differential advantage; and under such a system there should apparently be little chance of the dispassionate pursuit of such a non-invidious interest as that of workmanship. The prime mover in this cultural scheme appears to be invidious self-aggrandisement, without fear or favour; and its goal appears to be the conspicuous waste of goods and services. Yet in point of fact the technological advance under these modern conditions has been larger and more rapid than in any other cultural situation. Therefore the circumstances under which these modern gains in technology have been made will merit somewhat more detailed attention; as also the cultural consequences that have followed from this technological advance or been conditioned by it. And at the risk of some tedious repetition it seems pertinent summarily to recall these peculiar circumstances that have conditioned the modern culture and have presumably shaped its technological output.

By and large this modern technological era runs its course within the frontiers of Occidental civilisation, and in the period subsequent to the feudal age. Roughly, its centre of diffusion is the region of the North Sea, and its placement in point of time is in that period of comparative peace spoken of as "modern times." Such of the peoples comprised within this Western culture as have continued to be actively occupied with fighting during this modern period have had no creative share in this technological era, and indeed they have had little share of any kind. The broad centre of diffusion of this technology coincides in a curious way with that of the singularly competent and singularly matter-of-fact neolithic culture of northern Europe; and the racial elements that have been engaged in this modern technological advance are still substantially the same, and mixed in substantially the same proportions, as during that prehistoric technological era of the lower barbarism or the higher savagery. This implies, of course, that the spiritual (instinctive) endowment of the peoples that have made the modern technological era is still substantially the same as was that of their forebears of the Danish stone age.

The peoples that have taken the lead in this cultural growth, and more particularly in the technological advance, have never lived under a full grown and consistently worked out patriarchal system, nor have they, therefore, ever fully assimilated that peculiarly personal and arbitrarily authoritative scheme of anthropomorphic beliefs that commonly goes with the patriarchal system. In the earlier phases of their cultural experience, and until recently, they have lived in small communities, under more or less of local self-government, and have in great part shown some degree of religious scepticism and insubordination. They have had some experience of the sea and of that impersonal run of phenomena which the sea offers; which call on those who have to do with the sea for patient observation of how such impersonal forces work, and which constrain them to learn by trial and error how these forces may be turned to account. Latterly, in the days of their most pronounced technological advance, these peoples have had experience of an economic and industrial system organised on an unexampled scale, such as to constitute a very wide and inclusive industrial community within which intercourse has been increasingly easy and effective.

These circumstances have determined the range of their habituation in its larger features; and these peoples have come under the discipline of this situation with a spiritual endowment apparently differing in some degree from what any other group of peoples has ever brought to a similar task. How much of the outcome, cultural and technological, is to be set down naïvely and directly to a peculiar temperamental bent in this human raw material would be hazardous to conjecture. Something seems fairly to be credited to that score. The particular mixture of hybrids that goes to make up these peoples, and in which the dolicho-blond enters more or less ubiquitously, appears to lack a certain degree of subtlety, such as seems native to many other peoples that have created civilisations of a different complexion,—a subtlety that shows itself in a readiness for intrigue and far-sighted appreciation of the springs of human nature, and which often shows itself also in high-wrought and stupendous constructions of anthropomorphic myth and theology, religion and magic, as well as in such large and fertile systems of creative art as will commonly accompany these anthropomorphic creations. Those peoples that are infused with an appreciable blond admixture have on the other hand, not commonly excelled in the farther reaches of the spiritual life, particularly not in the refinements of a sustained and finished anthropomorphism. Their best efficiency has rather run to those bull-headed deeds of force and those mechanic arts that touch closely on the domain of the inorganic forces.

Of such a character is also this modern technological era. It is in the mechanic arts dealing with brute matter that the modern technology holds over all else, in matter-of-fact insight, in the naïveté of the questions with which its adepts search the facts of observation, and in the crudity (anthropomorphically speaking) of the answers with which they are content to go back to their work. Outside of the mechanic arts this technology must be rated lower than second best. In subtlety of craftsmanlike insight and contrivance or in delicacy of manipulation and adroit use of man's physical aptitudes the peoples of this Western culture are not now and never have been equal to the best.

Such a characterisation of the modern technology may seem too broad and too schematic,—that it overlooks features of the case that are sufficiently large and distinctive to call for their recognition even in the most general characterisation. So, e. g., in the light of what has been noted above in speaking of the domestication of the crop plants and animals, the question may well suggest itself: Is not the patent success of these modern industrial peoples in the use and improvement of crops and cattle to be accepted as evidence of a genial anthropomorphic bent, of the same kind and degree as took effect in the original domestication of plants and animals? For some two hundred years past, it is true, very substantial advances have been made in tillage and breeding, and this is at the same time the peculiar domain in which the anthropomorphic savages of the stone age once achieved those things which have made civilisation physically possible; but the modern gains made in these lines have, in the main if not altogether, been technologically of the same mechanistic character as the rest of the modern advance in the industrial arts, with little help or hindrance due to any such anthropomorphic bias as guided the savage ancients. It is rather by virtue of their having come competently to apprehend these facts of animate nature in substantially inanimate terms, mechanistic and chemical terms, that the modern technological adepts in tillage and cattle-breeding have successfully carried this line of workmanship forward at a rate and with an effect not approached before. The live-stock expert is soberly learning by trial and error what to attempt and how to go about it in his breeding experiments, and he deals as callously as any mechanical engineer with the chemistry of stock foods and the use and abuse of ferments, germs and enzymes. The soil specialist talks, thinks and acts in terms of salts, acids, alkalies, stratifications, 200-mesh siftings, and nitrogen-fixing organisms. The crop-plant expert looks to hand-made cross-fertilisation and to the Mendelian calculus of hybridisation, with no more imputation of anthropomorphic traits than the metallurgist who analyses fuels and fluxes, mixes ores, and with goggled eye scrutinises the shifting tints of the incandescent gases in the open hearth. It is from such facts so construed that modern technology is made up, and it is by such channels that the sense of workmanship has gone to the making of it.

So the question recurs, How has it come about that this pecuniary culture—with its institutions drawn in terms of differential advantage and moved by sentiments that converge on emulative gain and the invidiously conspicuous waste of goods—has yet furthered the growth of such a technology, even permissively? In its direct incidence, the discipline of this pecuniary culture is doubtless inimical to any advance in workmanlike insight or any matter-of-fact apprehension and use of objective phenomena. It is a civilisation whose substantial core is of a subjective kind, in the narrowly subjective, personal, individualistic sense given by the self-regarding sentiments of emulous rivalry.[1] But when all is said it is after all a peaceable culture, on the whole; and indeed the rules of the business game of profit and loss, forfeit and sequestration, require it to be so. It has at least that much, and perhaps much else, in common with the great technological era of the north-European neolithic age. The discipline to which its peoples are subject may be exacting enough, and its exactions may run to worldly wisdom rather than to matter-of-fact; but its invidious distinctions run in terms of price, that is to say in terms of an objective, impersonal money unit, in the last resort a metallic

[1] Such is tacitly assumed to be the nature of modern economic life in the current theoretical formulations of the economists, who make the theory of exchange value the central and controlling doctrine in their theoretical systems, and who with easy conviction trace this value back to an individualistic ground in the doctrines of differential utility—"marginal utility."

weight; and the traffic of daily life under this price system affords an unremitting exercise in the exact science of making change, large and small. Even the daydreams of the pecuniary day-dreamer take shape as a calculus of profit and loss computed in standard units of an impersonal magnitude, even though the magnitude of these standard units may on analysis prove to be of a largely putative character. The imputation under the price system is of an impersonal kind. In the current apprehension of the pecuniary devotee these magnitudes are wholly objective, so that in effect the training that comes of busying himself with them is after all a training in the accurate appreciation of brute fact.

At the same time, the instinct of workmanship, being not an acquired trait, has not been got rid of by disuse; and when the occasion offers, under the relatively tranquil conditions of this peaceable or quasi-peaceable pecuniary régime, the ancient proclivity asserts itself in its ancient force, uneager and asthenic perhaps, but pervasive and resilient. And when this instinct works out through the Bœotic genius of the north-European hybrid there is a good chance that the outcome of such observation and reflection will fall into terms of matter-of-fact, of such close-shorn naïveté, indeed, as to afford very passable material for the material sciences and the machine technology.

So also, the ancient and time-worn civil institutions of the north-European peoples have apparently not been of the high-wrought invidious character that comes of long and strenuous training in the practices and ideals of the patriarchal system; nor are their prevailing religious conceits extremely drastic, theatrical or ceremonious, as compared with what is to be found in the cults of the great dynastic civilisations of the East. On the whole, it is only through the Middle Ages that these peoples have been subject to the rigorous servile discipline that characterises a dynastic despotism, secular or religious; and much of the ancient, pagan and prehistoric preconceptions on civil and religious matters appear to have stood over in the habits of thought of the common people even through that interval of submergence under aristocratic and patriarchal rule. In the same connection it may be remarked that the blond-hybrid peoples of Christendom were the last to accept the patriarchal mythology of the Semites and have also been the first and readiest to shuffle out of it in the sequel; which suggests the inference that they have never fully assimilated its spirit; perhaps for lack of a sufficiently strict and protracted discipline in its ways and ideals, perhaps for lack of a suitable temperamental ground.

There is, indeed, a curiously pervasive concomitance, in point of time, place, and race, between the modern machine technology, the material sciences, religious scepticism, and that spirit of insubordination that makes the substance of what are called free or popular institutions. On none of these heads is the concomitance so close or consistent as to warrant the conclusion that race and topography alone have made this modern cultural outcome. The exceptions and side issues are too broad and too numerous for that; but it is after all a concomitance of such breadth and scope that it can also not be overlooked.

The course of mutations that has brought on this

modern technological episode may be conceived to have run somewhat in the following manner. For lack of sufficient training in predatory habits of thought (as shown, e. g., in the incomplete patriarchalism of the north-Europeans) the predatory culture failed to reach what may be called a normal maturity in the feudal system of Europe, particularly in the North and West, where the blond admixture is stronger; by "normal" being here intended that sequence of growth, institutionalisation, and decay shown typically by the great dynastic civilisations erected by Semitic invaders in the East. In the full-charged predatory culture, in its earlier phases, there appear typically to be present two somewhat divergent economic principles (habits of thought) both of which have something of an institutional force: (*a*) The warrant of seizure by prowess,[1] which commonly comes to vest in the dynastic head in case a despotic state is established; and (*b*) the prescriptive tenure of whatever one has acquired. These two institutional factors are at variance, and according as one or the other of the two finally takes precedence and rules out or masters its rival postulate, the predatory culture continues on lines of coercive exploitation, as in these Asiatic monarchies; or it passes into the quasi-peaceable phase marked by secure prescriptive tenure of property and a settled nobility, and presently into a commercialised industrial situation. Either line of development may, of course,

[1] Apart from scattered and progressively inconsequential manifestations of this canon of pecuniary equity in the European community at large, there occurs a quaint and well-defined application of it in the practice of "*hôlmgangr*" in late pagan and early Christian times among the Scandinavian peoples. The "wager of battle" is probably of the same derivation, at least in part.

be broken off without having reached a consummation.

Within the region of the Western Civilisation, both in north Europe and repeatedly in the Ægean, the course of events has fallen out in the line of the latter alternative; the growth of institutions has shifted from the footing of prowess to that of prescriptive ownership. So soon as this shift has securely been made, the development of trade, industry and a technological system has come into the foreground, and these habitual interests have then reacted on the character of the institutions in force, thereby accelerating the growth of conditions favourable to their own further advance. There is, of course, no marked point of conjuncture in the cultural sequence at which this transition may definitely be said to have been effected, but in a general way it may be held that the point of transition has been passed so soon as the current political and economic speculations uncritically give precedence to the "commonweal" as against the fiscal interests of the crown or the "state," whereby the crown and its officers come, in theory and public pronouncement, to be rated as guardians of the community's material welfare rather than autocratic exploiters of the community's productive capacity. Roughly from the same period there will duly set in something of an acceleration in rate of improvement in the state of the mechanic arts. This movement seems plainly to come on the initiative of the lower or industrial classes and to be carried by their genius, rather than by that of the ruling classes, whether secular or spiritual. It shows itself, typically, in a growth of handicraft and petty trade.

So the sense of workmanship and its associated sentiments again come, by insensible degrees, to take the first place among the factors that determine the run of habituation and therefore the character of the resulting culture,—so making the transition from barbarism to civilisation, in the narrower sense of the term; which is accordingly to be characterised, in contrast with the predatory barbarian culture, as a qualified or mitigated (sophisticated) return to the spirit of savagery, or at least as a spiritual reversion looking in that direction, though by no means abruptly reaching the savage plane. The new phase has this in common with the typical savage culture that workmanship rather than prowess again becomes the chief or primary norm of habituation, and therefore of the growth of institutions; and that there results, therefore, a peaceable bent in the ideals and endeavours of the community. But it is workmanship combined and compounded with ownership; that is to say workmanship coupled with an invidious emulation and consequently with a system of institutions embodying a range of prescriptive differential benefits.

II. The Competitive System

Dominated by the tradition handed down from the beginning of the nineteenth century, current economic theory has habitually made much of accumulated goods as the prime requisite of industry. In industrial enterprise as it was then carried on the prevailing unit of organisation was the private firm, with partnership concerns making up a secondary and less commonplace element in the business community. Ordinarily and typically these private firms and partnerships owned a certain material equipment employed in industry, and they took the initiative in industrial enterprise on the ground of this ownership; hiring the workmen, buying materials and supplies, and selling the products of the establishment. Credit relations, such as go to the creation and conduct of a modern corporation, were still of secondary consequence, being resorted to rather as an expedient in emergencies than as the initial move and the substantial ground of business organisation; the measure of the concern's magnitude and consequence was still (typically) its unencumbered ownership of the material equipment, the size of the plant and the numbers of its hired workmen. It follows by easy consequence that in the practical business conceptions of that time the equipment of material means, which embodies the concern's assets and affords the ground of its initiative and its rating in the business community, should commonly be rated as the prime mover in industry and the chief productive factor. So, also, the theoretical speculation that drew on that business traffic for its working concepts came unavoidably to accept these tangible assets, the community's material equipment,—implements, livestock, raw materials, means of subsistence,—as the prime agency in the community's economic life. As is true for the working conceptions and principles of industrial business, so also in the theoretical formulations of the economists, the community's immaterial equipment of technological proficiency is taken for granted as a circumstance of the environment conditioning the community's economic life,—the state of the industrial arts and the current workmanlike aptitudes and efficiency.

As the phrase runs, "given the state of the industrial arts."

This is good, homely, traditional common sense; it reflects the habitual practical run of affairs in the industrial community of that recent past. Such was the attitude of practical men toward industrial matters at the time when the current economic situation took its rise. But such a conception is no longer so true to the practical exigencies of the immediate present, nor do the men of affairs to-day habitually see these matters in just this light; although the principles of the law that govern industrial enterprise still continue to embody these time-worn conceptions, to which the economists also continue to yield allegiance. Like other elements of habitual knowledge this conception of things is drawn from past experience—chiefly from a past not too remote for ready comprehension—and it carries over the frame of mind out of which it arose.

In the earlier days of the machine industry, then,—say, in the closing quarter of the eighteenth century,—the conduct of industrial affairs was in the hands of business men who owned the material equipment and who directed the use of this equipment and turned it to account for their own gain, on the prescriptive ground of such ownership. Discretion and initiative vested in the capitalist-employer, who at that time, (typically) combined ownership of the plant with a somewhat immediate supervision and control of the industrial processes. The directive control of industry, covering both the volume and the character of the procesess and output, was in the typical case directly bound up with the ownership of the material equipment as such,—as tangible assets, not as corporation stock-holdings. Since then changes have come over the business situation, particularly through an extensive recourse to credit, such that this time-worn conception will no longer answer the run of current business practice, particularly not as touches that large-scale enterprise that now rules industrial affairs and that is currently accepted as the type of modern business enterprise.

Among the assumptions of a hundred years ago was the premise, self-evident to that generation of thoughtful men, that the phase of commercialised economic life then prevailing was the immutably normal order of things. And the assumptions surrounding that preconception were good and competent for a formulation of economic theory that takes such an institutional situation for granted and assumes it to be unchanging, or to be a *terminus ad quem.* But for anything like a genetic account of economic life, early or late, capitalistic or otherwise, such assumptions and the theoretical propositions and analyses that follow from them are defective in that they take for granted what requires to be accounted for. Theoretical speculation that presupposes the (somewhat old-fashioned) institutions formerly governing ownership and business traffic, and assumes them to have the immutable character and indefeasible force *de facto* which is assigned them *de jure*, and that likewise assumes as immutable a passing phase in the "state of the industrial arts," may serve passably for a theory of how business affairs should properly arrange themselves to fit the conditions so assumed; and such, indeed, has commonly been the character of theoretical formulations touching industry and business. And as should fairly be expected, in the speculations of the economists, these theoretical formulations have also commonly been accompanied by a parallel line of remedial advice designed to show what preventive measures should be applied to prevent the run of business practice from doing violence to these assumed conditions that are held to be immutably normal and indefeasibly right.

Now, since in the received theories the accumulated "productive goods" are conceived to be the most consequential factor in industry, and therefore in the community's material welfare and in the fortunes of individuals, it logically follows that the discretionary ownership of them has come to be accounted the most important relation in which men may stand to the production of wealth and to the community's livelihood; and the pecuniary transactions whereby this ownership is arranged, manipulated and redistributed are held to be industrially the most productive of all human activities. It is only during the nineteenth century that this doctrine of pecuniary productivity has been worked out into finished shape and has found secure lodgment in the systematic structure of economic theory—in the current theory of "the Function of the Entrepreneur;"[1] but it is also only during this period that business enterprise (pecuniary management) has come to dominate the economic situation in a substantially unmitigated degree, so that the material fortunes of the community have come to depend on these pecuniary negotiations into which its "captains of industry" enter for their own

[1] Cf. Frederic Barnard Hawley, *Enterprise and the Productive Process*, for an extreme, mature and consistent development of this tenet.

gain.[1] In the sense that no other line of activity stands in anything like an equally decisive relation of initiative or discretion to the industrial process, or bears with a like weight on the material welfare of the community, these business negotiations in ownership are unquestionably the prime factor in modern industry. But that such is the case is due to the peculiar institutions of modern times and to the peculiar current state of the industrial arts; and the former of these peculiar circumstances is conditioned by the latter.

It is not practicable to assign a hard and fast date from which this modern era began, with its peculiar scheme of economic life and the economic conceptions that characterise it. The date will vary from one country to another, and even from one industrial class to another within the same country. But it can be said that historically the modern era begins with the rise of handicraft; it is along the line of growth marked out by the development of handicraft that the modern technology has emerged, together with that industrial organisation and those pecuniary conceptions of economic efficiency and serviceability that have gradually come to their current state of maturity on the ground afforded by this technology. What historically lies back of the era of handicraft is not of a piece with the economic situation of modern times; nor is it characteristic of the Western civilisation, as contrasted with the agricultural and predatory civilisations of antiquity.

[1] See *The Theory of Business Enterprise*, ch. iv, vi, vii, for a more detailed discussion of this business traffic and the working principles which govern it. See also H. J. Davenport, *The Economics of Enterprise* (New York, 1913).

As indicated in an earlier chapter, in speaking of the decay of the predatory (feudalistic) régime and its servile agricultural organisation of industry, when peace and order supervene the instinct of workmanship by insensible degrees and in an uncertain measure supplants the invidious self-regarding sentiments that actuate the life of prowess and servility characteristic of that culture; so that workmanship comes again into the foreground among the instinctive propensities that shape the community's habitual interest and so bend the course of its institutional growth and determine the bias of its common sense.

The habitual outlook and the bias given by the handicraft system are of a twofold character—technological and pecuniary. The craftsman was an artificer engaged in mechanical operations, working with tools of which he had the mastery, and employing mechanical processes the mysteries of which were familiar to his everyday habits of thought; but from the beginning of the era of handicraft and throughout his industrial life he was also more or less of a trader. He stood in close relation with some form of market, and his proficiency as a craftsman was brought to a daily practical test in the sale of his wares or services, no less than in the workmanlike fashioning of them. Also, the price as well as the workmanlike quality of the goods presently became subject of regulation under the rules of the crafts; and the petty trade which grew up as an occupation accessory to the handicraft industry was itself organised on lines analogous to the crafts proper and was regulated by similar principles; the trader's work being accounted serviceable, or productive, in the same general sense as that of any other craftsman and being recognised as equitably entitling those who pursued it to a fair livelihood.

The handicraft system was an organised and regulated system of workmanship and self-help; and under the conditions imposed by its technology proficiency in the latter respect was no less indispensable and no less to the purpose than in the former. Both counted equally and in combination toward the successful working of the system, which is a practicable plan of economic life only so long as the craftsmen combine both of these capacities in good force and only so long as the technological exigencies admit the exercise of both in conjunction. The system broke down so soon as the state of the industrial arts no longer enabled the workmen to acquire the necessary technological proficiency and do the required work at the same time that they each and several were able to oversee and pursue their individual pecuniary interests. With the coming on of a wider and more extensively differentiated technological scheme, and with wider and remoter market relations, due in the main to increased facilities of transportation, these necessary conditions of a practicable handicraft economy gradually failed, and the practice of industrial investments and the larger commerce then gradually supplanted it.

The discipline of everyday life under the handicraft economy was a discipline in pecuniary self-help as well as in workmanship. In the popular ideal as well as in point of practical fact the complete craftsman stood shrewdly on his individual proficiency in maintaining his own pecuniary advantage, as well as on his trained workmanship; and the gilds were organised to maintain the craft's advantages in the market, as well as to regulate the quality of the output. The craft rules governing the quality of the output of goods were in the main enforced with a view to the maintenance of price, and so with a view to securing an adequate livelihood for the craftsmen. Efficiency in the crafts came in this way presently to be counted very much as the modern "efficiency engineers" would count it,—proximately in terms of mechanical performance, ultimately in terms of price, and more particularly in terms of net gain. So that the habits of life ingrained in the gildsman, and in the community at large where the gild system prevailed, comprised as a main fact a meticulous regard for details of ownership and for pecuniary claims and obligations. It is out of this insistent, pervasive, and minutely concrete discipline in the practice and logic of pecuniary detail that there have arisen those "natural rights" of property and those "business principles" that have been taken over by the later era of the machine industry and capitalistic investment.

The rules of the gild, as well as the larger legislative provisions that had to do with gild regulations, were avowedly drawn with a view to securing the gildsman in a fair customary livelihood, and the measures logically adopted to this end were designed to secure him in the enjoyment and disposal of the returns of his work as well as in his right to pursue his trade within the rules laid down for the collective welfare by the gild. With due training in this logic of the handicraft system it became a plain matter of common sense that the craftsman should equitably be entitled to whatever he can get for his work under the conventionally settled rules of the trade, and should be free to make the most of his capacities in all that pertains to his pursuit of a livelihood; and the like principles (habits of thought) apply to the traffic of the petty trade; which, being presently interpreted in terms of contract and investment, has come to mean the right to do business and to enjoy and dispose of the returns from all bargains made in due form.

Presently, as the technological situation gradually changed its character through extensions and specialisation in appliances and processes—perhaps especially through changes in the means of communication and in the density of population—the handicraft system with its petty trade outgrew itself and broke down in a new phase of the pecuniary culture. The increasingly wide differentiation between workmanship and salesmanship grew into a "division of labour" between industry and business, between industrial and pecuniary occupations,—a disjunction of ownership and its peculiar cares, privileges and proficiency from workmanship. By this division of labour, or divergence of function, a fraction of the community came to specialise in ownership and pecuniary traffic, and so came to constitute a business community occupied with pecuniary affairs, running along beside the industrial community proper, with a development of practices and usages peculiar to its own needs and bearing only indirectly on the further development of the industrial system or on the state of the industrial arts.

Master-workmen with means would employ other workmen without means, and might or might not themselves continue to work at the trade. Petty traders or hucksters, nominally members of some craft gild, would grow wealthy with the increasing volume of traffic and would organise a more and more extensive household (sweatshop) industry to meet the increasing demands of their market; or they might become jobbers, carry on more far-reaching trade operations over a longer term, withdraw more distantly from the actual work of the craft, and in the course of a generation or two (as, e. g., the Fuggers) would grow into merchant princes and financiers who maintained but a remote and impersonal relation to the crafts. Or, again, the associated merchants (as, e. g., those of the Hansa) would establish depots and agents, "factories," that would gradually assemble something of a working force of craftsmen to sort, warehouse and finish the products which they handled, at the same time that they would exercise an increasingly close and extensive oversight of the industries from which these products were derived; until these depots, under the management of the factors, in some cases grew into factories in somewhat the modern acceptance of the term. In one way and another this trading or huckstering traffic, which had been intimately associated with the handicraft industry and gild life, branched off in the course of time as the industries advanced to a larger scale and a more extensive specialisation; and this increasing "division of labour" between workmanship and salesmanship led presently to such a segregation of the traders out of the body of craftsmen as to give rise to a business community devoted to pecuniary management alone.

But the principles on which the new and larger business was conducted were the same as those on which the earlier petty trade had been carried on, and therefore the same in point of derivation and tenor as had been worked out by long experience within the handicraft system proper. Business traffic was an outgrowth of the handicraft system, and it was in as secure a position in respect of legitimacy and legal and customary guaranty as the industrial system from which its principles were derived and from which its gains were drawn.

The source from which the new line of businessmen drew the accumulations of wealth by force of which they were enabled to do business is somewhat in dispute; but however interesting a question that may be in its own right, it does not particularly concern the present inquiry, and the like is true for the still more interesting and spectacular phenomena that marked the growth and decline of that early business era that ran its course within the life-history of the handicraft system.[1] Throughout that great period of business activity on the continent of Europe that gathered head in the sixteenth century and that closed in decay and collapse in the seventeenth, the principles (habits of thought) which underlay, authenticated and animated the business community and its pecuniary traffic continued to be much the same as animated the body of craftsmen in their pecuniary relations from the beginning of the era of handicraft to its close. Such, in its turn, was also the case with the later business era that set in with the great industrial advance of England in the Eighteenth Century, and such continued to be the case through the greater part of its life-history in the Nineteenth Century. Of the latterday and latest de-

[1] Cf., e. g., Ehrenberg, *Das Zeitalter der Fugger;* Sombart, *Der Moderne Kapitalismus*, bk. i.

velopments in business practice and principles the like cannot unhesitatingly be said, but this too is a matter that does not immediately concern the inquiry at this point. But the principles of the new and larger business were the same as had been slowly worked out under the system of petty trade. These business principles have proved to be very tenacious and stable, even in the face of apparently adverse technological circumstances, coming as they do out of a long and rigorous habituation of very wide sweep and having acquired the authenticity due to formal recognition in legal decisions and to the painstaking definition given them in the course of a protracted and exacting struggle against the institutional remnants of the feudal system. These circumstances attending the genesis and growth of modern business principles have led to their being formulated in a well-defined conceptual scheme of customary right and also to their embodiment in statutory form. To this, perhaps, they owe much of their tenacious resistance to latterday exigencies that have tended to modify or abrogate them. In their elements, of course, these business principles are even older than the era of handicraft, being substantially of the same nature as that sentimental impulse to self-aggrandisement that lies at the root of the predatory culture and so makes the substantial core of all pecuniary civilisations.

The distinguishing mark of any business era, as contrasted with the handicraft economy, is the supreme dominance of pecuniary principles, both as standards of efficiency and as canons of conduct. In such a businesslike community efficiency is rated in terms of pecuniary gain; and in so far as business principles rule, efficiency in any other direction than business traffic can claim recognition only in the measure in which it may be reduced to terms of pecuniary gain. Workmanship, therefore, comes to be rated in terms of salesmanship. And the canons of workmanship, and even of technological efficiency, fall more and more into pecuniary lines and allow pecuniary tests to decide on points of serviceability.

The instinct of workmanship is accordingly contaminated with ideals of self-aggrandisement and the canons of invidious emulation, so that even the serviceability of any given action or policy for the common good comes to be rated in terms of the pecuniary gain which such conduct will bring to its author. Any pecuniary strategist—"captain of industry"—who manages to engross appreciably more than an even share of the community's wealth is therefore likely to be rated as a benefactor of the community at large and an exemplar of the social virtues; whereas the man who works and does not manage to divert something more from the aggregate product to his own use than what one man's work may contribute to it is visited not only with dispraise for having fallen short of a decent measure of efficiency but also with moral reprobation for shiftlessness and wasted opportunities. So also, to the current common sense in a community trained to pecuniary rather than to workmanlike discrimination between articles of use, those articles which serve their material use in a conspicuously wasteful manner commend themselves as more serviceable, nobler and more beautiful than such goods as do not embody such a margin of waste.[1]

[1] Cf. *The Theory of the Leisure Class*, ch. iv, v, vi.

Under this system of business principles, in one way and another, the sense of workmanship is contaminated in all its ramifications by preconceptions of pecuniary merit and invidious distinction. But what is here immediately in question is its deflection into the channels of gainful business, together with the more obvious consequences that follow directly from the substitution of differential gain in the place of material serviceability as the end to which the instinctive propensity of workmanship so comes to drive men's ideals and efforts under the discipline of the pecuniary culture.

For the purposes of a genetic inquiry into this modern business situation and its bearing on the sense of workmanship and on the technological phenomena in which that instinct comes to an expression, it is necessary summarily to recall certain current facts pertinent to the case: (*a*) It is a competitive system; that is to say it is a system of pecuniary rivalry and contention which proceeds on stable institutions of property and contract, under conditions of peace and order. (*b*) It is a price system, i. e., the competition runs in terms of money, and the money unit is the standard measure of efficiency and achievement; hence competition and efficiency are subject to a rigorous accountancy in terms of a (putatively) stable money unit, which is in all business traffic assumed to be invariable. (*c*) Technologically this situation is dominated by the mechanical industries; so much so that even the arts of husbandry have latterly taken on much of the character of the mechanic arts. Hence a somewhat thoroughgoing standardisation of processes and products in mechanical terms; which for business purposes has with a fair degree of success been made convertible into terms of price, and so made subject to accountancy in terms of price. (*d*) Hence consumption is also standardised, proximately in mechanical terms of consumable products but finally, through the mechanism of the market, in terms of price, and like other price phenomena consumption also is competitively subject to and enforced by the like accountancy in terms of the money unit. (*e*) The typical industries, which set the pace for productive work, for competitive gains, and through the standard rates of gain ultimately also for competitive consumption, are industries carried on on a large scale; that is to say they are such as to require a large material equipment, a wide recourse to technological insight and proficiency, and a large draught on the material resources of the community. (*f*) This material equipment—industrial plant and natural resources—it held in private ownership, with negligible exceptions; the noteworthy exceptions to this rule, as e. g., harbours, highways, and the like, serving chiefly as accessory means of industry and so come in chiefly as a gratuitous supplement to the industrial equipment held in private ownership and used for competitive gain. (*g*) Technological knowledge and proficiency is in the main held and transmitted pervasively by the community at large, but it is also held in part—more obviously because exceptionally—by specially trained classes and individual workmen. Relatively little, in effect a negligible proportion, of this technological knowledge and skill is in any special sense held by the owners of the industrial equipment, more particularly not by the owners of the typical large-scale industries. That is to say, the technologically proficient workmen do not in the typical case own or control any appreciable proportion of the material equipment or of the natural resources to which this technological knowledge and skill applies and in the use of which it takes effect. (*h*) It results that the owners of this large material equipment, including the natural resources, have a discretionary control of the technological proficiency of the community at large, as well as of those special lines of insight and skill that are vested in these specially trained expert men in whom a specialised proficiency is added to the general proficiency that is diffused through the community at large. (*i*) In effect, therefore, the owners of the necessary material equipment own also the working capacity of the community and the usufruct of the state of the industrial arts. Except for their effective ownership of these elements of productive efficiency their ownership of the material equipment of industry would be of no effect. But the usufruct of this productive capacity of the community and its trained workmen vests in the owners of the material equipment only with the contingent qualification that if the community does this work it must be allowed a livelihood, whereby the gross returns that go in the first instance to these owners suffer abatement by that much. This required livelihood is adjusted to a conventional standard of living which, under the current circumstances of pecuniary emulation, is in great part—perhaps chiefly—a standardised schedule of conspicuous waste.

In what has just been said above, the view is implied that the owners of the material means, who are in great part also the employers of workmen and are sentimentally spoken of as "captains of industry," have, in effect and commonly, but a relatively loose grasp of the technological facts, possibilities, and requirements of modern industry, and that by virtue of their business training they are able to make but a scant and uncertain use of such loose ideas as they have on these heads. To anyone imbued with the commonplaces of current economic theory it may seem that exception should dutifully be taken to this view, as being an understatement of the businessmen's technological merits. In current theoretical formulations the businessman is discussed under the caption of "entrepreneur," "undertaker," etc., and his gains are spoken of as "wages of superintendence," "wages of management," and the like. He is conceived as an expert workman in charge of the works, a superior foreman of the shop, and his gains are accounted a remuneration for his creative contribution to the process of production, due to his superior insight and initiative in technological matters. This conception of the businessman and his relation to industry has stood over from an earlier period, the period of the small-scale industry of handicraft and petty trade, when it still was true that the owner-employer, in the typical case, kept a personal oversight of his workmen and their work, and so filled the place of master-workman as well as that of buyer and seller of materials and finished goods. And such a characterisation of the businessman and his work will still hold true in the modern situation in so far as he still is occupied with industry conducted on the same small scale and continues to fill the place of a foreman of the shop. But under current conditions—the conditions of the past half century—and more particularly under the conditions of that large-scale industry that is currently accounted the type of modern industry, the businessman has ceased to be foreman of the shop, and his surveillance of industry has ceased effectually to comprise a technological management of its details; and in corresponding measure this traditional theoretical conception of the businessman has ceased to apply.

The view here spoken for, that the modern businessman is necessarily out of effectual touch with the affairs of technology as such and incompetent to exercise an effectual surveillance of the processes of industry, is not a matter of bias or of vague opinion; it has in fact become a matter of statistical demonstration. Even a cursory survey of the current achievements of these great modern industries as managed by businessmen, taken in contrast with the opportunities offered them, should convince anyone of the technological unfitness of this business management of industry. Indeed, the captains of industry have themselves latterly begun to recognise their own inefficiency in this respect, and even to appreciate that a businessman's management of industrial processes is not good even for the business purpose—the net pecuniary gain. And it is all the more ineffectual for the purposes of workmanship as distinct from the businessmen's gains. So, a professional class of "efficiency engineers" is coming into action, whose duty it is to take invoice of the preventable wastes and inefficiencies due to the business management of industry and to present the case in such concrete and obvious terms of price and percentage as the businessmen in charge will be able to comprehend. These men, in a way, take over the functions assigned in economic theory to the "entrepreneur;" in that they are men of general technological training and insight, who go into their inquiry on the ground of workmanship, take their data in terms of workmanship and convert them into terms of business expediency, somewhat to the same purpose as the like work of conversion was done by the owner-employers under that small-scale system of industrial enterprise from which the current theoretical concept of the "entrepreneur" was derived. It is then the duty of these efficiency engineers to present the results so obtained, for the conviction and guidance of the business-men in charge, who thereupon, if their business training has left them enough of a sense of workmanship, will give permissive instructions to the expert workmen in direct charge of the industrial processes to put these statistically indicated changes into effect. It is the testimony of these efficiency engineers that relatively few pecuniary captains in command of industrial enterprises have a sufficient comprehension of the technological facts to understand and accept the findings of the technological experts who so argue for the elimination of preventable wastes, even when the issue is presented statistically in terms of price. These men go about their work of ascertaining the efficiency, actual and potential, of any given plant, process, working force, or parcel of material resources, by the methods of precise physical measurement familiar to mechanical engineers, and as an outcome they have no hesitation in speaking of preventable wastes amounting to ten, twenty, fifty, or even ninety per-cent, in the common run of American industries.[1]

[1] Cf. Harrington Emerson, *Efficiency as a Basis for Operation and Wages.*

The work of the efficiency engineers being always done in the service of business and with a view to business expediency, their findings bear directly on the business exigencies of the case alone, and give definitive results only in terms of price and profits. How much greater the ascertained discrepancies in the case would appear if these findings could be reduced to terms of serviceability to the community at large, there is no means of forming a secure conjecture. That the discrepancy would in such case prove to be appreciably greater than that shown by the price rating is not doubtful. Under such an appraisal, where the given industrial enterprises would be brought to the test of net serviceability to the community instead of the net gain of the interested businessmen, many industrial enterprises would doubtless show a waste of appreciably more than one hundred per cent of their current output, being rather disserviceable to the community's material welfare than otherwise.

That the business community is so permeated with incapacity and lack of insight in technological matters is doubtless due proximately to the fact that their attention is habitually directed to the pecuniary issue of industrial enterprise; but more fundamentally and unavoidably it is due to the large volume and intricate complications of the current technological scheme, which will not permit any man to become a competent specialist in an alien and exacting field of endeavour, such as business enterprise, and still acquire and maintain an effectual working acquaintance with the state of the industrial arts. The current technological scheme cannot be mastered as a matter of commonplace information or a by-occupation incidental to another pursuit. The same advance to a large and exhaustive technological system, in the machine industry, that has thrown the direction of industrial affairs into the hands of men primarily occupied with pecuniary management has also made it impossible for men so circumstanced at all adequately to exercise the oversight and direction of industry thereby required at their hands. And the ancient principles of self-help and pecuniary gain by virtue of which these men are held to their work of business enterprise make it also impossible for them adequately to surrender the discretionary care of the industrial processes to other hands or to permit the management of industry to proceed on other than these same business principles.

This technological infirmity of the businessmen assuredly does not arise from a lack of interest in industry, since it is only out of the net product of industry that the business community's gains are drawn—except so far as they are substantially gains of accountancy merely, due to an inflation of values. Perhaps no class of men have ever been more keenly alert in their interest in industrial matters than the modern businessmen; and this interest extends not only to the industrial ventures in which they may for the time be pecuniarily "interested," but also and necessarily to other lines of industry that are more or less closely correlated with the one in which the given businessman's fortunes are embarked; for under modern market conditions any given line of industrial enterprise is bound in endless relations of give and take with all the rest. But this unremitting attention of businessmen to the affairs of industry is a business attention, and, so far as may be, it touches nothing but the pecuniary phenomena connected with the ownership of industry; so that it comes rather to a training in the art of keeping in touch with the pecuniary run of business affairs while avoiding all undue intimacy with the technological facts of industry, —undue in the sense of being in excess of what may serve the needs of a comprehensive short-term outlook over market relations, and which would therefore divert attention from this main interest and befog the pecuniary logic by which businessmen are governed.

Probably, also, no class of men have ever bent more unremittingly to their work than the modern business community. Within the business community there is properly speaking no leisure class, or at least no idle class. In this respect there is a notable contrast between the business community and the landed interest. What there is to be found in this modern culture in the way of an idle class, considered as an institution, runs back for its origins and its specific traits to a more archaic cultural scheme; it is a survival from an earlier (predatory) phase of the pecuniary culture. In the nature of things an idle life of fashion is an affair of the nobility (gentry), of predatory antecedents and, under current conditions, of predatory-parasitic habits; and as regards those modern rich men who withdraw from the business community and fall into a state of *otium cum dignitate*, it is commonly their fortune to be assimilated by a more or less ceremonial induction into the body of this quasi-predatory gentry or nobility and so assume an imitative colouring of archaism.

The business community is hard at work, and there is no place in it for anyone who is unable or unwilling to work at the high tension of the average; and since this close application to pecuniary work is of a competitive nature it leaves no chance for any of the competitors to apply himself at all effectually to other than pecuniary work. This high tension of work is felt to be very meritorious in all modern communities, somewhat in proportion as they are modern; as is necessarily the case in any work that is substantially of an emulative character. It spends itself on salesmanship, not on workmanship in the naïve sense; although the all-pervading preoccupation with pecuniary matters in modern times has led to its being accounted the type of workmanlike endeavour. It concerns itself ultimately with the pecuniary manipulation of the material equipment of industry, though there is much of it that does not bear immediately on that point. The exceptions under this broad proposition are more apparent than real, although there doubtless are exceptions actual as well as apparent. In such a case the business transactions in question are likely to bear on the ownership of certain specific elements of the immaterial technological equipment, as e. g., habits of thought covered by patent-right or mechanical expedients covered by franchise. Beyond these there are elements of "good-will" that are subject of traffic and that consist in preferential advantages in respect of purely pecuniary transactions having to do not with the material equipment but with the right to deal with it and its management, as e. g., in banking, underwriting, insurance, and the phenomena of the money market at large.

But the mature business situation as it runs today is a

complex affair, large and intricate, wherein the effective relations in which business traffic stands to workmanship and to the community's immaterial equipment of technological knowledge at large are greatly obscured by their own convolutions and by the institutional arrangements and convictions to which this traffic has given rise. So that the matter is best approached by way of a genetic exposition that shall take as its point of departure that simpler business enterprise of early modern times out of which the larger development of the present has grown by insensible accretions and displacements.

Business enterprise came in the course of time to take over the affairs of industry and so to withdraw these affairs from the tutelage of the gilds. This shifting of the effectual discretion in the management of industrial affairs came on gradually and in varying fashion and degree over a considerable interval of time. But the decisive general circumstance that enforced this move into the modern way of doing was an advance in the scope and method of workmanship.[1] What threw the fortunes of the industrial community into the hands of the owners of accumulated wealth was essentially a technological change, or rather a complex of technological changes, which so enlarged the requirements in respect of material equipment that the impecunious workmen could no longer carry on their trade except by a working arrangement with the owners of this equipment; whereby

[1] Cf., e. g., Karl Bücher, *Die Entstehung der Volkswirtschaft*, (3d ed.), ch. iv, "Die gewerblichen Betriebssysteme," ch. v. "Der Niedergang des Handwerks;" W. J. Ashley, *English Economic History and Theory*, part ii, ch. i, sec. 25, ch. iii, especially sec. 44; W. Cunningham, *The Growth of English Industry and Commerce*, vol. ii, Introduction; Werner Sombart, *Der Moderne Kapitalismus*, bk. i, especially ch. iv–xii.

the discretionary control of industry was shifted from the craftsmen's technological mastery of the ways of industry to the owner's pecuniary mastery of the material means. In the change that so took place to a larger technological scale much was doubtless due to the extension of trade, itself in great part an outcome of technological changes, directly and indirectly. For the craftsmen and their work the outcome was that recourse must be had to the material equipment owned by those who owned it, and on such terms as would content the owners; whereby the usufruct of the workmen's proficiency and of the state of the industrial arts fell to the owners of the material equipment, on such terms as might be had.[1] So it fell to these owners of the material means and of the products

[1] To complete the sketch at this point, even in outline, it would be necessary to go extensively into the relations of ownership and control (largely indirect) in which the owners of land and natural resources, the Landed Interest, had stood to the industrial community of craftsmen before this transition to the business era got under way, as also into the further mutual relations subsisting between the landed interest, the craftsmen and the business community during this transition to a business régime. In the most summary terms the pertinent circumstances appear to have been that from the beginning of its technological era the handicraft community, with its workmanship and its technological attainments, was in an uncertain measure at the discretionary call of the landed interest, largely in an impersonal way through channels of trade and on the whole with decreasingly exacting effect as time went on; and the industrial community at large had by no means emancipated themselves from this control when the era of business enterprise set in; for the landed interest continued to draw its livelihood from the mixed agricultural and handicraft community, and the products of handicraft still continued to go chiefly as supplies to the landed interest in return for the means of subsistence controlled by the latter; and long after the businessmen had taken over the direction of industry the claims of the landed interest still continued paramount in the economic situation, and industry still continued to be carried on largely with a view to meeting the requirements of the landed interest.

of industry to turn this technological situation to account for their own gain, with as little abatement as might be, and at the same time it became incumbent on them each and several competitively to divert as large a share of the community's productive efficiency to his own profit as the circumstances would permit.

CHAPTER VI

The Era of Handicraft [1]

Owing, probably, to the peculiar topography of Europe, small-scale and broken, the pastoral-predatory culture has never been fully developed or naturalised in this region; nor has a monarchy of the great type characteristic of western Asia ever run its course in Europe. The nearest approach to such a despotic state would be the Roman Empire; which was after all essentially Mediterranean, largely Levantine, rather than peculiarly European. And owing probably to the same conditioning limitations of topography the subsequent sequence of institutional phenomena have also been characteristically different in this European region from that in the large and fertile lands of the near East. It is necessarily this run of events in the Western culture that is of chief interest to the present inquiry; which will therefore most conveniently follow the historical outlines of this culture in its later phases, in so far as these outlines are to be drawn in economic terms of a large generality.

In a passably successful fashion the peoples of Christendom made the transition from a frankly predatory

[1] "Handwerk (im engeren Sinne) ist diejenige Wirtschaftsform, die hervorwächst aus dem streben eines gewerblichen Arbeiters seine zwischen Kunst und gewöhnlicher Handarbeit die Mitte haltende Fertigkeit zur Herrichtung oder Bearbeitung gewerblicher Gebrauchsgegenstände in der Weise zu vertreten, dass er sich durch Austausch seiner Leistungen oder Erzeugnisse gegen entsprechende Äquivalente seinen Lebensunterhalt verschafft."—Sombart, *Moderne Kapitalismus*, bk. i, ch. iv.

and servile establishment, in the Dark Ages, to a settled, quasi-peaceable situation resting on fairly secure property rights, chiefly in land, by the close of the Middle Ages. This transition was accompanied by a growth of handicraft, itinerant merchandising and industrial towns, so massive as to outlive and displace the feudal system under whose tutelage it took its rise, and of so marked a technological character as to have passed into history as the "era of handicraft." Technologically, this era is marked by an ever advancing growth of craftsmanship; until it passes over into the régime of the machine industry when its technology had finally outgrown those limitations of handicraft and petty trade that gave it its character as a distinct phase of economic history. In its beginning the handicraft system was made up of impecunious craftsmen, working in severalty and working for a livelihood, and the rules of the craft-gilds that presently took shape and exercised control were drawn on that principle.[1] The petty trade which characteristically runs along with the development of handicraft was carried on after the same detail fashion and was presently organised on lines afforded by the same principle of work for a livelihood.

Presently, however, in early modern times, larger holdings of property came to be employed in the itinerant trade, and investment for a profit found its way into this trade as also into the handicraft system proper. The processes of industry grew more extensive and roundabout, the specialisation of occupations ("division of

[1] Cf. Sombart, *Der Moderne Kapitalismus*, bk. i; W. J. Ashley, *English Economic History and Theory*, bk. i, especially ch. iii; Karl Bücher, *die Entstehung der Volkswirtschaft*, ch. iv, v.

labour") increased, the scale of organisation grew larger, and the practice of employing impecunious workmen in organised bodies under the direction of wealthier masters came to be the prevailing form taken by the industry of the time.

From near the beginnings of the handicraft system, and throughout the period of its flourishing, the output of the industry was habitually sold at a price, in terms of money. In the earlier days the price was regulated on the basis of labour cost, on the principle that a competent craftsman must be allowed a fair livelihood, and much thought and management was spent on the determination and maintenance of such a "just price." But in the course of generations, with further development of trade and markets, this conception of price by degrees gave way to or passed over into the modern presumption that any article of value is worth what it will bring; until, when the era of handicraft and petty trade merges in the late-modern régime of investment and machine industry, it has become the central principle of pecuniary relations that price is a matter to be arranged freely between buyer and seller on the basis of bargain and sale.

The characteristic traits of this era are the handicraft industry and the petty trade which handled the output of that industry, with the trade gradually coming into a position of discretionary management, and even dominating the industry of the craftsmen to such an extent that by the date when the technology of handicraft begins to give way to the factory organisation and the machine industry the workmen are already somewhat fully under the control of the businessmen. Visibly, the ruling cause of this change in the relations between the craftsmen on the one hand and the traders and master-employers on the other hand was the increasing magnitude of the material means necessary to the pursuit of industry, due to such a growth of technology as required an ever larger, more finished and more costly complement of appliances. So that in the course of the era of handicraft the ancient relation between owners and workmen gradually re-established itself within the framework of the new technology; with the difference that the owners in whose hands the discretion now lay, and to whose gain the net output of industry now inured, were the businessmen, investors, the owners of the industrial plant and of the apparatus of trade, instead of as formerly the owners of the soil.

Under the handicraft system, and to the extent to which that system shaped the situation, the instinct of workmanship again came into a dominant position among the factors that made up the discipline of daily life and so gave their characteristic bent to men's habits of thought. In the technology of handicraft the central fact is always the individual workman, whether in the crafts proper or in the petty trade. In that era industry is conceived in terms of the skill, initiative and application of the trained individual, and human relations outside of the workshop tend also by force of habit to be conceived in similar terms of self-sufficient individuals, each working out his own ends in severalty.

The position of the craftsman in the economy of that time is peculiarly suited to induce a conception of the individual workman as a creative agent standing on his own bottom, and as an ultimate, irreducible factor in the community's make-up. He draws on the resources of his own person alone; neither his ancestry nor the favour of his neighbours have visibly yielded him anything beyond an equivalent for work done; he owes nothing to inherited wealth or prerogative, and he is bound in no relation of landlord or tenant to the soil. With his slight outfit of tools he is ready and competent of his own motion to do the work that lies before him, and he asks nothing but an even chance to do what he is fit to do. Even the training which has given him his finished skill he has come by through no special favour or advantage, having given an equivalent for it all in the work done during his apprenticeship and so having to all appearance acquired it by his own force and diligence. The common stock of technological knowledge underlying all special training was at that time still a sufficiently simple and obvious matter, so that it was readily acquired in the routine of work, without formal application to the learning of it; and any indebtedness to the community at large or to past generations for such common stock of information would therefore not be sufficiently apparent to admit of its disturbing the craftsman's naïve appraisal of his productive capacity in the simple and complacent terms of his own person.

The man who does things, who is creatively occupied with fashioning things for use, is the central fact in the scheme of things under the handicraft system, and the range of concepts by use of which the technological problems of that era are worked out is limited by the habit of mind so induced in those who have the work in hand and in those who see it done. The discipline of the crafts inculcates the apprehension of mechanical facts and processes in terms of workmanlike endeavour and achievement; so that questions as to what forces are available for use, and of how to turn them to account, present themselves in terms of muscular force and manual dexterity. Mechanical appliances for use in industry are designed and worked out as contrivances to facilitate or to abridge manual labour, and it is in terms of labour that the whole industrial system is conceived and its incidence, value and output rated.

Such a fashion of conceiving the operations and appliances of industry seems at the same time to fall in closely with men's natural bent as given by the native instinct of workmanship; and fostered by the consistent drift of daily routine under the handicraft system this attitude grew into matter of course, and has continued to direct men's thinking on industrial matters even long after the era of handicraft has passed and given place to the factory system and the large machine industry. So much so that throughout the nineteenth century, in economic speculations as well as in popular speech, the mechanical plant employed in industry has habitually been spoken of as "labour saving devices;" even such palpable departures from the manual workmanship of handicraft as the power loom, the smelting furnace, artificial waterways and highways, the steam engine and telegraphic apparatus, have been so classed.

There need be no question but that these phenomena of the machine era will bear such an interpretation; the point of interest here is that such an interpretation should have been resorted to and should have commended itself as adequate and satisfactory when applied to these mechanical facts whose effective place in technology and in its bearing on the economy of human life has turned out to be so widely different from that range of manual operations with which it is so sought to assimilate them.[1]

The discipline of the handicraft industry enforces an habitual apprehension of mechanical forces and processes in terms of manual workmanship,—muscular force and craftsmanlike manipulation. This discipline touches

[1] A classic passage of Adam Smith shows this handicraft conception of the mechanics of industry: "The annual labour of every nation is the fund which originally supplies it with all the necessaries and conveniencies of life which it annually consumes. . . ." "But this proportion [of the produce to the consumers] must in every nation be regulated by two different circumstances; first, by the skill, dexterity, and judgment with which its labour is generally applied; and, secondly, by the proportion between the number of those who are employed in useful labour, and that of those who are not so employed."—*Wealth of Nations*, Introduction, p. 1.

Adam Smith consistently speaks of industry in terms of manual workmanship, as the traditions and the continued habitual outlook of that generation unavoidably led him to do; and the sweeping way in which his interpretation of economic life finds acceptance with his contemporaries shows that in so doing he is speaking in full consonance with the prevailing conceptions of his time. He writes during the opening passages of the machine era, but he speaks in terms of the past industrial era, from which his outlook on the economic situation and his conception of normal economic relations had been derived. It may be added that his conception of natural liberty in economic matters is similarly derived from the traditional situation, whose discipline during the later phases of the handicraft era inculcated freedom of ownership as applied to the workman's product and freedom of bargain and sale as touches the traffic of the typical petty trader. And so thoroughly had this manner of conceiving industry and the economic situation been worked into the texture of men's thinking, that the same line of interpretation continues to satisfy economic theory for a hundred years after Adam Smith had formulated this canon of economic doctrine, and after the situation to which it would apply had been put out by the machine industry and large business management.

first, and most intimately and coercively, the classes engaged in the manual work of industry, but it also necessarily pervades the community at large and gathers in its net all individuals and classes who have to do with the facts of industry, near or remote. It gives its specific character to the habits of life of the community that lives under its dispensation and by its means, and so it acts as an overruling formative guide in shaping the current habits of thought.

The consequences of this habitual attitude, for the technology of the machine era that presently follows, are worth noting. The mechanical inventions and expedients that lead over from the era of handicraft, through what has been called the industrial revolution, to the later system of large industry, bear the marks of their handicraft origin. The early devices of the machine industry are uniformly contrivances for performing by mechanical means the same motions which the craftsmen in the given industries performed by hand and by man power; in great part, indeed, they set out with being contrivances to enable the workmen to perform the same manual operation in duplicate or multiple—(as in the early spinning and weaving machinery) or to perform a given operation with larger effect than was possible to the unaided muscular work (as in the beginnings of steam power). In their beginnings the new mechanical appliances are conceived as improved tools, which extend the reach and power of the workman or which facilitate or lighten the manual operations in which he spends himself. They are, as they aim to be, labour saving devices, designed to further the workmanlike efficiency of the men in whose hands they are placed.

The early history of steam power shows how closely this workmanlike conception limited the range of invention. It was first employed to pump water out of mines. In this use the pressure of the air on a piston, in a low-pressure cylinder, was brought to bear on a lever so suspended as to yield formally the same motion as a like lever previously moved by human muscle. After a long interval, sufficiently long to make the use of this intermittent pressure and the resulting reciprocating motion familiar and impersonal in men's habitual apprehension, the reciprocating motion was turned to use to produce a rotary motion,—after the fashion suggested by the treadle of a lathe or spinning wheel, which was already familiar enough to have been divested of something of that fog of personality that had doubtless surrounded it at its first invention.[1] The next serious

[1] The case of the treadle applied to the production of rotary motion is typical of what happens to a technological element of the general class here under discussion. Such a new technological expedient appears at the outset to be apprehended in terms of manual workmanship; but presently it comes, through habitual use, to take its place as a mechanical functioning of the tools in whose use it takes effect,—to be associated in current apprehension with the mechanical appliances employed in its production and, by so much, dissociated from the person of the workman. In a measure, therefore, it falls into the category of impersonal facts that are available as technological raw material with which to go about the work in hand. With further use, and particularly with the interjection of further mechanical expedients between the workman and this given technological element, it will be conceived in progressively more objective fashion, as a fact of the mechanics of brute matter rather than an extension of the workman's manual reach; until it passes finally into the category of mechanical fact simply, obvious and commonplace through routine use; in which there remains but a vanishing residue of imputed personality, such as attaches to all conceptions of action. The given technological element in this way may be said to pass by degrees out of the workman's "quasi-personal fringe" of manual effects, into the do-

move in the development of the steam engine is the invention of the automatic valves, for admission and escape of steam from the cylinder. According to the ancient myth, a boy whose work it was to shift the valves by hand, contrived to connect them by cords with the moving parts of the machine in such a way as to lift them at the proper moment by the motion of the machine itself; so making the machine perform what had in the original concept of the valve mechanism been a manual operation. Later still, after the due interval for externalisation and assimilation of this mechanical valve movement as an impersonal fact of the machine process, further improvement and elaboration of the elements so gained has worked out in the highly finished mechanism familiar to later times.

Detail scrutiny of any one of the greater mechanical inventions, or series of inventions, will bring out something of the same character as is seen in the sequence of successive gains that make up the history of the steam engine. It is to be noted in this connection that time appears to be of the essence of the process of mechanical

main of raw material available for use in workmanship; where it will, in apprehension, be possessed of only such imputed quasi-personal or anthropomorphic characteristics as are necessarily imputed to external facts at large.

Concretely, the concept of the treadle seems in its beginnings to be a variant of the same conception that leads to the use of the bow-drill. Both inventions comprise at least two distinct forms. In each the simpler and presumably more primitive form converts a reciprocating longitudinal motion into a reciprocating rotary motion; and it is apparently only after an interval of familiarity and externalisation of this mechanical achievement that the next move takes place in the direction of the perfected treadle, which converts a reciprocating longitudinal into a continuous rotary motion.

invention in any field; so much so, indeed, that it will commonly be found that any single inventor contributes but one radical innovation in any one particular connection; which may then presently be taken up again as a securely objective element by a later inventor and pushed forward by a new move as radical as that to which this original invention owed its origin. This time interval which plays such a part in mechanical inventions appears necessary only as an interval of habituation, for the due externalisation of the element, to relieve it, by neglect, of the personal equation with which it is contaminated as it first comes into use, and so to leave it such an objective concept as may be turned to account as mere technological raw material.

It appears, then, that the accumulation of technological experience is not of itself sufficient to bring out a consecutive improvement of the industrial arts, particularly not such an advance in the industrial arts as is embodied in the machine technology of late-modern times. In this modern machine technology the ruling norm is the highly impersonal, not to say brutal, concept of mechanical process, blind and irresponsible. The logic of this technology, accordingly, is the logic of the machine process,—a logic of masses, velocities, strains and thrusts, not of personal dexterity, tact, training, and routine. In the degree in which the information that comes to hand comes encumbered with a teleological bias, a connotation of personal bent, it is unavailable or refractory under this logic. But all new information is infused with such an anthropomorphic colouring of personality; which may presently decay and give place to a more objective habitual apprehension of the facts in case use and wont play up the mechanical character and bearing of these facts in subsequent experience of them; or which may on the other hand end by giving its definitive character and value to the acquired information in case it should happen that the facts of experience are by use and wont bent to an habitual anthropomorphic rating and employment. To serve the needs of this machine technology, therefore, the information which accumulates must in some measure be divested of its naïve personal colouring by use and wont; and the degree in which this effect is had is a measure of the degree of availability of the resulting facts for the uses of the machine technology. The larger the available body of information of this character, and the more comprehensive and unremitting the share taken by the discipline of the machine process in the routine of daily life, therefore, the greater, other things equal, will be the rate of advance in the technological mastery of mechanical facts.

But much else goes to the makeup of use and wont besides the routine of industry and the ultilisation of those mechanical processes and that output of goods which the modern machine industry places at men's disposal. To put the same thing in terms already employed in another connection, the sense of workmanship is still subject to contamination with other impulsive elements of human nature working under the constraining limitations imposed by divers conventional canons and principles of conduct; besides being constantly subject to self-contamination in the way of an anthropomorphic interpretation that construes the facts of experience in terms of a craftsmanlike bent.

As bearing on the effectual reach of this self-contamination of the sense of workmanship it is pertinent to recall that craftsmanship ran within a class, and so had the benefit of that accentuated sentiment of self-complacency that comes of class consciousness. From its beginnings down to the period of its dissolution the handicraft industry is an affair of the lower classes; and, as is well known, class feeling runs strong throughout the era, particularly through the centuries of its best development. Whether their conceit is wholly a naïve self-complacency or partly a product of affectation, the sentiment is well in evidence and marks the attitude of the handicraft community with a characteristic bias. The craftsmen habitually rate themselves as serviceable members of the community and contrast themselves in this respect with the other orders of society who are not occupied with the production of things serviceable for human use. To the creative workman who makes things with his hands belongs an efficiency and a merit of a peculiarly substantial and definitive kind, he is the type and embodiment of efficiency and serviceability. The other orders of society and other employments of time and effort may of course be well enough in their way, but they lack that substantial ground of finality which the craftsman in his genial conceit arrogates to himself and his work. And so good a case does the craftsman make out on this head, and so convincingly evident is the efficiency of the skilled workman, and so patent is his primacy in the industrial community, that by the close of the era much the same view has been accepted by all orders of society.

Such a bias pervading the industrial community must

greatly fortify the native bent to construe all facts of observation in anthropomorphic terms. But the training given by the petty trade of the handicraft era, on the other hand, is not altogether of this character. The itinerant merchant's huckstering, as well as the buying and selling in which all members of the community were concerned, would doubtless throw the personal strain into the foreground and would act to keep the self-regarding sentiments alert and active and accentuate an individualistic appreciation of men and things. But the habit of rating things in terms of price has no such tendency, and the price concept gains ground throughout the period. Wherever the handicraft system reaches a fair degree of development the daily life of the community comes to centre about the market and to take on the character given by market relations. The volume of trade grows greater, and purchase and sale enter more thoroughly into the details of the work to be done and of the livelihood to be got by this work. The price system comes into the foreground. With the increase of traffic, book-keeping comes into use among the merchants; and as fast as the practice of habitual recourse to the market grows general, the uncommercial classes also become familiar with the rudimentary conceptions of book-keeping, even if they do not make much use of formal accounts in their own daily affairs.[1]

The logic and concepts of accountancy are wholly impersonal and dispassionate; and whether men's use of its logic and concepts takes the elaborate form of a set of books or the looser fashion of an habitual rating

[1] Cf. Sombart, *Moderne Kapitalismus*, bk. i, Exkurs zu Kapitel 7, bk. ii, ch. xv.

of gains, losses, income, and outgo in terms of price, its effect is unavoidably in some degree to induce a statistical habit of mind. It makes immediately for an exact quantitative apprehension of all things and relations that have a pecuniary bearing; and more remotely, by force of the pervasive effect of habituation, it makes for a greater readiness to apprehend all facts in a similarly objective and statistical fashion, in so far as the facts admit of a quantitative rating. Accountancy is the beginning of statistics, and the price concept is a type of the objective impersonal, quantitative apprehension of things. Coincidently, because they do not lend themselves to this facile rating, facts that will not admit of a quantitative statement and statistical handling decline in men's esteem, considered as facts, and tend in some degree to lose the cogency which belongs to empirical reality. They may even come to be discounted as being of a lower order of reality, or may even be denied factual value.

Doubtless, the price system had much to do with the rise of the machine technology in modern times; not only in that the accountancy of price offered a practical form and method of statistical computation, such as is indispensable to anything that may fairly be classed as engineering, but also and immediately and substantially in that its discipline has greatly conduced to the apprehension of mechanical facts in terms not coloured by an imputed anthropomorphic bent. It has probably been the most powerful factor acting positively in early modern times to divest mechanical facts of that imputed workmanlike bent given them by the habits of thought induced by the handicrafts.

This reduction of the facts of observation to quantitative and objective terms is perhaps most visible not in the changes that come over the technology of industry directly, in early modern times, but rather in that growth of material science that runs along as a concomitant of the expansion of the mechanical industry during the later era of handicraft. The material sciences, particularly those occupied with mechanical phenomena, are closely related to the technology of the mechanical industries, both in their subject matter and in the scope and method of the systematisation of knowledge at which they aim; and it is in these material sciences that the concomitance is best seen, at the same time that it is the advance achieved in these sciences that most unequivocally marks the transition from mediæval to modern habits of thought. This modern interest in matter-of-fact knowledge and the consequent achievements in material science, comes to an effectual head wherever and so soon, as the handicraft industry has made a considerable advance, in volume and in technological mastery, sufficient to support a fair volume of trade and make thoughtful men passably familiar with the statistical conceptions of the price system.

It is accordingly in the commercial republics of Italy that the modern growth of material science takes its first start,[1] about the point of time when industry and commerce had reached their most flourishing state on the Mediterranean seaboard and when the attention of these communities was already swinging off from these material interests to high-handed politics and religious reaction. The higher interests of church and state came to the front, and science, industry, and presently commerce dwindled

[1] Outside of the Orient, where something similar is to be seen back in the Arabic and earlier cultural eras.

and decayed in the land that had promised so handsomely to lead Western civilisation out of the underbrush of piety and princely intrigue.

Next followed the Low Countries, with the south German industrial centres, where again industry of the handicraft order grew great, gave rise to trade on a rapidly increasing scale, and presently to an era of business enterprise of unprecedented spirit and scope. But the age of the Fuggers closed in bankruptcy and industrial collapse when the princely wrangles of the era of statemaking had used up the resources of the industrial community and exhausted the credit of that generation of captains of industry. Here too religious contention came in for its share in the set-back of industry and commerce. In their economic outlines the two cases are very much of the same kind. Central Europe ran through much the same cycle of industrial growth, commercial enterprise, princely ambitions, dynastic wars, religious fanaticism, exhaustion and insecurity, and industrial collapse and decay,—substantially repeating, on an enlarged scale and with much added detail, the sequence that had brought South Europe into arrears. Meantime the material sciences had come forward again in the West, and flourished at the hands of the Netherlanders, South Germans and French scholars, who under the favouring discipline of this new advance in industry and commerce had slowly come abreast of the same matter-of-fact conceptions that had once made Italy the home of modern science. And here again, as before, princely politics, with the attendant war, exactions and insecurity, followed presently by religious controversies and persecutions, not only put an end to the advance of industry and business but also checked the attendant development of science nearly to a standstill.

So that when a further move of the kind is presently made it is the British community that takes the lead. Great Britain had been in arrears in all those respects that make up civilisation of the Occidental kind, and not least in the material respect; until the time when the peoples of the Continent by their own act fell into the rear in respect of those material interests—technology and business enterprise—which afford the material ground out of which the Occidental type of civilisation has grown. In Great Britain the sequence of these cultural phenomena has not been substantially different, taken by and large, from that which had previously been run through by the Continental communities; except that the same outcome was not reached, apparently because the sequence was not interrupted by collapse at the same critical point in the development.

The run of events under the handicraft system in England differs in certain consequential features from that among the Continental peoples,—consequential for the purposes of this inquiry, whether of similarly grave consequence from the point of view given by any other and larger interest. These peculiar traits of the British era of handicraft yield a side light on the methods and reach of the handicraft discipline as a factor in civilisation at large, at the same time that a consideration of them should go to show how slender an initial difference may come to be decisive of the outcome in case circumstances give this initial difference a cumulative effect.

As regards the ultimately substantial grounds of the British situation, in the way of racial make-up, natural resources, and cultural antecedents, the British community has no singular advantage or disadvantage as against its Continental competitors. What is true of England in respect of peculiarly favourable natural resources later on, about and after the close of the era of handicraft, does not hold for the beginnings or the best days of that era. Racially there is no appreciable difference between the English population of that time and the population of the Low Countries, of the Scandinavian peninsulas, or even of the nearer lying German territories; and no markedly characteristic national type of temperament had at that time been developed in Great Britain, as against the temperamental make-up of its Continental neighbours,—whatever may be conceived to have become the case in the nearer past.

The characteristic, and apparently decisive, peculiarities of the British situation may all confidently be traced to the insular position of the country. Owing to the isolation so given to the Island the British community was notably in arrears in early modern times, as contrasted with the more cultured, populous and wealthier peoples of the Continent; and this backward state of England in the earlier period of the era of handicraft is no less marked in respect of technology than in any other. As is well known, England borrowed extensively and persistently from its Continental neighbours throughout the era, and it was only by help of these borrowed elements that the English were able to overtake and finally to take the lead of their competitors. Similarly, the British commercial development also comes on late as compared with the Continent; so much so that the British had substantially no share in the great expansion of business enterprise that has been called the Age of the Fuggers. This late start of the English, coupled with their peculiar advantage in being able to borrow what their neighbours had worked out, conduced to a more rapid rate and shorter run of industrial advance and expansion in the Island, and so, among other consequences, hindered the rounded system of handicraft, industrial towns, and gild organisation from attaining the same degree of finality, and ultimately of obstructive inertia, that resulted in many of the Continental countries.

Again, owing to the same geographic isolation that long held England culturally in arrears, the English community lay, in great measure, outside of that political "concert of nations" that worked out the exhaustion and collapse of industry and business on the Continent. Not that the English took no interest in the grand whirl of politics and princely war that occupied the main body of Christendom in that time. The English crown, or to use a foreign expression, the English State, was deeply enough implicated in the political intrigues of late mediæval and early modern Europe; but as modern time has advanced the English community has visibly hung back with an ever growing reluctance. And whatever may be conceived to be the share of the English crown in the political complications of the Continent, it remains true that the English community at large, during the mature and concluding phases of the era of handicraft, stood mainly and habitually outside of these princely concerns.[1] In effect, after the handicraft era

[1] The adventures of Charles I and James II sufficiently illustrate this insular temper of the industrial and commercial community as contrasted with the crown and the court party.

was well under way, England is never for long or primarily engaged in international war, nor, except for the civil war of the Commonwealth period, in destructive war of any kind. Hence the era runs to a different outcome in England from what it does elsewhere. It ends not in the exhaustion of politics, but in the industrial revolution. The close of the handicraft system in England comes by way of a technological revolution, not by collapse.

To this attempted explanation of the English case, as due to its geographic isolation, the objection may well suggest itself that other cases which parallel the British in this respect do not show like results. So, for instance, the Scandinavian countries enjoyed an isolation nearly if not quite as effective as that of Great Britain during this period of history; whereas the outcome in these countries is notoriously not the same. The Scandinavian case, however, differs in at least one essential respect, which seems decisive even apart from secondary circumstances. These countries were too small to make up a self-supporting community under the conditions required by the system of handicraft. They had neither the population nor the natural resources on such a scale as a passably full development of the handicraft system required. At any advanced stage of its growth the system can work out into a self-balanced technological organisation, with full specialisation of labour and local differentiation of industry, only in a community of a certain (considerable) size. This condition was not met by the Scandinavian countries. Hence they remained in a relatively backward state, on the whole, through the handicraft era, and never reached anything like an independent position in the industrial world of that time, either technologically or in point of commercial development; hence also they failed to achieve or maintain that degree of independence, or isolation, in their political relations that left England free to pursue a self-directed course of material development.

At an earlier period, as, for instance, from neolithic times down to the close of paganism, under the slighter, less differentiated, less complex technological conditions of a more primitive state of the industrial arts, the Scandinavian countries had, each and several, proved large enough for a very efficient industrial organisation; and, again, during the early historical period, they had also proved to be of a sufficient and suitable size to make up national units of a thoroughly competent sort, autonomous politically as well as industrially and working out their own fortunes in severalty,—very much as the British community does later on, in the days of the later handicraft era and the early growth of the machine industry. But during the era of handicraft, and indeed somewhat in a progressive fashion as the technology of that era grew to a fuller development and required larger territorial dimensions, the Scandinavian countries lost ground, relatively to the larger communities of Great Britain and the Continent; in a degree they progressively lost autonomy both in the political and the industrial respect, and much the same is to be said for their position in point of general culture. This falling into arrears and dependence is least marked in the case of Sweden, the largest and still passably isolated community among them; and it is most marked in the case of Norway and Iceland, the most isolated but at the same time the least sizable units of the Scandinavian group. In material sciences, that most characteristic trait of the Western culture, the case of these peoples is much the same as in the matter of technology and cultural autonomy at large; the largest of them has the most to show.

Great Britain, on the other hand, fulfilled the conditions of size and isolation demanded in order to a free development of the industrial arts during this era, when the traffic in dynastic politics stood ready to absorb all accessible resources of industry and sentiment. And England accordingly takes the lead when the era of handicraft goes out and that of the new technology comes in.

Material science of the modern sort has been drawn into the discussion as a cultural phenomenon closely bound up with the state of the industrial arts under the handicraft system. This modern science may, indeed, be taken as the freest manifestation of that habit of mind that comes to its more concrete expression in the technology of the time. To show the pertinency of such a recourse to the state of science as an outcome of the discipline exercised by the routine of life in the era of handicraft some further detail touching the state and progress of scientific inquiry during that period will be in place.

In its beginnings, the theoretical postulates and preconceptions of modern science are drawn from the scholastic speculations of the late Middle Ages; the problems which the new science undertook to handle, on the other hand, were, by and large, such concrete and material questions as the current difficulties of technology brought to the notice of the investigators. These traditional postulates, preconceptions, canons, and logical methods that stood over from the past were essentially of a theological complexion, and were the outcome of much time, attention and insight spent on the systematisation of knowledge in a cultural situation whose substantial core was the relation of master and servant, and under the guidance of a theological bias worked out on the same ground. The postulates of this speculative body of knowledge and the preconceptions with which the scholastic speculators went to their work of systematisation, accordingly, are of a highly anthropomorphic character; but it is not the anthropomorphism of workmanship, at least not in the naïve form which the sense of workmanship gives to anthropomorphic interpretation among more primitive peoples.[1] It may be taken as a matter of course that the sense of workmanship is present in its native, direct presentment throughout the intellectual life of the middle ages, as it necessarily is under all the permutations of human culture; but it is equally a matter of course that the promptings of an unsophisticated sense of workmanship do not afford the final test of what is right and good in a cultural situation drawn on rigid lines of mastery and submission.

During the middle ages the faith had taken on an extremely authoritative and coercive character, to answer to the similar principles of organisation and control that ruled in secular affairs; so that at the transition to modern times the religious cult of Christendom was substantially a cult of fearsome subjection and arbitrary authority. Much else, of a more genial character, was of course comprised in the principles of the faith of that

[1] See ch. ii and iii, above.

time, but when all is said the fact remains that even in its genial traits it was a cult of irresponsible authority and abject submission,—a cult of the pastoral-predatory type, adapted and perfected to answer the circumstances of feudal Europe, and so embodying the principles (habits of thought) that characterised the feudal system.

Notoriously, the fashions of religious faith change tardily. Such change is always of the nature of concession. And since the conceptions of the cult are of no material consequence, taken by themselves and in their direct incidence, they are subject, as such, to no direct or deliberate control or correction in behalf of the community's material interests or its technological requirements. It is almost if not altogether by force of their consonance or dissonance with the prevailing habits of thought inculcated by the routine of life that any given run of religious verities find acceptance, command general adherence to their teaching, or become outworn and are discarded; and such lack of consonance must become very pronounced before a radical change of the kind in question will take effect. Barring conversion to a new faith, it is commonly by insensible shifts of adaptation and reconstruction that any wide-reaching change is worked out in these fundamental conceptions. Such was the character of the move by which the Mediæval cult merged in the modernised theological concepts of a later age.

Gradually, by force of unremitting habituation to a new scheme of life, and marked by long-drawn theological polemics, a change passed over the spirit of theological speculation, whereby the fundamentals of the faith were infused with the spirit of the handicraft system, and the preconceptions of workmanship insensibly supplanted those of mastery and subservience in the working concepts of devout Christendom. Meantime, while the routine of the era of handicraft was slowly reconstructing the current conceptions of divinity on lines consonant with the habit of mind of workmanship, the ancient conceptions continued with gradually abating force to assert their prescriptive dominion over men's habitual thinking. This gradually loosening hold of the ancient conceptions is best seen in the speculations of the philosophers and in the higher generalisations of scientific inquiry in early modern times.

In the mediæval speculations whether theological, philosophical or scientific, the search for truth runs back to the authentic ground of the religious verities,—largely to revealed truth; and these religious verities run back to the question, "What hath God ordained?" In the course of the era of handicraft this ultimate question of knowledge came to take the form, "What hath God wrought?" Not that the creative office of God in the divine economy was overlooked or in any degree intentionally made light of by the earlier speculators; nor that the sovereignty of God was denied or in any degree questioned by those devout inquirers who carried forward the work in later time. But in that earlier phase of faith and inquiry it is distinctly the suzerainty of God, and His ordinances, that afford the ground of finality on which all inquiry touching the economy of this world ultimately come to rest; and in the later phase, as seen at the close of the era of handicraft, it is as distinctly His creative office and the logic of His creative design that fill the place of an ultimate term in human inquiry—as that inquiry conventionally runs within the spiritual frontiers of Christendom. God had not ceased to be the Heavenly King, and had not ceased to be glorified with the traditional phrases of homage as the Most High, the Lord of Hosts etc., but somewhat incongruously He had also come to be exalted as the Great Artificer—the preternatural craftsman. The vulgar habits of thought bred in the workday populace by the routine of the workshop and the market place had stolen their way into the sanctuary and the counsels of divinity.

Similarly, in the best days of scholastic learning scientific inquiry ran back for a secure foundation to the authentic ordinances of the Heavenly King; under the discipline of the era of handicraft it learned instead to push its inquiries to the ground of efficient cause, ultimately of course, in the philosophical liquidation of accounts in that devout age, to the creative efficiency of the First Cause. In the scientific inquiries of the earlier age the test of truth was the test of authenticity, and the logic of systematisation by use of which knowledge in that time was digested and stored away was essentially a logic of subsumption under securely authentic categories that could be run back at need to the ascertained requirements of the glory of God. The canon of truth is that of the revealed word, reënforced and filled out with the quasi-divine Aristotelian scheme of things. It is a logic of hierarchical congruity in respect of potencies and qualities, suggestively resembling the devolution of powers and dignities under the finished scheme of feudalism. In the later age the good of man gradually, insensibly supplants the glory of God as the ultimate ground of systematisation. The sentimental ground of conviction comes to be the recognised serviceability of the ascertained facts for human use, rather than their conformity with the putative exigencies of a self-centred divine will. The Providential Order that means so much in the scheme of knowledge in the mature years of the era of handicraft is an order imposed by a providentially beneficent Creator who looks to the good of man; as it has been expressed, it is a scheme of "humanism."

By the close of the era this beneficent providential order had worked out in an Order of Nature, indued with the same meliorative trend; and in the sentimental conviction of the inquiring spirits of that age it lay in the nature of this beneficent order of the universe that in the end, in the finished product of its working, it would bring about the highest practicable state of well-being for man,—very much as any skilled workman of sound sense and a good heart would turn out good and serviceable goods. And in this Order of Nature, as it runs in the matter-of-course convictions of thoughtful men at the close of the era, the person of the deity, even as a workmanlike creative Providence, had fallen into the background. The Order of Nature, with its scheme of Natural Law, is felt as the work of a consummately skilful and ingenious workmanlike agency that looks to a serviceable end to be accomplished; and the profoundly thoughtful scientific inquiry of that time harbours no doubt that this workmanlike agency of Nature at large rules the world of visible fact and will achieve its good work in good time. But this quasi-personal Nature is not reverenced for anything but its workmanlike qualities; the awe which it inspires is not the fear of God, such as that fear has played its part under the feudalistic rule of the church and sent men hunting cover from the imminent wrath to come. As he stands in the presence of this eighteenth-century Nature, man is not primarily a sinner seeking a remission of penalties at all costs, but rather a focus of workmanlike attention upon whose welfare all the forces of the visible universe beneficently converge.

How this workmanlike Nature goes about her [1] work is no more plain to the casual spectator than are the recondite processes of high-wrought handicraft to the uninstructed. But Nature after all accomplishes her ends in a workmanlike fashion, and by staying by and patiently watching the operations of Nature and construing the facts of observation by the sympathetic use of a rational common sense, men may learn much of the methods of her manipulation as well as of the rules of procedure under whose guidance the works of Nature are accomplished. For it is a matter of course to that generation that Nature is essentially rational in her aims and logic as well as in the technology of her work; very much after the fashion of the master craftsman, who goes to his work with an intelligent oversight of the available

[1] The imputation of the feminine in this personification of Nature is probably nothing more than a carrying over of the Latin gender of the word, but there is commonly involved in this quasi-personal conception of Nature a notable imputation of kindliness and gentle solicitude that well comports with her putative womanhood. By extraordinarily easy gradation *Natura naturans* passes over into Mother Nature. The contrast in this respect, simply on its sentimental side, between the conception of Nature, say in the eighteenth century, on the one hand, and the patriarchal Heavenly King, remote and austere, of the Mediæval cult on the other hand is striking enough. In point of sentimental content this conception of Nature is more nearly in touch with the mediæval Mother of God than with the Heavenly King.

means and the purpose to be wrought out, as well as with a firm and facile touch on all that passes under his trained hand. Like the perfect craftsman, "Nature never makes mistakes," "never makes a jump," "never does anything in vain," "never turns out anything but perfect work."

The means whereby this work of Nature is brought to its consummate issue are forces of Nature working under her Laws by the method of cause and effect. The principle, or "law," of causation is a metaphysical postulate; in the sense that such a fact as causation is unproved and unprovable. No man has ever observed a case of causation, as is a commonplace with the latterday psychologists. But such a doubt does not present itself seriously in the days of handicraft; it would be out of touch with the spirit of the time and the discipline of that craftsmanship out of which the spirit of the time arises. To the inquiring minds of that era it is a matter of course and of common sense that the forces of Nature are seen to work out the effects which emerge before their eyes. What they see in fact may be, as the modern psychologists would perhaps say, a certain concomitance and sequence in the observed phenomena; but what those observers see in effect is always a certain cause working out a certain effect. The imputation of causal efficiency to the observed phenomena is so thoroughly a matter of course that there is no sense of imputation in the observer's mind.

Observation simply, without imputation of anthropomorphic qualities and efficacies, should yield nothing more to the purpose than idle concomitance and sequence of phenomena, but there is, in effect, none of this early scientific work done in terms of simple concomitance or sequence alone; nor for that matter, has any of the effective (theoretical) work of modern science been carried to an issue by the use of such objective terms of concomitance and sequence alone, whether in that or in a later age, without the help of a putative causal nexus. Through the early modern scientific period there runs an increasingly free and frequent recourse to statistical argument,—in the material sciences a recourse to punctilious measurement, enumeration and instruments of precision; but it is of the essence of the case that the phenomenal facts which so are subjected to measurement and statistical computation are facts selected for the purpose on the strength of their (putatively) known causal implication in the problem whose solution is sought, and that the facts which emerge from these measurements, computations, and instruments of precision, are turned to account in an argument of cause and effect; they have served their purpose only when and in so far as they enable the inquirer to determine the course of efficient transition from a putative cause to a putative effect, or conversely.

The relation of cause and effect, as commonly conceived by the vulgar and as commonly employed by the scientist, is a putative relation between phenomena which can not be said to stand in any observed relation of efficiency to one another. Efficiency, as understood in this connection, is not a fact of observation, but of imputation; and efficiency, performance of work, is the substance of the causal relation as that concept is universally employed in modern science. It may well be said that this recourse to the concept of efficient cause—a metaphysical postulate touching a putative fact—is the distinguishing characteristic of modern science as contrasted with any other scheme of systematised knowledge.[1]

Not only does the development of modern science rest on this postulate of causality, but the concept of causation which so characterises the modern sciences is of a particular and restricted kind. At least on the face of things it seems unquestionable that the peculiar temper and limitations of this modern European concept of causation are to be credited to the habits wrought out by a life under the handicraft system. It has been noted already that the ubiquitous prevalence of trade and of the price system in modern times has given to the modern apprehension of facts a certain objectivity, a degree of

[1] This, of course, does not overlook the fact that in the course of scientific inquiry there has been an increasing use of statistical methods and results, and that this recourse to statistics has been of an increasingly objective character, both in its methods and in the items handled. It is also to be noted that from time to time serious and consequential attempts have been made to reduce scientific argument at large to similarly objective terms of quantity, quantivalence and concomitance. Karl Pearson's *Grammar of Science*, for instance is a shrewd and somewhat popularly known endeavour of this kind. So, again, the philosophical views associated with the names of Leibnitz and of Berkely are of this nature, and there is not a little of the same line of scepticism in the speculations of Hume. But it is equally to be noted that except on the remote plane of generality that belongs to philosophical speculation, and except in the works of pure mathematics, this method of handling facts has not proved available for scientific ends. The "idle curiosity" which finds employment in scientific inquiry is not content with the vacant relation of concomitance alone among the facts which it seeks and systematises. In scientific theory no headway has been made hitherto without the use of this indispensable imputation of causality.—In this connection cf. a paper on "The Evolution of the Scientific Point of View," *University of California Chronicle*, November, 1908, especially footnote, p. 396.

impersonality, which is at least a characteristic of modern knowledge, whether scientific or commonplace, even if it cannot be said to be a unique distinction of modern science as contrasted with other deliberate systems of knowledge. But it is the unique distinction of modern science, particularly as it comes into view in its early phases, that its concept of causality is drawn not simply in terms of workmanship but specifically in terms of craftsmanship. There need probably be no argument spent on the thesis that the sense of causality is, by and large, a particular manifestation of the sense of workmanship. But the sense of workmanship in its native scope apparently covers something more than the manual efficiency of the skilled workman simply. And in other times and under other cultural (technological) circumstances the sense of workmanship has apparently given rise to concepts of causation of a wider, or at least of a looser, scope. In the naïve rating of savage peoples workmanship appears to cover, perhaps uncertainly, notions of generation, nurture, tendance, and the like, without any sharp line being drawn between these various lines of effective endeavour on the one side and manual efficiency on the other. And so, on the other hand, in the cosmological knowledge (or quasi-knowledge) current among these peoples explanation in terms of generation and growth are accepted as final along with explanations in terms of what the modern man would conceive to be the stricter sense of cause and effect. Even in the speculations of the sages of classical antiquity, and again in the cosmologies and natural history of the far-Oriental peoples, many questions of cause and effect are found to be sufficiently disposed of when worked out in the like terms of generation, growth and quasi-physiological mutation.

To modern inquiry explanations in these terms, other than those of physically effective work, are provisional at the best, and are held to only as awaiting a final solution in a materially, mechanistically competent way. And what is alone materially competent in the modern scientific apprehension is such an explanation as will make things plain in terms of matter and motion, working a change in the constitution of things by displacement through contact and pressure. Causation is conceived as manual work,—to use a French term, it is a *remaniement* of raw materials at hand. Physiological or chemical explanations must finally be recast in terms of physics, to satisfy the modern scientist's sense of finality, and physics must be made to run in terms of impact, pressure, displacement in space, regrouping of material particles, coördinated movements and a shifting of equilibrium.

Through all this runs the concomitant requirement of quantivalence, statable in statistical form. The scientist's results are not finally merchantable, on the scientific exchange, until they have been reduced to such terms of accountancy as would be comprehensible to the man trained in the merchandising traffic of the petty trade, for whose conviction things must be punctiliously rated in exchange value. But, as has been noted above, it is only as an expedient of scientific accountancy that the facts under inquiry are kept account of in an itemised bill of values. This meticulous statistical accountancy is necessary to safeguard the accuracy of the work done and its conformity with the facts in hand; but the work so done handles these facts as active factors which go efficiently to the production of the results observed. The cause is conceived to produce the effect, somewhat after the fashion in which a skilled workman produces a finished article of trade. But when the scientist has set forth the operations and working conditions that have brought forth the effects which he is engaged in explaining, he must also, in order to the conviction of his fellow craftsmen, show a statistically itemised statement of receipts and expenditures covering the facts engaged,—in quantitative values he must show that the costs are balanced by the values that emerge in the finished product of that workmanlike process of causation whose recondite nature and course he has so laid bare to the light of understanding.

This attempted characterisation of modern scientific inquiry and its working concepts applies immediately to the earlier phases and down to a date well past the advent of the machine industry,—so far past that date as to allow time and experience to work the new habits of thought peculiar to the machine technology into the texture of men's preconceptions. In time, but tardily, as is the case with the pervasive effects of any new line of habituation, the discipline of the machine has wrought a further, though, hitherto less profound and decisive, change in the aims and methods of science; a discussion of which is deferred until it comes up again in its connection with the new technology. Less cogently and with qualifications, however, the above characterisation will apply to the later phases of modern science, as well as to that initial stage that marks the era of handicraft.

Something further is due to be said of the cultural

consequences of this discipline in workmanship during the era of handicraft, besides its guidance in the growth of technology and the related field of material science. As has been intimated above, habituation to the working conceptions of handicraft had much to do with that revision of the religious cult and its theological tenets that has shaped the spiritual life of modern times in contrast with the mediæval life of faith. But it is an ungrateful, perhaps ungraceful, office to turn the dry light of matter-of-fact on the sacred verities, and a degree of parsimony will best be observed in any layman's discussion of these intimate movements of the spirit. Yet it seems necessary to call to mind at least one point of singular concomitance between the state of the industrial arts and fortunes of the Christian faith.

Characteristic of modern times has been the Protestant rehabilitation of the cult and its tenets. In this rehabilitation, which has not been without effect even within the Catholic church, much of the ancient spirit of subjection has been lost, replaced in part with a certain attitude of self-help and autonomy on the part of the laity. There is a degree of democratic initiative and a gild-like spirit of lay discretion in spiritual affairs. As already noted above, the tenets of the faith have also in some degree been revised and reconstructed in terms consonant with the workmanlike conceptions of the handicraft system. Such a protestant or quasi-protestant reconstruction of the cult and its tenets set in, as is well known, successively in the several leading countries of Europe, somewhat in the same order as these several countries successively advanced to a high level of technological and commercial enterprise. As noted above, in the south in the so-called Latin countries, this era of industrial and commercial enterprise was presently checked; the like being true in a less pronounced fashion for the peoples of Central Europe. Wherever the advance was seriously checked, so that the era of handicraft closed in collapse or reaction on its secular side, there the reconstruction of the religious cult also came to an incomplete issue at the most. So that by the definitive close of the era of handicraft those peoples of Christendom that had maintained the advance achieved in this secular respect were also the ones that had accepted and continued to hold the revised form of the faith. Where this era of industrial and business enterprise closed in exhaustion and collapse, there the ancient form of the faith also triumphed over the heretics. It is, indeed, to be remarked as a sufficiently striking coincidence that even now the centre of diffusion of the modern industry is at the same time the centre of diffusion of religious protestantism and heresy. And the antique forms and fervour of the faith are found in better preservation progressively outward from this centre of diffusion; and even in somewhat minute detail it appears to hold true not only that the more advanced industrial peoples are the less amenable to religious control and less given to superstitious observances of the archaic sort, but also that within these industrial countries the industrial centres in the narrower sense of the word are less devout, or devout in a less archaic fashion, than the non-industrial population at large. Something of the kind, indeed, has been visibily true ever since a relatively early phase of the handicraft system; though nothing like undevoutness can be alleged of the industrial town population during the handicraft era proper. The handicraft population was devout, but not consistently orthodox; and the industrial towns of that time were devout enough in their way, but it was in a way obnoxious to the received dogmas of the church. They were centres of devout heresy. It is only in late modern times that the malady has progressed so far that it may fairly be called a degree of apostacy. This concomitance between technological mastery and religious dissent is doubtless susceptible of a good and serviceable explanation at the hands of the religious experts; it is here cited without prejudice as having at least a negative bearing on the question of how the discipline of the handicraft industry may be conceived to affect men's spiritual attitude in a field so remote as that of the life of faith.[1]

What is known to economic history as the era of handicraft is for the purposes of the political historian spoken of as the era of statemaking. The two designations may not cover precisely the same interval, but they coincide in a general way in point of dates, and the phenomena which have given rise to the two designations have much more than an accidental connection. It is not simply that the development of handicraft happens to fall in the same general period of history that is characterised by the dynastic wars that went to the making of the larger states. The growth of handicraft had much to

[1] In this connection it is worth noting, for what it may be worth, that there is a similarly rough concomitance between the diffusion of the blond racial stock in Europe and the modern forms of protestantism and religious heresy. Whether this fact strengthens or weakens any argument that may be drawn from the concomitance of heresy and industry cited above may perhaps best be left an open question.

do with making the large states practicable and with supplying the material means of large-scale warfare; while the traffic of dynastic politics in that time had in its turn very much to do with bringing that era of industrial and commercial enterprise to an inglorious close. The new industry supplied the sinews of war, and the wars ate up the substance of the industrial community.

The new industry gave rise to a growth of industrial towns and commercial centres, primarily occupied by the traffic of the itinerant traders. One of the immediate consequences of this extension of merchandising enterprise was the improvement of means of communication, both in the way of an extension and improvement of shipping—itself a technological fact—and in the way of improved routes of communication. A secondary consequence was a growth of population, coupled with its concentration in urban centres, together with a growth of wealth, in good part drawn together in the same centres. These changes enabled the powers in control to extend an effectual coercion over larger distances and over larger aggregations of population and wealth; it became practicable, mechanically, to swing a larger political aggregation and to hold it together in closer coördination than before. The physical conditions requisite to the formation and enduring maintenance of large political organisations were in this way supplied by the new industrial era as an incidental result of its technological efficiency.

More direct and obvious, though of no graver importance, is the contribution made by the new technology to the means of coercion placed at the disposal of the warlords, in the way of improved weapons and armour, defences and warlike appliances. The improvements worked out in the means of warfare during the early half of the era of handicraft exceed in material effect and in boldness of conception all the traceable improvements wrought in that line by all the warlike peoples of classical antiquity and all the fighting aggregations of Asia and Africa, from the beginning of the bronze age down to modern times. The craftsmen spent their best endeavours and their most brilliant ingenuity on this production of arms and munitions, with the result that these articles still lie over in the modern collections as the most finished productions of workmanship which that era has to show. The (unintended) result at large was that these improved appliances enabled the war-lords and their fighting men to control the industrial classes for their own ends and to levy exactions on trade and industry up to the limit of what the traffic would bear, or perhaps more commonly somewhat over that limit. It was, in this way, their own technological mastery that furnished the means of their own undoing, directly (mechanically speaking) and indirectly (in the resulting growth of warlike sentiment).

That the craftsmen went so diligently into this production of ways and means for their own discomfort and abiding defeat is due not to any innately perverse bent of the sense of workmanship as it comes to expression in the spirit of the handicraft community, but rather to the exigencies created by the price system, with its principles of self-help,—a secondary, conventional product of the handicraft industry. As has been noted already, with perhaps tedious iteration, there runs through the handicraft community a highwrought spirit of individual self-sufficiency. So soon as the petty trade has grown to effective dimensions the individual workman comes into somewhat direct relations with the market, and except for the collective interest and action embodied in the gild organisations the craftsmen stand in little else than a pecuniary relation to one another and bear little else than a pecuniary responsibility to their fellow craftsmen or to the community. It is the place of each to gain a livelihood by honest work through his own individual skill and enterprise. Notoriously, the craftsmen were in effect lacking in that sense of solidarity that makes an efficient organisation for defence or offence; concerted action, outside the regulative activity of the gild, was to be had only with extreme difficulty on any other basis than individual pecuniary advantage. Each worked for himself, with an eye steadily to the main chance. And the main chance, from an early date in this era, meant gain in terms of price. So the craftsman worked for such customers as would pay his price, and he spent his skill and ingenuity on such goods as were in demand. The trade in arms and weapons was good at that time. These appliances were a means of livelihood to the men at arms and a means of income and prestige to their princely employers. So the traffic went busily on, and the individual craftsmen put forth their best efforts toward enhancing the efficiency of the ruling and fighting classes, whose endeavours, without much collusion but by the inevitable drift of circumstance, converged on the subjection of the community of craftsmen at large and on the exhaustion of the community's resources.

Through its side issue in the commercial enterprise

which it fostered the handicraft industry brought to the hands of the politicians a further means of trouble. The trade brought on the price system, and so made it possible for ambitious princes to buy what they needed in their warlike negotiations; with funds in hand stores and munitions could be bought where they were needed, so enabling warlike operations to be carried on with greater facility at a greater distance than was feasible under the earlier rule of contributions in kind. The price system also enabled the warlords to hire mercenaries, and so to organise and maintain a standing force of skilled fighting men, mobile and irresponsible. But to hold one's own in the competitive use of this new arm the prince must have funds; which led incontinently to all available manner of exactions on trade and commerce, since it was from these sources almost solely that funds could be had. But it led also and equally to an increasing traffic between the princes and the captains of industry, for the use of funds. Funds had become the sinews of war, since the handicraft industry had come to turn out goods for sale and the merchandising trade had made funds accessible in sufficient volume to be worth while. So the princes dealt with the captains of industry, selling what they could and hypothecating what they could not sell, in a competitive struggle to outdo one another at war and diplomacy. The game was then as always an emulative one, in which any advantage was a differential advantage only. Hence the princes engaged, each and several, needed all the funds they could get the use of, and their need was ever present, not to be deferred. Hence they borrowed what they could and where they could, their borrowings being floated by the help of all manner of expedients. Some of these fiscal expedients brought monopolistic advantage to the captains of industry, and so contributed to their further gain and to the concentration of wealth in fewer hands. Meantime, the princely chancelries, being in debt as far as possible, extorted further loans from the captains by seizure and by threats of bankruptcy; and whatever was borrowed was expeditiously used up in the destruction of property, population, industrial plant and international commerce. So, when all available resources of revenue and credit, present and prospective, had been exhausted, and all the accessible material had been consumed, the princely fisc went into bankruptcy, followed by its creditors, the captains of industry, followed by the business community at large with whose funds they had operated and by the industrial community, whose stock of goods and appliances was exhausted, whose trade connections were broken and whose working population had been debauched, scattered and reduced to poverty and subjection by the wars, revenue collectors and forced contributions. Meantime, too, habituation to the sentiments, ideals, standards and manner of life suitable to a state of predation had swamped the handicraft spirit and put abnegation and dependence on arbitrary power in the place of that initiative and pertinacious self-reliance that had made the era of handicraft. It was from this eventuality that England in great measure escaped by favour of her insular position and the inability of her princes to draw a reluctant industrial community into the traffic of dynastic intrigue that filled the Continent.

It will have been remarked that one of the essential

moves in this sequence of events, from the beginnings of handicraft in impecunious and self-reliant workmanship to its eventual collapse in exhaustion, is the gradual accumulation of commercial and industrial wealth in relatively few hands. This accumulation of wealth, or rather its segregation in few hands, appears, as already indicated, to have entered as a potent factor in the course of things that lead the system of handicraft through maturity to collapse, as on the Continent, or to decay, as in England. It will accordingly be in place to go somewhat more narrowly into the circumstances of its beginnings and growth and the manner in which it plays its part in the organisation of the handicraft industry.

It appears that this uneven distribution of wealth arises out of the technological exigencies of handicraft and of the petty trade which characteristically runs along with the handicraft industry in its early stages.[1] In its earliest, impecunious beginnings, handicraft as known in mediæval Europe was like its congener, the manual arts of the savage and lower barbarian peoples, in that the whole material equipment requisite to its pursuit consisted of a skilled workman and an extremely slender kit of tools. The tradition countenanced by historical students says that the beginnings of the handicraft system, with its specialised industry and trained workmanship, is due to such workmen, possessed of substantially nothing but their own persons, who escaped in one way and another from the bonds of the manorial system, or its equivalent, and found shelter on sufferance near some

[1] See chapter v, above.

feudal protector or religious corporation that found some advantage in this novel arrangement.[1]

On looking into this inchoate working arrangement between these masterless workmen and their patrons, and generalising the run of facts as may be permitted an inquiry that aims at theoretical presentation rather than historical description, the probable causal relation running through these obscure events will appear somewhat as follows. It happened in Europe, as it has happened now and again elsewhere, that the ownership of the soil in advanced feudal times took shape as a Landed Interest living at peace and under settled relations with the community from which they drew their livelihood and their means of controlling the community. Under these circumstances there grew up an ever-widening industrial system, under manorial auspices, in which the foremost place is taken by the mechanic arts, in the way of specialised crafts and mechanical processes and appliances. The tranquil conditions that prevail under such a settled, pacific or sub-predatory scheme of control bring out an increased volume of consumable products, particularly since these same settled conditions admit a larger and more economical use of all industrial appliances. The immediate consequence is that an increased net product accrues to the propertied class; which calls them to an intensified consumption of goods; which requires increased elaboration and diversity of products; which calls for an increasing diversity and volume of appliances and more prolonged and elaborate technological processes. The needs of the propertied

[1] Cf. Ashley, *English Economic History and Theory*, bk. i, ch. i; Karl Bücher, *Entstehung der Volkswirtschaft*, ch. iii.

class, particularly in the way of superfluities, reach such a degree of diversity that it is no longer practicable to supply these needs by specialised work within the industrial framework of the manor or its equivalent. The itinerant trade comes in to help out in this difficult passage by bringing exotic luxuries, curious articles of great price; but that is not sufficient to cover the requirements of the case, since there is much needed work of elaboration that cannot be taken care of by way of an importation of finished goods.

Here comes the opportunity of the skilled masterless workman. The growth of wealth has provided a place for him in the economy of the time, and having once got a foothold he and his followers congregate in industrial towns and find a living by the work of their hands.

The point should be kept in mind in any consideration of the era of handicraft that its beginnings are made by these "masterless men," who broke away (or were broken out) from the bonds of that organisation in which the arbitrary power of the landed interest held dominion. By tenacious assertion of the personal rights which they so arrogated to themselves, and at great cost and risk, they made good in time their claim to stand as a class apart, a class of ungraded free men among whom self-help and individual workmanlike efficiency were the accepted grounds of repute and of livelihood. This tradition never dies out among the organised craftsmen until the industrial system which had so been inaugurated went under in the turmoil of politics and finance or was supplanted by the machine era that grew out of it. With this class-tradition of initiative and democratic autonomy is associated, as an integral fact in the system, the concomitant tradition that work is a means of livelihood.

In these early phases of the system the individual workman is (typically) competent to work out his livelihood with the use of such a slight equipment of tools as could readily be acquired in the course of his employment. In great part, indeed, the craftsman of the early days made his tools and appliances as he went along. But it follows necessarily that further training in the skilled manipulations of the crafts led to the use of improved and specialised tools as well as to the use of larger appliances useful in the technological processes employed, such as could scarcely be called tools in the simpler sense of the word but would rather be classed as industrial plant. With the advance of technology the material equipment so requisite to the pursuit of industry in the crafts increases in volume, cost and elaboration, and the processes of industry grow extensive and complex; until it presently becomes a matter of serious difficulty for any workman single-handed to supply the complement of tools, appliances and materials with which his work is to be done. It then also becomes a matter of some moment to own such wealth.

As under any earlier and simpler industrial régime, so in this early-advanced phase of the handicraft system the workman must also have command of that immaterial equipment of technological information at large that is current in the community, in so far as it affects his particular occupation; and he must in addition acquire the special trained skill necessary in his own branch of craft. The former he will, at that stage of technological growth, still come by without particular deliberate application, in the ordinary routine of life; it is made up of general information and familiarity with current ways of doing, simply, and on the level of general information which then prevailed no special training or schooling seems to have been needed to place the young man abreast of his time. In other words, the common stock of technological knowledge had not by that time grown so unwieldy as to require special pains to assimilate it. As for the latter, the special skill which would make him a craftsman, that was also accessible at the cost of some application; but under the rules of handicraft the early apprentice gained this trained skill at no cost beyond application to the work in hand. But the like does not continue to hold true of the material equipment; which presently was no longer to be compassed as a matter of course and of routine application to the work in hand. It was becoming increasingly important and increasingly difficult to be provided with these means with which to go to work, and the ownership of such means gave an increasingly decisive advantage to their owner.

What adds further force to this position of affair is the fact that in many of the crafts the work could no longer be carried on to full advantage in strict severalty; the best approved processes required a gang or corps of workmen in coöperation, and required also something in the way of a "plant" suitable for the employment of such a corps rather than of a single individual. Such a condition, of course, came on earlier and more urgently in some crafts, as, e. g., in tanning, or brewing, or some of the metal-working trades, than in others, as, e. g., the building trades, locksmithing, cobbling, etc. But an advance of this kind, and the exigencies which such an advance brings, came on gradually and with such a measure of general prevalence through the crafts that the general statement made above may fairly stand as a free characterisation of the state of the industrial arts in the crafts at large at the period in question. The growing resort to working methods requiring organised groups of workmen together with something in the way of collective industrial plant would greatly hasten the concentration of the ownership of the material equipment. Ownership in all ages is individual ownership; and then as ever any single item of property, such as a workshop and its appliances, would presently fall into the possession of an individual owner. The owners of the plant became employers of their impecunious fellow craftsmen and so came into a position to dispose of their working capacity and their product.

When and in so far as the advanced state of the industrial arts, therefore, made it impracticable for the individual craftsman readily to acquire the material means for work in his craft, any proficiency in the craft would be of no effect except by arrangement with some one who could supply these material means. The possession of the material equipment, therefore, placed in the discretion of its owners the utilisation of such technological knowledge and skill as the members of the given crafts might possess. The usufruct of the handicraft community's technological proficiency in this way came to vest in the owners of the plant, in the same measure as this plant was necessary to the pursuit of industry under the technological scheme then in force. This effect would be had so soon and in such measure as it became a matter of appreciable difficulty to acquire and maintain the material equipment requisite to the workmanlike pursuit of industry; and it would become generally decisive of the relation between master and workman so soon as the outfit of material means required for effective work had grown larger than the common run of workmen could acquire in the course of such training as would fit them to do the work in the particular branch of industry in which they engaged.

The change brought on in this way by the growth of technology was neither abrupt nor sharply defined. Like other changes in the technological scheme it was an outgrowth of the knowledge and methods already previously current, and it took effect in detail and in a very concrete way, leading on through fluctuating usage to a gradually settled general practice which came at length to differ substantially from the situation out of which it had grown. By insensible gradations it came into such general prevalence and everyday recognition, and established such stable methods of procedure, as presently left it standing as an established institutional fact. It grew into the prevalent habits of thought without a visible break, and made its way more or less thoroughly in the several branches of industry which it touched, until it came to be accepted as the type of handicraft organisation to which other, outlying branches of industry would then also tend to conform, even when there was no direct provocation for these outlying members of the industrial system to take on the typical form so given. But given the tranquil conditions necessary to the accumulation of such industrial appliances and to the invention and employment of long and roundabout processes in industry, and the resulting change that sets in will be of a cumulative character, affecting an ever increasing proportion of the industrial arts, and permeating the industrial system at large in a progressive fashion.

Under these circumstances, and in proportion as these technological exigencies take effect in one branch of industry and another, the usufruct of the industrial community's current productive efficiency comes to vest effectually in those who own the material means of industry. Their effectual exploitation of the community's industrial efficiency will extend to such industries, and with such a degree of thoroughness and security, as the state of the industrial arts may decide. This effectual engrossing of the technological heritage by the owners will extend to any branch of the industrial arts in which so considerable a material equipment is required, in appliances and raw materials, that the workmen who go into this given line of employment cannot practically create or acquire it as they go along. In an uncertain measure, therefore, and varying in degree somewhat from one industry to another, the owner of the plant becomes in effect the owner of the community's technological knowledge and workmanlike skill, and thereby the owner of the workman's productive capacity.

In the small beginnings of the handicraft industry the craftsman typically passed by a simple routine from the status of apprentice to that of master, picking up the slight necessary outfit as he went along; in the closing phases of the era handicraft methods had reached a high degree of specialisation and made use of extensive processes and appliances, and it was then only by exception that any craftsman could pass from apprenticeship through the intervening stages to the position of a working master, without the help of inherited means or special favour. Toward the close of the era the masters were, typically, employers of skilled labour and foremen in their own shop, except in the frequent case where they altogether ceased to work at the trade and gave their whole attention to the business side of the industry. Many of these nominal master craftsmen were in fact mere traders, captains of industry, businessmen, who never came in manual contact with the work.[1]

So capitalism emerged from the working of the handicraft system, through the increasing scale and efficiency of technology. And on the ground afforded by this capitalistic phase of the system arose that era of business enterprise that ruled the economic fortunes of Europe in the fifteenth and sixteenth centuries, with its captains of industry and great financial houses. Whether the large means with which these captains of industry operated were primarily drawn from the gains of the petty trade that had gone before, or were drawn into this field of business from outside, is a debated question which need not detain the present inquiry. The fact remains that, by whatever means, this development of the situation comes out of that growth of handicraft whereby the ownership and control of the industrial plant passed out of the hands of the body of working craftsmen.

When this business situation collapsed, therefore, as already spoken of above, the handicraft industry at its best was organised on capitalistic lines and managed for capitalistic ends,—with a view to profits on investment, not primarily with a view to the livelihood of the working

[1] Cf. R. Ehrenberg, *Das Zeitalter der Fugger.*

craftsmen. The new situation which then presented itself, as a consequence of the collapse of the business community, was industrially and commercially better suited to the simpler and ruder methods of handicraft that had succeeded in the early days of the system; but the current preconceptions and trade relations that actually ruled at the time were of a capitalistic kind, and the current state of the industrial arts, even where industry had fallen into a fragmentary state, was such as technologically required the large-scale organisation in order to its due working. Between the impossibility of going forward on the accustomed lines and the impracticability of an effectual rehabilitation of more primitive methods, there resulted a period of poverty and confusion, helped out by the continued mismanagement of the dynastic politicians; so that the industrial situation of the Continent never recovered until it was overtaken by the new era of the machine industry inaugurated by the English.

The circumstances of life for the common man underwent more than one substantial change during the era of handicraft, and these changes were not all in the same sense. The dominant note changes from workmanship in the earlier phases of the era to pecuniary competition and political anxiety toward the close, particularly as regards the industrial communities of the Continent. The era is a long period of history, all told, running over some five or six centuries, from an advanced stage of the feudal age to the eighteenth century, or to various earlier dates in those countries where the handicraft system came to a provisional close in the era of statemaking; and the discipline of life does not run to the same effect in the earlier of these phases of the development as in the later. Not that handicraft ceased to be the prevailing method in the mechanical industries of these countries when the reaction overtook them, but the technological advance had been seriously checked, and such handicraft industry as still went on had ceased to dominate the economic situation and no longer held the primacy among the factors that shaped the life of the communities in question. Its place as a dominant force was taken by the new political interests and by such commercial enterprise as still went on.

But through the centuries of its earlier growth the handicraft industry, simply as a routine of workmanship, shaped the conditions of life for the common people more pervasively and consistently than any other one factor. Its discipline, therefore, was of protracted duration and touched the current habits of thought in an intimate and enduring fashion; so as to leave a large and enduring effect on the institutions of the peoples among whom it prevailed. The English-speaking community shows these effects in a larger measure and a more evident manner than any other,—visible only in a less degree in the Low Countries, and more equivocally in the Scandinavian countries. These peoples had not been subjected to the handicraft discipline for a longer time or in a more exacting fashion than their Continental neighbours, but they had on the other hand escaped the full measure of the political activity of the era of state-making that did so much to neutralise the effects of the handicraft system in the larger Continental countries.

Something has been said above of the way in which the

discipline of life under the rule of handicraft shaped and coloured men's thinking in those materialistic sciences whose early growth runs parallel with the technological advance in modern times. It has also been evident that this training in the manner of conceiving things for the purposes of technology wrought certain broad changes in the theological and philosophical conceptions that guided the inquiring spirits of the same and subsequent generations. This effect wrought by the routine of life under the handicraft system on scientific and philosophical conceptions is of a very pervasive character, being of the nature of an habitual bent, an attitude or frame of mind, whose characteristic mark is the acceptance of creative workmanship as a finality. It became an element of common sense in the apprehension of thoughtful men whose frame of mind was formed under the traditions of that era that creative workmanship is an ultimate, irreducible factor in the constitution of things, accepted as a matter of course and used unsparingly and with ever-growing conviction as a *terminus a quo* and *ad quem.*[1]

Creative workmanship, fortified in ever-growing measure by the conception of serviceability to human use, works its way gradually into the central place in the theoretical speculations of the time, so that by the close of the era it dominates all intellectual enterprise in the thoughtful portions of Christendom. Hence it becomes not only the instrument of inquiry in the sciences, but a

[1] Seen, as indicated above, in the matter-of-course resort of the scientists to the conception of efficient cause as a solvent of problems touching material phenomena, as well as in the theologians' and philosophers' resistless drift toward creative efficiency as the ultimate term of their speculations.

major premise in all work of innovation and reconstruction of the scheme of institutions. In that extensive revision of the institutional framework that characterises modern times it is the life of the common people, their rights and obligations, that is forever in view, and their life is conceived in terms of craftsmanlike industry and the petty trade. By and large, the outcome of this revision of civil and legal matters under handicraft auspices is the system of Natural Rights, including the concept of Natural Liberty. The whole scheme so worked out is manifestly of the same piece with that Order of Nature and Natural Law that dominated the inquiries of the scientists and the speculations of the philosophers.

It lies in the nature of the case that the English-speaking community should take the lead in the final advance in all these matters and should work out the most finished, secure and enduring results within these premises, both in the field of scientific inquiry and in that of the theory of institutions. It lies in the nature of the case because the English-speaking community had the benefit of the technological gains made before their time, because they had a long and passable uneventful experience of the handicraft routine in industry and in the workday life to whose wants the handicraft industry ministered, and because the discipline of the handicraft era was not in their case neutralised in its closing phase by the turmoil, insecurity and civic debaucheries of an epoch of war and political intrigue. And here again the neighbouring peoples come into the case as copartners in this work with England in much the same measure in which their experience through this period was of the same general nature.

The scheme of Natural Rights, and of Natural Liberty, which so emerges is of a pronounced individualistic tenor, as it should be to answer to the scheme of experience embodied in the system of handicraft. In the crafts, particularly during the protracted early phases of the system, it is the individual workman, working for a livelihood by use of his own personal force, dexterity and diligence, that stands out as the main fact; so much so, indeed, that he appears to have stood, in the apprehension of his time, as the sole substantial factor in the industrial organisation. Similarly under the canon of Natural Liberty the individual is thrown on his own devices for his life, liberty and pursuit of happiness. The craftsman by immemorial custom traditionally disposed of his work and its product as he chose, under the rules of his gild. He was by prescription in full possession of what he made, subject only to the gild regulations imposed for the good of his neighbours who were similarly placed. The most sacred right included in the scheme of Natural Rights is that of property in whatever wealth has been honestly acquired, subject only to the qualification that it must not be turned to the detriment of one's fellows. In the days of the typical handicraft system the petty trade runs along with the handicraft industry, in such a way that every master craftsman is more or less of a trader, disposing of his goods or services in plenary discretion, and even the apprentices and journeymen similarly bargain for their terms of work and at times for the disposal of their product; while the professional itinerant trader is a member of this industrial community on much the same footing as the craftsmen proper. So it is a secure item in the scheme of Natural Rights that all persons not under tutelage have an indefeasible right to dispose by purchase and sale not only of products of their own hands but of whatever items they have come by through alienation by its producer or lawful owner. And ownership is in natural-rights theory always to be traced back to the creative workmanship of its first possessor.[1]

In the sequel this natural right freely to dispose of one's person and work, when it had found lodgment among the principles of civil rights in the eighteenth century, contributed substantially to the dissolution of that organ of surveillance and control that the craftsmen of an earlier generation had instituted in the gild system. The case is but an instance of what is continually happening and bound to happen in the field of institutional growth. Institutional principles, such as this item of civil rights, emerge from use and wont, resulting as a settled line of convention from usage and custom that grow out of the exigencies of life at the time. But use and wont is a matter of time. It takes time for habituation to attain that secure degree of conventional recognition and authenticity that will enable it to stand as an indefeasible principle of conduct, and by the time this consummation is achieved it commonly happens that the exigencies which enforced the given line of use and wont have ceased to be operative, or at least to

[1] Cf. Locke, *Of Civil Government*, ch. v, "Though the earth and all inferior creatures be common to all men, yet every man has a property in his own person; this nobody has a right to but himself. The labour of his body and the work of his hands we may say are properly his. Whatsoever, then, he removes out of the state that Nature hath provided and left it in, he hath mixed his labour with, and joined to it something that is his own, and thereby makes it his property."

be so imperative as in their earlier incidence. The control which the gilds were initially designed to exercise was a control that should leave the gildsmen free in the pursuit of their work, subject only to a salutary surveillance and standardisation of the output, such as would maintain the prestige of their workmanship and facilitate the disposal of the goods produced. The initial purpose seems, in modern phrase, to have been a creation of intangible assets for the benefits of the body of gildmen. Under the new conditions that came to prevail when capitalistic management took over the direction of industry these gild regulations no longer served their purpose, but they seem on the contrary to have become an obstacle to the free employment of skilled workmen.

A similar fortune was about the same time beginning to overtake this principle of Natural Liberty itself, and that even in the particular bearing which seems at the outset to have been its primary and most substantial aim. Initially, it seems, the point of interest, and indeed of contention, was the freedom of the masterless workman to dispose of his person and workmanship as he saw fit and as he best could and would,—to take care of his life, liberty and pursuit of happiness without let or hindrance from persons vested with authority or prerogative. With the passage of time, use and wont erected this conventional rule into an inalienable right. But included with it, as an integral extension of the powers which this inalienable right safeguarded, was the right of purchase and sale, touching both work and its product, the right freely to hold and dispose of property. Presently, toward the close of the handicraft era, or more specifically in the late eighteenth century in England, industry fell under capitalistic management. When this change had taken passably full effect the workman was already secure in his civil (natural) right to dispose of his workmanship as he thought best, but the circumstances of employment under capitalistic management made it impossible for him in fact to dispose of his work except to these employers, and very much on their terms, or to dispose of his person except where the exigencies of their business might require him. And the similarly inalienable right of ownership, which had similarly emerged from use and wont under the handicraft system, but which now in effect secured the capitalist-employer in his control of the material means of industry,—this sacred right of property now barred out any move that might be designed to reinstate the workman in his effective freedom to work as he chose or to dispose of his person and product as he saw fit.

The connection so shown between the growth of handicraft and the system of Natural Rights does not purport to be a complete account of the rise of that system, even in outline. The more usual account traces this system to the concept of *jus naturale*, of the late Roman jurists. There is assuredly no call here to question or disparage the work of those jurists and scholars who have busied themselves with authenticating the system of Natural Rights by showing it to be founded in the *jus gentium* and the *jus naturale* of the Latin Codes. Their work is doubtless historically exact and competent. But as is commonly the case with such work at the hands of jurists and scholars, especially in that past age, it contents itself with tracing an authentic pedigree, rather than go into questions of the causes that led to the vogue of these concepts at the time of their acceptance or the circumstances which gave these Natural Rights that particular scope and content which they have assumed in modern theory of law and civil relations. The thesis which is here offered is to the effect that the habituation of use and wont under the handicraft system installed these rights, in an inchoate fashion, in the current preconceptions of the community, and that this habituation is traceable, causally rather than by process of ratiocination, to the sense of workmanship as it took form and went into action under the particular conventional circumstances of the early era of handicraft; that the preconceptions that so went into effect determined the current attitude of thoughtful men toward questions of civil rights and legal principle; and that the jurists who had occasion to take notice of these current preconceptions touching human rights found themselves constrained to deal with them as elementary facts in the situation as it lay before them, and therefore to find a ground for them in the accepted canons, such as would satisfy the legal mind of their authenticity by ancient prescription, or such as should determine the scope of their application in conformity with legal principles having a prior claim and authoritative sanction. The thesis, therefore, is not that the jurists founded these modern principles of legal theory on the popular prejudices current in their time and due in point of habituation to the routine of handicraft, nor that they stretched the ancient principles of *jus naturale* to meet the demands of popular prejudice, but that on prompting of legal exigencies to which the practical acceptance of these principles had given rise, the jurists found in the capitularies of the code what was necessary to authenticate these principles of legal theory and give them the sanction of authority, — a work of reasoning all the more congenial and convincing to the jurists since they in common with the rest of their generation were by habit and tradition imbued with the penchant to find these principles right and good, and consequently to find none other in the codes that might fatally traverse those whose authentication was due. But these are matters of pedigree, and this work of the great jurists and philosophers is in great part of the nature of accessory after the fact, so far as bears on that sweeping acceptance of these principles and that incontestable efficiency that marks the course of their life-history in modern times. The jurists and philosophers have sought and shown the sufficient reason for accepting this scheme of principles, as well as for the particular fashion in which they have been formulated; but the insensible growth of habits of thought induced by the conditions of life in (early) modern times must be allowed to stand as the efficient cause of their dominant control over modern practice, speculation, and sentiment touching all those relations that have been standardised in their terms. By use and wont the range of conventional elements included in the scheme had become eternal and indubitable principles of right reason, ingrained in the intellectual texture of the jurists as well as in their lay contemporaries; and the task of the jurists therefore was to work out their authentication in terms of sufficient reason; it was not for them to trouble with any question of the causes to which these principles owed their eternal fitness in the scheme of Nature at that particular time.

The Natural Rights which so found authentication at the hands of the jurists were of the individualistic kind which the discipline of the handicraft system had inculcated, and the authentication found in the *jus naturale* does not range much beyond the individualistic bounds so prescribed, nor are other lines of ancient prescription, at variance with these rights, brought at all prominently into the light by the legal inquiries of the jurists. Whereas it is no matter of serious question that the chief bearing of the ancient findings embodied in the code is not of this individualistic character. The causes which brought on the modern acceptance of this scheme of Natural Rights are a matter of use and wont, quite distinct from that line of argument by which the jurists established them on grounds of sufficient reason resting on ancient prescription.

The extreme tenacity of life shown by the system of Natural Rights may raise a reasonable doubt as to the adequacy of any account that assigns their derivation to the discipline of use and wont peculiar to any particular cultural era, even when the era in question is of so consistent a character and such protracted duration as the era of handicraft. What adds force to such a question is the fact that something like these preconceptions of natural right is not uncommon in the lower cultures. So that on the face of the returns there appears to be good ground in the nature of things for designating these conventional rights "natural." Something of the kind is current in an obvious fashion among the peaceable communities on the lower levels of culture, among whom the scheme of accepted rights and obligations bears more than a distant resemblance to the Natural Rights of the eighteenth century. But something of the kind will also be found among peoples on a higher level, both peaceable and predatory; though departing more notably in point of contents from the eighteenth-century system.

The point of similarity, or of identity, among all these systems of conventionally fundamental and eternal human rights is to be found in their intrinsic sanction—they are all and several right and good as a matter of course and of common sense; the point of divergence or dissimilarity is to be found in the contents of the code, which are not nearly the same in all cases. In the mediæval natural common-sense scheme of rights, prerogative, personal and class exemption, is of the essence of the canon; but the scheme is none the less intrinsically mandatory on those who had been bred into a matter-of-course acceptance of it by the routine of life in that age. Differential rights, duties and privilege give the point of departure in this mediæval system of civil relations; whereas in the system worked out under the auspices of the handicraft industry the denial of differential advantage, whether class or individual, is the beginning of wisdom and the substance of common sense as applied to civil relations. The one of these schemes comes out of an economic situation drawn on lines of predation, ancient, prescriptive and settled, and its first principle is that of master and servant; the other comes of a situation grounded in workmanlike efficiency, and its first principle is that of an equitable livelihood for work done.

That some of the working systems of civil rights in customary force among the peaceable communities of the lower culture have more in common with modern Natural Rights than this mediæval scheme, should logically be due to a similarity in the conditions of life out of which they have arisen. In these savage or lower barbarian communities, too, the principle of organization is work for a livelihood, and the conventional ground of economic relations is that of workmanship, as it is under the early handicraft system; but with the difference that whereas the technology of handicraft throws the skilled workman into perspective as a self-sufficient individual, and so throws self-help into the foreground as the principle of economic equity, among these savages and lower barbarians living by means of a technology of a less highly specialised character, with a material situation not admitting of the same degree of severalty in work or livelihood, the prime requisite in the relations governing the rights and duties of the members of the group is not the individual livelihood of the skilled workman but that of the group at large. The individual's personal claims come in only as secondary and subservient to the needs of the group at large; rights of ownership are loose and vague, and they lack that tenacity of life that characterises the like rights under the handicraft system. It is true, the product of industry belongs primarily to the producer of it, it is his in some sense that might pass into ownership if the technological situation admitted of work for a livelihood in strict and consistent severalty; but in the actual case as found on these lower levels the product commonly escapes somewhat easily from his individual possession and comes to inure to the use of the group. Except for such articles as continue to pertain to him by virtue of intimate and daily use, the producer's possessive control of his product is likely at the best to be transient and dubious, readily giving way before any urgent call for its use by other members of the group.[1]

A fact of some incisive effect in this connection is doubtless the characteristic trait of handicraft that, in its early phases wholly and obviously and in its later development also somewhat evidently, it was the affair of a class; whereas in the savage communities with which it is here compared, the technology and the livelihood in question are those of the community at large, not of a class that stands in contrast and in some degree of competition with the community at large. The craftsmen were a fraction of the community by work for whose needs they got their livelihood, even though, in the course of time, they became the dominant element within the local community (municipality) whose fortunes they shared. And as between this fraction of the population and outside classes with whom they carried on their traffic, particularly the well-to-do and land-holding classes, there could be no constraining sense of a solidarity of interest. The ancient bond of master and servant had been broken by something like an overt act of class secession on the part of the craftsmen, and nothing like a bond of fellowship had taken its place. The fellowship ran within the lines of craftsmanship, while the traffic of each craftsman typically ran across the line that divided the craftsman from the old order and population outside of this industrial system.

[1] Illustrative instances of such a customary code of "natural" rights and obligations are numerous in the late literature of ethnology. Good illustrations are afforded by various papers in the *Reports* of the *Am. Bureau of Ethnology*, on the culture of the Pueblos, Eskimo, and the Indians of the North-West Coast; so also in Skeat and Blagden, *Pagan Races of the Malay Peninsula*, or in Seligmann, *The Veddas*.

That the eighteenth-century system of Natural Rights shows such a degree of approximation to the scheme of rights and obligations observed among many primitive peoples need flutter no one's sense of cultural consistency. Return to Nature was more or less of a password in the closing period of the era of handicraft and after, and in respect of this system of civil relations it appears that the popular attitude of that time was in effect something of a reversion to primitive habits of thought; though it was at best a partial return to a "state of nature" in the sense of a state of peace and industry rather than a return to the unsophisticated beginnings of society. That such a partial reversion takes effect in the habits of thought of the time appears to be due to a similarly partial return to somewhat analogous habits of life. The correspondence in the habits of thought is no greater than that in the habits of life out of which these habits of thought emerged.

The primitive peoples that show this suggestive resemblance of the system of Natural Rights typically are living under a routine of workmanship and in a state of habitual peace,—in these respects being placed somewhat similarly to the handicraft community. The handicraft system comes true to the same characterisation in so far that it was dominated by a routine of workmanship and so far as, in effect, its life-history falls in an era of prevailingly peaceable conditions; and such a characterisation holds true of the industrial community proper through the period during which handicraft is the ruling factor in the community's habitual range of interest. It is not that the era of handicraft was an era of reversion to savagery, but only that the tone-giving factor in the community of that time reverted, by force of the state of the industrial arts, to habits of peace and industry, in which direct and detailed manual work takes a leading place. There is also the further point of economic contact with the savage state that in the handicraft community distinctions of wealth are neither large nor of decisive consequence during the long period of habituation that brought the preconceptions of that era into the settled shape and that gave them the character of a finished and balanced system of principles.

It may be added, at the risk of tedious repetition, that the habits of life characteristic of the era, as well as the frame of mind suited to this characteristic routine of life, seem peculiarly suited to the native endowment of the European peoples,—perhaps in an especial degree suited to the native bent of those sections of the population in which there is an appreciable admixture of the dolicho-blond stock. That such may be the case is at least strongly suggested by the tenacious hold which this system of Rights apparently still has on the sentimental allegiance of these Western peoples, after the conditions to which these Rights owe their rise, and to which they are suited, have in the main ceased to exist; as well as by the somewhat blind fervour with which these peoples, and more especially the English-speaking section of them, go about the idyllic enterprise of rehabilitating that obsolescent "competitive system" that embodied the system of Natural Rights, and that came up with the era of handicraft and went under in its dissolution.

CHAPTER VII

The Machine Industry

The era of the machine industry has been designated variously, to answer to the varying point of view from which it has been considered by divers writers. As an historical era it shows divers traits, more or less characteristic, and it has been designated by one or another of these traits according to the particular line of interest that may have directed the attention of those who have had occasion to name it. It is spoken of as the era of the factory system, of large-scale industry, as the age of Capitalism or of free competition, or again as an era of the credit economy. But as seen from the point of view of technology, and more specifically from that of workmanship as it underlies the technological system, it is best characterised as the era of the machine industry, or of the machine process. As a technological period it is commonly conceived to take its rise in the British industrial community about the third quarter of the eighteenth century, the conventional date of the Industrial Revolution,—those who have a taste for precise dates assigning it more specifically to the sixties of that century, to coincide with the earliest practical use of certain large mechanical inventions of that age.[1]

Such a precise date is scarcely serviceable for any other

[1] Cf., e. g., C. Beard, *The Industrial Revolution*, ch. ii; Spencer Walpole, *History of England from 1815*, vol. i; C. W. Taylor, *The Modern Factory System*, ch. i, ii.

than a mnemonic purpose. If the matter is taken in historical perspective the era of the machine process will be seen to have been coming on in England through the earlier years of the century, and even from before that time; whereas notable mechanical inventions, and engineering exploits of the like general bearing in technology, had begun to affect the industrial situation in some of the Continental countries at an appreciably earlier period. So, *e. g.*, practical improvements had gone into effect in water-wheels, pumps and wind mills, in the use of sails and the designs of shipping, in wheeled vehicles (though the early modern improvements in this particular may easily be over-rated) and in such appliances as chimneys; and, again, there is the peculiar but highly instructive field of applied mechanics represented by the invention and improvement of firearms. Such engineering enterprises as the drainage systems of Holland also belong here and are to be counted among the notable achievements in applied mechanics.

Even the most casual review of the technological situation in Europe, say in the seventeenth century, will bring out characteristic features that cannot be denied honourable mention as applications of mechanical science, although the reserve caution is immediately to be entered that these early mechanical expedients and their employment stand out as sporadic facts of mechanical contrivance in an age of manual work, rather than as characteristic traits of the industrial system in which they are found. The beginnings of the machine industry are of this sporadic character. They come up as an outgrowth of the handicraft technology, particularly at conjunctures where that technology is called on to deal with such large mechanical problems as exceed the force of manual labour or that elude the reach of the craftsman's tools.

So, *e. g.*, in England, say from the sixteenth century onward, there are improvements in highways and waterways and in the drainage of agricultural lands; and, as an instance more obviously related to the machine industry as commonly apprehended, there comes early in the eighteenth century the "horse-hoing cultivation" on which Jethro Tull spent his enthusiasm. Along with this obviously mechanical line of endeavour and innovation is also to be noted the deliberate efforts to improve the races of sheep and cattle that were in progress about the same time. These are perhaps not to be rated as mechanical inventions in the simple and obvious sense of the phrase, but they have this trait in common with the inventions of the machine era that they turn ascertained facts of brute nature to account for human use by a logic that has much of that character of impersonal incidence that marks the machine technology. The machine industry comes on gradually; its initial stages are visible in the early eighteenth century, but it is only toward the close of that century that its effects on the industrial system become so pronounced that the era of the machine technology may fairly be said to have set in; and it is only in Great Britain that it can be said to prevail at that period.

Of the other features above alluded to as characteristic of this period of history none are of so substantial a character or so distinctive of this particular period as its technological peculiarities. Free competition, *e. g.*, belongs as much to the era of handicraft as to that of the machine, having prevailed—more extensively in theory than in practice—under the former régime as under the latter; and in point of fact it gradually falls under increasing restrictions as the machine age advances, until in the more highly developed phases of the current situation it has largely ceased to be a practicable line of policy in industrial business. So, also, Capitalism did not take its rise coincident with the industrial revolution, although its best development and largest expansion may lie within the machine age. It had its beginnings in the prosperous days of handicraft, and one capitalistic era had already run its course, on the Continent, before the machine industry came in. The "credit economy," associated with the capitalistic management of industry, is also of older growth, so far as regards the days of its early vigour, although the larger and more far-reaching developments of credit come effectually into play only in the later decades of the machine age. Much the same is true of the so-called large-scale organisation of industry and the factory system. Its highest development comes with the advanced stages of the machine technology and is manifestly conditioned by the latter, but it was already a force to be counted with at the time of the industrial revolution. The large-scale industry contemplated, with a degree of apprehension, by Adam Smith, *e. g.*, was not based on the machine technology but on handicraft with an extensive division of labour, and on the "household industry" as that was gaining ground in his time. The latter was, in form, what has since come to be known as the "sweatshop" industry.

In this new era technology comes into close touch with

science; both the science and the technology of the new age being of a matter-of-fact character, beyond all precedent. So much so that by contrast, the technology of handicraft would appear to have stood in no close or consistent relation with the avowed science of its time. Not that anthropomorphic imputation is altogether wanting or inoperative in this latter-day scientific inquiry, or in the technological utilisation of the facts in hand; but in the later conceptions anthropomorphism has at the best been repressed and sterilised in an unprecedented degree. And it holds true for the machine technology beyond any other state of the industrial arts that the facts of observation can effectually be turned to account only in so far as they are apprehended in a matter-of-fact way. The logic of this technology, by which its problems are to be worked out, is the logic of a mechanical process in which no personal or teleological factors enter. The engineer or inventor who designs processes, appliances and expedients within these premises is required to apprehend and appreciate the working facts after that dispassionate, opaque, unteleological fashion in which the phenomena of brute matter occur; and he must learn to work out their uses by the logic of brute matter instead of construing them by imputation and by analogy with the manifestations of human workmanship. Less imperatively, but still in a marked degree, the same spirit must be found in the workmen under whose tendance these processes and appliances are to work out the designed results.

Under the simpler technology of more primitive industrial systems recourse to anthropomorphic imputation has also always been a hindrance to workmanlike mastery, more particularly in the mechanic arts proper, and only less pronounced in those industrial arts, like husbandry, that have to do immediately with plants and animals. Knowledge of brute facts as interpreted in terms of human nature appears never to have been serviceable in full proportion to their content. But in these more primitive industrial systems—as also in the better days of handicraft—the workman is forever in instant control of his tools and materials; the movements made use of in the work are essentially of the nature of manipulation, in which the workman adroitly coerces the materials into shapes and relations that will answer his purpose, and in which also nothing (typically) takes place beyond the manual reach of the workman as extended by the tools which his hands make use of. Under these conditions it is a matter of relatively slight effect whether the workman does or does not rate the objects which he uses as tools and materials in quasi-personal terms or imputes to them a degree of self-direction, since they are at no point allowed to escape his manual reach and are by direct communication of his force, dexterity and judgment coerced into the forms, motions and spatial dispositions aimed at by him. His imputing some bias, bent, initiative or spiritual force or infirmity to brute matter will doubtless incapacitate him by so much for efficiently designing processes and uses for the available material facts; his creative imagination proceeds on mistaken premises and goes wrong in so far; and so this anthropomorphic interpretation must always count as a material drawback to technological mastery of the available resources and in some degree retard the possible advance in the industrial arts. But within the premises given by the industrial arts as they stand, he may still do effective work as a mechanic skilled in the manual operations prescribed by the given state of the arts. For in the mechanic industries of all these other and more archaic industrial systems the workman does the work; it may be by use of tools, and even by help of more or less extended processes in which natural forces of growth, fermentation, decay, and the like, play à material part; but the decisive fact remains that the motions and operations of such manual industry take effect at his hands and by way of his muscular force and manual reach. Where natural processes, as those of growth, fermentation or combustion, are drawn into the routine of industry, they lie, as natural processes, beyond his discretionary control; at the most he puts them in train and lets them run, with some hedging and shifting as they go on, to bring them to bear in such a way as shall suit his ends; he takes his precautions with them and then he takes the chance of their coming to the desired issue. They are not, and as he sees the work and its conditions they need not be, within his control in anything like the fashion in which he controls his tools and the materials employed in his manual operations; they work well or ill, and what comes of it is in some degree a matter of his fortune of success or failure, such as comes to the man who has done his best under Providence. In case of a striking outcome for good or ill from the operation of such natural processes the devout craftsman is inclined to rate it as the act of God; very much as does the devout husbandman who depends on rain rather than on irrigation. It is the part of the wise workman in such a case to take what comes, without elation or repining, in so far as these factors of success and failure are not comprised in his presumed workmanlike proficiency.

The matter lies differently in the machine industry. The mechanical processes here engaged are calculable, measurable, and contain no mysterious element of providential ambiguity. In proportion as they work to the best effect, they are capable of theoretical statement, not merely approachable by rule of thumb. The designing engineer takes his measures on the basis of ascertained quantitative fact. He knows the forces employed, and, indeed, he can employ only such as he knows and only so far as he knows them; and he arranges for the processes that are to do the work, with only such calculable margin of error as is due to the ascertained average infirmity of the available materials. He deals with forces and effects standardised in the same opaque terms. He will be proficient in his craft in much the same degree in which he is master of the matter-of-fact logic involved in mechanical processes of pressure, velocity, displacement and the like; not in proportion as he can adroitly impart to the available materials the workmanlike turn of his own manual force and dexterity, nor in the degree in which he may be able shrewdly to guess the run of the season or the variations of temperature and moisture that condition the effectual serviceability of natural processes in handicraft.

The share of the operative workman in the machine industry is (typically) that of an attendant, an assistant, whose duty it is to keep pace with the machine process and to help out with workmanlike manipulation at points where the machine process engaged is incomplete.[1]

[1] In a general way, the relation in which the skilled workman in the

His work supplements the machine process, rather than makes use of it. On the contrary the machine process makes use of the workman. The ideal mechanical contrivance in this technological system is the automatic machine. Perfection in the machine technology is attained in the degree in which the given process can dispense with manual labour; whereas perfection in the handicraft system means perfection of manual workmanship. It is the part of the workman to know the working of the mechanism with which he is associated and to adapt his movements with mechanical accuracy to its requirement. This demands a degree of intelligence, and much of this work calls for a good deal of special training besides; so that it is still true that the workman is useful somewhat in proportion as he is skilled in the occupation to which the machine industry calls him.

In the new era the stress falls rather more decidedly on general intelligence and information, as contrasted with detail mastery of the minutiæ of a trade; so that familiarity with the commonplace technological knowledge of the time is rather more imperative a requirement under the machine technology than under that of handicraft. At the same time this common stock of technological information is greatly larger in the current state of the industrial arts; so much larger in volume, and at the same time so much more exacting in point of accuracy and detail, that this commonplace information that is requisite to any of the skilled occupations can no

large industries stands to the machine process is analogous to that in which the primitive herdsman, shepherd or dairymaid stand to the domestic animals under their care, rather than to the relation of the craftsman to his tools. It is a work of attendance, furtherance and skilled interference rather than a forceful and dexterous use of an implement.

longer be acquired in the mere workday routine of industry, but is to be had only at the cost of deliberate application and with the help of schools.

On this head, as regards the requirements of industry in the way of general information on the part of the skilled workmen, the contrast is sufficiently marked, *e. g.*, between Elizabethan times and the Victorian age. At the earlier period illiteracy was no obstacle to adequate training in the skilled trades. In the seventeenth century Thomas Mun includes among the peculiar and extraordinary acquirements necessary to eminent success in commerce, matters that are now easily comprised in the ordinary common-school instruction; and in so doing he plainly shows that these acquirements were over and above what was usual or would be thought useful for the common man. Even Adam Smith, in the latter half of the eighteenth century, shrewd observer as he was, does not include any degree of schooling or any similar pursuit of general information among the requisites essential to the efficiency of skilled labour. Even at that date it appears still to have been true that the commonplace information and the general training necessary to a mastery of any one of the crafts lay within so narrow a range that what was needful could all be acquired by hearsay and as an incident to the discipline of apprenticeship. Within a century after the first inception of the machine industry illiteracy had come to be a serious handicap to any skilled mechanic; the range of commonplace information that must habitually be drawn on in the skilled trades had widened to such an extent, and comprised so large a volume of recondite facts, that the ability to read came to have an industrial value; the higher proficiency in any branch of the mechanic arts presumed such an acquaintance with fact and theory as could neither be gained nor maintained without habitual recourse to printed matter. And this line of requirements has been constantly increasing in volume and urgency, as well as in the range of employments to which the demand applies, until it has become a commonplace that no one can now hope to compete for proficiency in the skilled occupations without such schooling as will carry him very appreciably beyond the three R's that made up the complement of necessary learning for the common man half a century ago.

It follows as a consequence of these large and increasing requirements enforced by the machine technology that the period of preliminary training is necessarily longer, and the schooling demanded for general preparation grows unremittingly more exacting. So that, apart from all question of humanitarian sentiment or of popular fitness for democratic citizenship, it has become a matter of economic expediency, simply as a proposition in technological efficiency at large, to enforce the exemption of children from industrial employment until a later date and to extend their effective school age appreciably beyond what would once have been sufficient to meet all the commonplace requirements of skilled workmanship.[1]

[1] It follows also, among other secondary consequences, that the effective industrial life of the skilled workman will, in order to the best average effect, begin at an appreciably more advanced age, and will therefore be shortened by that much. The period of preparation becomes more protracted, more exacting and more costly, and the effective life cycle of the workman grows shorter. Although it does not, perhaps, belong in precisely this connection, it may not be out of place to recall that the increasingly exacting requirements of the machine industry, particularly

The knowledge so required as a general and commonplace equipment requisite for the pursuit of these modern skilled occupations is of the general nature of applied mechanics, in which the essence of the undertaking is a ready apprehension of opaque facts, in passably exact quantitative terms. This class of knowledge presumes a certain intellectual or spiritual attitude on the part of the workman, such an attitude and animus as will readily apprehend and appreciate matter of fact and will guard against the suffusion of this knowledge with putative animistic or anthropomorphic subtleties, quasi-personal interpretations of the observed phenomena and of their relations to one another. The norm of systematisation is that given by the logic of the machine process, and the

in the way of accurate, alert and facile conformity to the requirements of the machine process, interrupt the industrial life of the skilled workman at an earlier point in the course of senile decay. So that the industrial life-cycle of the workman is shortened both at its beginning and at its close, at the same time that the commonplace preparation for work grows more costly and exacting.

Child labour, which once may, industrially speaking, have been an economical method of consuming the available human material, is no longer compatible with the highest industrial efficiency, even apart from any question of hardship or deterioration incident to an excessive or abusive recourse to child labour; it is incompatible with the community's material interests. Therefore the business community—the body of businessmen at large—for whose behoof the industries of the country are carried on, have a direct interest not only in extending the age of exemption from industrial employment but also in procuring an adequate schooling of the incoming generation of workmen. The business community is evidently coming to appreciate this state of the case, at least in some degree, as is evidenced by their inclination to favour instruction in the "practical" branches in the public schools, at the public expense, as well as by the wide-reaching movement that aims to equip private and state schools that shall prepare the youth for work in the various lines of industrial employment.

scope of it is that inculcated by statistical computation and the principle of material cause and effect.

In some degree the routine of the machine industry necessarily induces such an animus in its employees, since such is the scope and method of its own working; and the closer and more exacting the application to work of this kind, the more thorough-going should be the effects of its discipline. But this routine and its discipline extend beyond the mechanical occupations as such, so as in great part to determine the habits of all members of the modern community. This proposition holds true more broadly for the current state of the industrial arts than any similar statement would hold, *e. g.*, for the handicraft system. The ordinary routine of life is more widely and pervasively determined by the machine industry and by machine-like industrial processes today, and this determination is at the same time more rigorous, than any analogous effect that was had under the handicraft system. Within the effective bounds of modern Christendom no one can wholly escape or in any sensible degree deflect the sweep of the machine's routine.

Modern life goes by clockwork. So much so that no modern household can dispense with a mechanical timepiece; which may be more or less accurate, it is true, but which commonly marks the passage of time with a degree of exactness that would have seemed divertingly supererogatory to the common man of the high tide of handicraft.[1] Latterly the time so indicated, it should be called to mind, is "standard time," standardised to coincide over wide areas and to vary only by large and standard

[1] *Cf.*, *e. g.*, Adam Smith's reflections on the uses of an accurate watch. *Theory of the Moral Sentiments*, part iv, ch. 2.

units. It brings the routine of life to a nicely uniform schedule of hours throughout a population which exceeds by many fold the size of those communities that once got along contentedly enough without such an expedient under the régime of handicraft. In this matter the demands of the machine have even brought on a revision of the time schedule imposed by the mechanism of the heavenly bodies, so that not only "solar time," but even the "mean solar time" that once was considered to be a sufficient improvement on the ways of Nature, has been superseded by the schedule imposed by the railway system.

The discipline of the timepiece is sufficiently characteristic of the discipline exercised by the machine process at large in modern life, and as a cultural factor, as a factor in shaping the habits of thought of the modern peoples, it is itself moreover a fact of the first importance. Of the standardisation of the time schedule just spoken of, the earlier, the adoption of "mean solar time," was due immediately to the exigencies of the machine process as such, which would not tolerate the seasonal fluctuations of "apparent" solar time. This epithet "apparent," by the way, carries a suggestion that the time schedule so designated is less true to the actualities of the case than the one which superseded it. And so it is if the actualities to which regard is had are those of the machine process; whereas the contrary is true if the actualities that are to decide are those of the seasons, as they were under the earlier dispensation. "Standard time" has gone into effect primarily through the necessities of railway communication,—itself a dominant item in the mechanical routine of life; but it is only in a less degree a requirement of the other activities that go to make up the traffic of modern life. The railway is one of the larger mechanical contrivances of the machine age, and its exigencies in this respect are typical of what holds true at large. Communication of whatever kind, as well as the supply of other necessaries, is standardised in terms of time, space, quantity, frequency, and indeed in all measurable dimensions; and the "consumer," as the denizens of these machine-made communities are called, is required to conform to this network of standardisations in his demand and uses of them, on pain of "getting left." To "get left" is a colloquialism of the machine era and describes the commonest form of privation under the régime of the machine process. It is already a timeworn colloquialism, inasmuch as it is now already some time since the ubiquitous routine of the machine process first impressed on the common man the sinister eventuality covered by the phrase.

The relation in which the consumer, the common man, stands to the mechanical routine of life at large is of much the same nature as that in which the modern skilled workman stands to that detail machine process into which he is dovetailed in the industrial system. To take effectual advantage of what is offered as the wheels of routine go round, in the way of work and play, livelihood and recreation, he must know by facile habituation what is going on and how and in what quantities and at what price and where and when, and for the best effect he must adapt his movements with skilled exactitude and a cool mechanical insight to the nicely balanced moving equilibrium of the mechanical processes engaged. To live—not to say at ease—under the exigencies of this machine-made routine requires a measure of consistent training in the mechanical apprehension of things. The mere mechanics of conformity to the schedule of living implies a degree of trained insight and a facile strategy in all manner of quantitive adjustments and adaptations, particularly at the larger centres of population, where the routine is more comprehensive and elaborate.

And here and now, as always and everywhere, invention is the mother of necessity. The complex of technological ways and means grows by increments that come into the scheme by way of improvements, innovations, expedients designed to facilitate, abridge or enhance the work to be done. Any such innovation that fits workably into the technological scheme, and that in any appreciable degree accelerates the pace of that scheme at any point, will presently make its way into general and imperative use, regardless of whether its net ulterior effect is an increase or a diminution of material comfort or industrial efficiency. Such is particularly the case under the current pecuniary scheme of life if the new expedient lends itself to the service of competitive gain or competitive spending; its general adoption then peremptorily takes effect on pain of damage and discomfort to all those who fail to strike the new pace. Each new expedient added to and incorporated in the system offers not only a new means of keeping up with the run of things at an accelerated pace, but also a new chance of getting left out of the running. The point is well seen, e. g., in the current competitive armaments, where equipment is subject to constant depreciation and obsolescence, not through decline or decay, but by virtue of new improvements. So also in the increase and acceleration of advertising that has been going on during the past quarter of a century, due to increased facilities and improved methods in printing, paper-making, and the other industrial arts that contribute to the appliances of publicity.

It is of course not hereby intended to imply that these modern inventions meet no wants but such as they themselves create. It is beyond dispute that such mechanical contrivances, for instance, as the telephone, the typewriter, and the automobile are not only great and creditable technological achievements, but they are also of substantial service. At the same time it is at least doubtful if these inventions have not wasted more effort and substance than they have saved,—that they are to be credited with an appreciable net loss. They are designed to facilitate travel and communication, and such is doubtless their first and obvious effect. But the net result of their introduction need by no means be the same. Their chief use is in the service of business, not of industry, and their great further use is in the furtherance, or rather the acceleration, of obligatory social amenities. As contrivances for the expedition of traffic both in business and in social intercourse their use is chiefly, almost wholly, of a competitive nature; and in the competitive equipment and manœuvres of business and of gentility the same broad principle will be found to apply as applies to competitive armaments and improvements in the technology of warfare. Any technological advantage gained by one competitor forthwith becomes a necessity to all the rest, on pain of defeat. The typewriter is, no doubt, a good and serviceable contrivance for the expedition of a voluminous correspondence, but there is also no reasonable doubt but its introduction has appreciably more than doubled the volume of correspondence necessary to carry on a given volume of business, or that it has quadrupled the necessary cost of such correspondence. And the expedition of correspondence by stenographer and typewriter has at the same time become obligatory on all business firms, on pain of losing caste and so of losing the confidence of their correspondents. Of the telephone much the same is to be said, with the addition that its use involves a very appreciable nervous strain and its ubiquitous presence conduces to an unremitting nervous tension and unrest wherever it goes. The largest secure result of these various modern contrivances designed to facilitate and abridge travel and communication appears to be an increase of the volume of traffic per unit of outcome, acceleration of the pace and heightening of the tension at which the traffic is carried on, and a consequent increase of nervous disorders and shortening of the effective working life of those engaged in this traffic. But in these matters invention is the mother of necessity, and within the scope of these contrivances for facilitating and abridging labour there is no alternative, and life is not offered on any other terms.[1]

[1] On the other hand the aphorism often cited, that "Necessity is the Mother of Invention," appears to be nothing better than a fragment of uncritical rationalism. It offers a rationalised, *ex post facto* account of changes that take place, and reflects that ancient preconception by help of which the spokesmen of edification were enabled to interpret all change as an improvement due to the achievement of some definitely foreknown end. It appears also to be consistently untrue, except so far as "invention" is to be taken as a euphemistic synonym for "prevarica-

Other kinds of routine, standardised and elaborate, have been or still are in force, besides this machine-like process of living as carried on under modern technological conditions; and one and another of these will at times rise to a degree of exigence quite comparable with that of the machine process. But these others are of a different character in that their demands are not enforced by sanctions of an unmediated mechanical kind; they do not fall on the delinquent with a direct mechanical impact, and the penalties of non-conformity are of a conventional nature. So, *e. g.*, the punctilios of religious observance may come to a very rigid routine, to be observed on pain of sufficiently grave consequences; but in so far as these eventual (eschatological) consequences are statable in terms of material incidence (of fire, sulphur, or the like) the mechanically trained modern consumer will incline to hold that they are of a putative character only. So, again, in the matter of fashion and decorum the schedule of observances may be sufficiently rigorous, but here too failure to articulate with the sweep of a punctilious routine with all the sure and firm touch of the expert is not checked with an immediate disastrous impact of mechanical shock. Conformity in the technological respect with the routine of living under other technological systems than that of the machine process had also something of this character of conventional prescription; and the discipline exercised by the

tion." Doubtless, the felt need of ways and means has brought on many changes in technology, but doubtless also the ulterior consequences of any one of the greater mechanical inventions have in the main been neither foreseen nor intended in the designing of them. The more serious consequences, especially such as have an institutional bearing, have been enforced by the inventions rather than designed by the inventors.

routine of living in these more archaic technological eras was also something more in the nature of a training in conventional expedients. The resulting growth of habits of thought in such a community should then also differ in a similar way from what comes in sight in the present.

Both in its incidence on the workman and on the members of the community at large, therefore, the training given by this current state of the industrial arts is a training in the impersonal, quantitative apprehension and appreciation of things, and it tends strongly to inhibit and discredit all imputation of spiritual traits to the facts of observation. It is a training in matter-of-fact; more specifically it is a training in the logic of the machine process. Its outcome should obviously be an unqualified materialistic and mechanical animus in all orders of society, most pronounced in the working classes, since they are most immediately and consistently exposed to the discipline of the machine process. But such an animus as best comports with the logic of the machine process does not, it appears, for good or ill, best comport with the native strain of human nature in those peoples that are subject to its discipline. In all the various peoples of Christendom there is a visible straining against the drift of the machine's teaching, rising at time and in given classes of the population to the pitch of revulsion.

It is apparently among the moderately well-to-do, the half-idle classes, that such a revulsion chiefly has its way; leading now and again to fantastic, archaising cults and beliefs and to make-believe credence in occult insights and powers. At the same time, and with the like tincture of affectation and make-believe, there runs through much of the community a feeling of maladjustment and discomfort, that seeks a remedy in a "return to Nature" in one way or another; some sort of a return to "the simple life," which shall in some fashion afford an escape from the unending "grind" of living from day to day by the machine method and shall so put behind us for a season the burdensome futilities by help of which alone life can be carried on under the routine of the machine process.

All this uneasy revulsion may not be taken at its face value; there is doubtless a variable but fairly large element of affectation that comes to expression in all this talk about the simple life; but when all due abatement has been allowed there remains a substantial residue of unaffected protest. The pitch and volume of this protest against "artificial" and "futile" ways of life is greatest in the advanced industrial countries, and it has been growing greater concomitantly with the advance of the machine era. What is perhaps more significant of actualities than these well-bred professions of discomfort and discontent is the "vacation," being a more tangible phenomenon and statable in quantitative terms. The custom of "taking a vacation" has been on the increase for some time, and the avowed need of a yearly or seasonal holiday greatly exceeds the practice of it in nearly all callings. This growing recourse to vacations should be passably conclusive evidence to the effect that neither the manner of life enforced by the machine system, nor the occupations of those who are in close contact with this technology and its due habits of thought, can be "natural" to the common run of civilised mankind.

According to accepted theories of heredity,[1] civilised mankind should by native endowment be best fit to live under conditions of a moderately advanced savagery, such as the machine technology will not permit.[2] Neither in the physical conditions which it imposes, therefore, nor in the habitual ways of observation and reasoning which it requires in the work to be done, is the machine age adapted to the current native endowment of the race. And these various movements of unrest and revulsion are evidence, for as much as they are worth, that such is the case.

Not least convincing is the fact that a considerable proportion of those who are held unremittingly to the service of the machine process "break down," fall into premature decay. Physically and spiritually these modern peoples are better adapted to life under conditions radically different from those imposed by this modern technology.[3] All of which goes to show, what is the

[1] See pp. 18–21, above.

[2] Cf., however, what has been said above (pp. 21–23) of the variability and adaptability of a hybrid population and the possible selective establishment of a hybrid type more suitable to current conditions of life than any one of the racial stocks out of which the hybrid population is made up.

[3] So, *e. g.*, the modern technology has, directly and indirectly, brought on the growth of large cities and industrial towns, as well as an increasing density of population at large. This modern state of the industrial arts is a creation of the European community of nations, with the blond-hybrid populations leading. The population of these countries is drifting into these machine-made cities and towns, and this drift affects the blond-hybrids in a more pronounced degree than any other similarly distinguishable element in the population. At the same time the birth-rate is lower and the death-rate higher in these modern urban communities than

point here in question, that however exacting and however pervasive the discipline of the machine process may be, it can not, after all, achieve its perfect work in the way of habituation in the population of Christendom as it stands. The limit of tolerance native to the race, physically and spiritually, is short of that unmitigated materialism and unremitting mechanical routine to which the machine technology incontinently drives.

For anything like a comprehensive view of the effects which the machine technology has had on the scope and method of knowledge in modern times it is necessary to turn back to its beginnings. Historically the machine age succeeds the era of handicraft, but the two overlap very extensively. So much so that while the era of the machine technology is commonly held to have set in something like a century and a half ago it is still too early to assert that the industrial system has cleared

in the open country, in spite of the fact that more attention is given to preventive sanitation in the urban than in the rural communities, and it is in the urban communities that medical attendance is most available at the same time that its most efficient practitioners congregate there. This accelerated death-rate strikes the blond-hybrids of the towns in an eminent degree; and infant mortality in the towns, particularly, runs at such a figure as to be viewed with the liveliest apprehension. In its summary effects on the viability of the modern peoples this modern technology appears to be as untoward as would their removal to an unsuitable climate. Indeed the hygienic measures that are taken or advocated as a remedy for these machine-made conditions of urban life are of much the same character and require much the same degree of meticulous attention to details that are required to preserve the life of Europeans under the precarious climatic conditions of the low latitudes. So that, for these Europeans at least, the hygienic situation created by their own technology has much of that character of a comprehensive clinic that attaches to the British occupation of India or the later European occupation of West Africa or the Philippines.

itself of the remnants of handicraft or that the habits of thought suitable to the days of handicraft are no longer decisive in the current legal and popular apprehension of industrial relations. The discipline of the machine process has not yet had time, nor has it had a clear field. The best that can be looked for, therefore, in the way of habits of thought conforming to the ways and means of the machine process should be something of a progressive approximation; and the considerations recited in the last few paragraphs should leave it doubtful whether anything more than an imperfect approximation to the logic of the machine process can be achieved, through any length of training, by the peoples among whom the greatest advance in that direction has already been made.

The material sciences early show the bias of the machine technology, as is fairly to be expected, since these sciences stand in a peculiarly close relation to the technological side of industry,—almost a relation of affiliation. At no earlier period has the correlation between science and technology been so close. And the response in respect of the scope and method of these sciences to any notable advance in technology has been sufficiently striking. As has already been indicated above, modern science at large takes to the use of statistical methods and precise mechanical measurements, and in this matter scientific inquiry has grown continually more confident and more meticulous at the same time that this mechanistic procedure is continually being applied more extensively as the technological advance goes forward. How far this statistical-mechanistic bias of modern inquiry is to be set down to the account of the drift of technology toward mechanical engineering, and how far it may be due to an ever increasing familiarity with conceptions of accountancy enforced by the price system and the time schedule in daily life, may be left an open question. The main fact remains, that in much the same degree as niceties of calculation have come to dominate current technological methods and devices the like insistence on extreme niceties of mechanical measurement and statistical accuracy has also become imperative in scientific inquiry; until it may fairly be said that such meticulous scrutiny of quantitative relations as would have seemed foolish in the early days of the machine era has become the chief characteristic of scientific inquiry today.[1] It is of course not overlooked that in this matter of quantitative scruple the relation between current technology and the sciences is a relation of mutual give and take; but this fact can scarcely be urged as an objection to the view that these two lines of expression of the modern habit of mind are closely bound together, since it is precisely such a bond of continuity between the two that is here spoken for.

As shown in the foregoing chapter, in the course of the transition to modern times and modern ways of thinking the principle of efficient cause gradually replaced that of sufficient reason, as the final ground of certitude in conclusions of a theoretical nature. This shifting of the metaphysical footing of knowledge from a subjective ground to an objective one first and most unreservedly affects the material sciences, as it should

[1] The statisticians of a hundred years ago, *e. g.*, were content to work in round percentages where their latterday successors are doubtfully content with three-place decimals.

if it is at all to be construed as an outcome of the discipline exercised by the then current technology of handicraft. But the like effect is presently, though tardily, had in other lines of systematic knowledge that lie farther from the immediate incidence of technology and secular traffic. So that by the time of the industrial revolution the like mechanistic animus had come to pervade even the philosophical and theological speculations current in those communities that were most intimately and unreservedly touched by the discipline of craftsmanship and the petty trade.[1]

By this time,—the latter part of the eighteenth century,—the material sciences (overtly) admit no principle of systematisation within their own jurisdiction other than that of efficient cause. But at that date the concept of causation still has much of the content given it by the technology of handicraft. The efficient cause is still conceived after an individualistic fashion; without grave exaggeration it might even be said that the concept of cause as currently employed in the scientific speculations of that time had something of a quasi-personal complexion. The inquiry habitually looked to some one efficient cause, engaged as creatively dominant in the case and working to its end under conditioning circum-

[1] An eminently illustrative instance of the mechanistic bias in the moral sciences is afforded by the hedonistic conceptions of the early nineteenth century; and the deistic theology of that period and earlier is no less characteristic a symptom of the same animus.

Cf. also, for a view running to a conclusion opposed to that spoken for above, H. Bergson, *Creative Evolution* (translation by Arthur Mitchell, New York, 1911), ch. i, especially pp. 16–23; where the mechanistic conception is construed as an instinctive metaphysical norm and contrasted with the deliverances of reason and experience, which are then held to inculcate an anthropomorphic interpretation of the same facts.

stances that might greatly affect the outcome but that were not felt (or avowed) to enter into the case with the same aggressive thrust of causality that belonged to the efficient cause proper. The "contributory circumstances" were conceived rather extrinsically as accessory to the event; "accessory before the fact," perhaps, but none the less accessory. And scientific research took the form of an inquiry into the causal nexus between an antecedent (a cause or complex of causes) and its outcome in an event. The inquiry looked to the beginning and end of an episode of activity, the outcome of which would be a finished product, somewhat after the fashion in which a finished piece of work leaves the craftsman's hands. The craftsman is the agency productively engaged in the case, while his tools and materials are accessories to his force and skill, and the finished goods leave his hands as an end achieved; and so an episode of creative efficiency is rounded off.

From an early period in the machine era a new attitude toward questions of causation comes in evidence in scientific inquiry. The obvious change is perhaps the larger scale on which the sequence of cause and effect is conceived. It is no longer predominantly a question of episodes of causal efficiency, detached and rounded off. Such detail episodes still continue to occupy the routine of investigation; necessarily so, since these empirical sciences proceed step by step in the determination of the phenomena with which they are occupied. But in an increasing degree these detached phenomena are sought to be worked into a theoretical structure of larger scope, and this larger structure of theory falls into shape as a self-determining sequence of cumulative change.

The same concept of process that rules in the machine technology invades the speculations of the scientists and results in theories of cumulative sequence, in which the point of departure as well as the objective end of the sequence of causation gradually come to have less and less of a determinative significance for the course of the inquiry and for its results. In theoretical speculations based on the data of the empirical sciences, interest and attention come progressively to centre on this process of cumulative causation, so that the interest in the productive efficiency of a given cause which eventuates in a given consummation ceases gradually to be of decisive moment in the formulations of theory; which comes in this way to be an account of an unfolding process rather than a checking up of individual effects against individual causes. What once were ultimate questions have in modern science become ulterior questions and have lost their preferential place in the inquiry. Neither the seat of efficient initiative, that would be presumed to give this unfolding process of cumulative change its content and direction, nor its eventual goal, wherein it would be presumed to come to rest when the initial impulse has spent itself and its end has been compassed,—neither of these ultimates holds the attention or guides the inquiry of modern science.

It is only gradually, concomitant with the gradual maturing of the machine technology, that the systematisation of knowledge in scientific theory has come by common consent to converge on formulations of a genetic process of cumulative change. This science of the machine age is "evolutionary" in a peculiarly impersonal, indeed in a mechanistic sense of the term. In the consummate form, as it stands at the transition to the twentieth century, this evolutionary conception of genetic process is, at least ideally, void of all teleological elements and of all personality—except as personality may be concessively admitted as a by-product of the mechanistic sweep of the blind motions of brute matter. Neither the name nor the notion of a genetic evolution is peculiar to the machine age; but this current, impersonal, unteleological, mechanistic conception of an evolutionary process is peculiar to the late modern fashion of apprehending things.

It goes without saying that this mechanistic conception of process has worked clear of personation and teleological bias only gradually, by insensible decay and progressive elimination of those preconceptions of personal force and teleological fitness that ruled all theoretical knowledge in the days when the principle of sufficient reason held over that of efficient cause; and it should likewise be a matter of course that this shift to the mechanistic footing is by no means yet complete, that scientific inquiry is not yet clear of all contamination with animistic, anthropomorphic, or teleological elements; since the change is of the nature of habit, which takes time, and since the discipline of modern life to which the mechanistic habit of mind is traceable is by no means wholly consistent or unqualified in its mechanistic drift. Yet so far has the habituation to mechanistic ways of thinking taken effect, and so comprehensive and thorough has the discipline of the machine process been, that a mechanistic, unteleological notion of evolution is today a commonplace preconception both with scientists and laymen; whereas a hundred years ago such a conceit had intimately touched the imagination of but very few, if any, among the scientific adepts of the new era.

To what effect Lucretius and his like in classical antiquity, *e. g.*, may have speculated and tried to speak in these premises is by no means easy to make out; nor does it concern the present inquiry, since no vital connection or continuity of habit is traceable between their achievements in this respect and the theoretical preconceptions of modern science or of the machine technology. In the course of modern times conceptions of an evolutionary sequence of creation or of genesis come up with increasing frequency, and from an early period in the machine age these conceptions take on more and more of a mechanistic character, but it is not until Darwin that such a genetic process of evolution is conceived in terms of blind mechanical forces alone, without the help of imputed teleological bias or personalised initiative. It may perhaps be an open question whether the Darwinian conception of evolution is in no degree contaminated with teleological fancies, but however that may be it remains true that a purely mechanistic conception of a genetic process in nature had found no lodgment in scientific theory up to the middle of the nineteenth century. With varying success this conception has since been assimilated by the adepts of all the material sciences, and it may even be said to stand as a tacitly postulated commonplace underlying all modern scientific theory, whether in the material or the social sciences. It is accepted by common consent as a matter of course, although doubtless much antique detail at variance with it stands over both in the theoretical formulations of the adepts and in popular thought, and must continue to stand over until the course of habituation may conceivably in time enforce the sole competency of this mechanistic conception as the definitive norm of systematic knowledge. Whether such an eventuality is to overtake the scope and method of knowledge in Western civilisation should apparently be a question of how protracted, consistent, unmitigated, and how far congruous with their native bent the discipline of the machine process may prove in the further history of these peoples.

As has been shown above, in its beginnings the machine technology took over the working concepts of handicraft, and it has gradually shifted from the ground of manual operation so afforded to the ground of impersonal mechanical process; but this shifting of base in respect of the elementary technological preconceptions has not hitherto been complete, much of the personal attitude of craftsmanship toward mechanical forces and structures being still visible in the work of modern technologists. In like manner, and concomitant with the transition to the machine industry, there has gone forward a like shifting in respect of the point of view and the elementary preconceptions of science. This has taken effect most largely and gone farthest in the material sciences, as should be expected from the close connection that subsists between these sciences and the technology of the machine industry; but here again the elimination of craftsmanlike conceptions has hitherto not been complete. And, what is more instructive as to the part played by technological discipline in the growth of science, the character of this change in scientific scope, method and preconceptions is somewhat obviously such as would be given by habituation to the working of the machine process. Where later scientific inquiry has departed from or overpassed the limitations imposed by the habits of thought peculiar to craftsmanship the movement has taken the direction enforced by the machine technology.

So, *e. g.*, while the elements made use of by the machine technology, and characteristic of its work, are conceptions of mass, velocity, pressure, stress, vibration, displacement, and the like, these elements are made use of only under the rule that action in any of these bearings takes effect only by impact, by contact directly or through a continuum. The mathematical computations and elucidations that are one main instrumentality employed by the technologist do not and can not include this underlying postulate of contact, since it is an assumption extraneous to those magnitudes of quantity in terms of which this technology does its work. How far this preconception that action can take place only by contact is to be rated as an elementary concept carried over from handicraft, where it is obviously at home and fundamental in all work of manipulation, may perhaps be an idle question. In any case the machine technology is at one with craftsmanship on this head, even though there are many features in modern industrial processes that do not involve action by contact in any such obvious fashion as to suggest its necessary assumption, as, *e. g.*, in processes involving the use of light, heat or electricity. Yet it remains true that, by and large, the technology of the machine process is a technology of action by contact; and, apparently under stress of this wide though not necessarily universal application of the principle, the trained technologist does not rest content until he has in some tenable fashion construed any apparent exception as a special instance under the rule.

So also in modern scientific inquiry. The conceptual elements with which the scientist is content to work are precisely those that have commended themselves as competent in their technological use. Since action by contact is, on the whole, the working principle in the machine process, it is also accepted as the prime postulate in the formulation of all exact knowledge of impersonal facts. There is, of course, no inclination here to criticise or take exception to this characteristic habit of thought that pervades modern scientific inquiry. It has done good service, and to this generation, trained in the enexorably efficient ways of the machine process, the fact that it works is conclusive of its truth.[1] Yet the further fact is not to be overlooked that adherence to this principle is not due to unsophisticated observation simply. It is a principle, a habit of thought, not a fact of simple observation. Doubtless it is a fact of observation, direct and unambiguous, in respect of our own manual operations; and doubtless also it is a matter of such ready inference in respect of many external phenomena as to do duty as a fact of observation in good faith; but doubtless also there are many of these external phenomena that have to be somewhat painstakingly construed to bring them under the rule. Conceivably, even if such a habit of thought had not been handed down from the experience of handicraft it might have been induced by the discipline of the machine process, and might even have been ingrained in men exposed to this disci-

[1] "Pragmatism" is the term that has been elected to cover this metaphysical postulate of efficiency conceived as the bench-mark of actuality.

pline in sufficiently rigorous fashion to serve as a prime postulate of scientific inquiry; the machine process doubtless bears out such a principle in the main, and very rigorously. But in point of historical fact it is quite unnecessary to suppose this principle of action by contact to be a product *de novo* of the discipline of the machine, since it is older than the advent of the machine industry and is also quite consonant with the habits of work enforced by the technology of handicraft, more so indeed than with the technology of the machine industry. It appears fairly indubitable that this principle is a legacy taken over from the experience of life in the days of craftsmanship. And it may even be an open question whether the machine technology would not today be of an appreciably different complexion if it had, as it conceivably might have, developed without the hard and fast limitations imposed by this postulate. Doubtless, scientific inquiry, and the theoretical formulations reached by such inquiry, would differ somewhat notably from what they currently are if the scientists had gone to their work without such a postulate, or holding it in a qualified sense, as a principle of limited scope, as applying only within a limited range of phenomena, only so far as empirical evidence might enforce it in detail.

If, as seems at least presumably true, this principle of action by contact owes its origin to habits induced by manipulation, it will be seen to be of an anthropomorphic derivation. And if it further owes its acceptance as a principle universally applicable to material phenomena to the protracted discipline of life under the technology of handicraft, its universality must also take rank as an anthropomorphic imputation enforced by long habit. It is of the nature of habit, and moreover of workmanlike habit. Casting back into the past history of civilisation and into the contemporary lower cultures, it will appear that the principle (habit of thought) in question is prevalent everywhere and presumably through all human time; as it should be if it is traceable to so ubiquitous an experience as manipulation. But it will also appear that, except within the bounds, in time and space, of the high tide of craftsmanship and the machine technology, this principle does not arrogate to itself universal mandatory authority in the domain of external phenomena. Not only are the tenets of magic and theology at variance with the proposition that action can take place only by mechanical contact; but in the naïve thinking of commonplace humanity outside this machine-made Western civilisation, action at a distance is patently neither imbecile nor incomprehensible as a familiar trait of external objects in their everyday behaviour.

Nor is it by any means a grateful work of spontaneous predilection, all this mechanistic mutilation of objective reality into mere inert dimensions and resistance to pressure; as witness the widely prevalent revulsion, chronic or intermittent, against its acceptance as a final term of knowledge. Laymen seek respite in the fog of occult and esoteric faiths and cults, and so fall back on the will to believe things of which the senses transmit no evidence; while the learned and studious are, by stress of the same "aching void," drawn into speculative tenets of ostensible knowledge that purport to go nearer to the heart of reality, and that elude all mechanistic proof or disproof. This revulsion against thinking in uncoloured mechanistic terms alone runs suggestively parallel with that other revulsion, already spoken of, against the geometrically adjusted routine of conduct imposed on modern life by the machine process; the two are in great part coincident, or concomitant, both in point of the class of persons affected by each and in point of the uncertain measure of finality attending the move so made in either case. Neither the manner of life imposed by the machine process, nor the manner of thought inculcated by habituation to its logic, will fall in with the free movement of the human spirit, born, as it is, to fit the conditions of savage life. So there comes an irrepressible—in a sense, congenital—recrudescence of magic, occult science, telepathy, spiritualism, vitalism, pragmatism.[1]

[1] Of all these latterday revulsionary schemes of surcease from the void and irritation of the mechanistic conception, that spoken for by M. H. Bergson is doubtless the most felicitous, at the same time that it is, in its elements, the most engagingly naïve. Apart from, and without prejudice to, the (doubtless very substantial) merits of this system of speculative tenets, the vogue which it has achieved appears to be due in good part to its consonance with this archaic bent of civilised human nature, already spoken of. The immanent, or rather intrinsically dominant, creative bent inherent in matter and not objectively distinguishable from it, is sufficiently suggestive of that praeter-mechanical efficacy that seems so easy of comprehension to many of the peoples on the lower levels of culture, and that affords the substantial ground of magical practices and finds untroubled expression in the more naïve of their theoretical speculations. It would be a work of extreme difficulty, e. g., to set up a consistently tenable distinction between M. Bergson's *élan de la vie*, on the one hand, and the *mana* of the Melanesians (*Cf.* Codrington, *The Melanesians*, esp. ch. vii and xii), the *wakonda* of the Sioux (*Cf.* A. C. Fletcher and F. la Flesche, "The Omaha Tribe," *Bureau of Ethnology, Report xxvii* (1905–1906), esp. pp. 597–599), or even the *hamingia* of Scandinavian paganism, on the other hand.

It was noted above that action by contact is not included, except by subsumption, in the mathematical formulations of technology or science. It should now

In fact, the point of departure and support for M. Bergson's speculations appears to be nothing else than a projection, into objective reality, of the same human trait that has here been spoken of as the instinct of workmanship; this norm of initiative and efficiency which so is imposed on objective facts being then worked out with great subtlety and sympathetic insight, to make a comprehensive, cosmological scheme. The like projection of workmanlike initiative and efficiency, and its imputation to objective reality, both at large—as with M. Bergson—and in concrete detail, with more or less of personalisation, is one of the main, though frequently misunderstood, factors in the cosmologies that do duty as a body of science and philosophy among savages and the lower barbarians.

That the roots of this speculative scheme of "creative evolution" should reach so far into the background of human culture and draw on sources so close to the undisciplined prime-movers of human nature is, of course, in no degree derogatory to this system of theory; nor does it raise any presumption of unsoundness in the tenets that so are, in the course of elaboration, built up out of this metaphysical postulate. In point of fact, the characterisation here offered places M. Bergson's thesis, and therefore his system, precisely where he has been at pains to explain that he wishes to take his initial position in advocating his view,—at an even break with the mechanistic conception; the merits of which, as contrasted with his own thesis, will then be made to appear in the course of the further argument that is to decide between their rival claims to primacy. In point of formal and provisional legitimation, such an imputation of workmanlike efficacy at large rests on ground precisely even with that on which the mechanistic conception also rests,—viz. imputation by force of metaphysical necessity, that is to say by force of an instinctive impulse. The main theorem of causation, as well as its several mechanistic corollaries, are, in the last resort, putative traits of matter only, not facts of observation; and the like is true—in M. Bergson's argument admittedly so—of the *élan de la vie* as well. So far, therefore, as regards the formally determinable antecedent probability of the two rival conceptions, the one is as good as the other; but M. Bergson's argument, running on ground of circumstantial evidence in the main, makes out at least a cogently attractive likelihood that the conception for which he speaks is to be accepted as the more fundamental, underlying the be added that in all the concomitance and sequence with which the mathematical formulations of mechanical phenomena are occupied, the assumption of concomitance or sequence at a distance will fill the requirements of the formulæ quite as convincingly and commonly more simply than the assumption of concomitance by contact only. To realise the difficulties which beset this postulate of action by mechanical continuity solely, as well as the *prima facie* imbecility of the principle itself, it is only necessary to call to mind the tortuous theories of gravitation designed to keep it intact, and the prodigy of incongruous intangibilities known as the ether,—a rigid and imponderable fluid.

Associated with the principle of action by mechanical continuity alone is a second metaphysical postulate of science,—the conservation of energy, or persistence of quantity. Like its fellow it does not admit of empirical proof; yet it is likewise held to be of universal application. This principle, that the quantity of matter or of energy does not increase or diminish, or, perhaps better, that the quantity of mechanical fact at large is invariable, has a better presumptive claim to rank as a by-product of the machine technology; although such a claim could doubtless be allowed only with broad qualifications.

mechanistic conception, conditioning it and on occasion overruling its findings in matters that lie beyond its ascertained competence. Which would come, in a different phrasing, to saying that the imputation of creatively workmanlike efficiency rests on instinctive ground more indefeasibly intrinsic to human nature; presumably in virtue of its embodying the functioning of an instinctive proclivity less sophisticated and narrowed by special habituation, such special habituation, e. g., as that exercised by the technology of handicraft and the machine process in recent times.

Not that the principle was not known or not formally accepted prior to the machine age; long ago the Roman scholar and the scholastic philosophers after him declared *ex nihilo nihil, in nihilum nil posse reverti.* But throughout the era of handicraft there continued also to be devoutly held the postulate that the material universe had a beginning in an act of creation, as also that it would some day come to an end, a quantitative collapse. As the era of handicraft advanced and, apparently, as the discipline of life under that technology enforced the habitual acceptance of the proposition that the quantity of material fact is constant, much ingenuity and much ambiguous speech was spent in an endeavour to reconcile the mechanical efficiency of the creative fiat with the dictum, *ex nihilo nihil fit.* But down to the close of that era it remains true that, by and large, the peoples of Christendom continued to believe in the mechanically creative efficiency of the Great Artificer; although, it must be admitted, with an ever growing apprehension that in this tenet of the faith they were face to face with a divine mystery. The eighteenth-century scientists, and many even in the nineteenth century, continued to profess belief in a creative origin of material things, as well as also in a providential guidance of material events,—which latter must have been conceived to be exerted by some other means than action through mechanical contact, since one term of the relation was conceived not to be of a mechanical nature.

It is not until the machine age is well under way and the machine technology has come to occupy the land, that faith in the theorem of the conservation of energy has grown robust enough to let the scientists lose interest in all questions of creation. The tenet has died by neglect, not by confutation. That it has done so among the adepts of the material sciences, and that it is doing so among the lay population at large in the modern industrial communities, is probably to be credited to the discipline of the machine process and the technological conceptions to which that discipline conduces. It conduces to this outcome in more than one way. This modern technology is a technology of mechanical process; it looks to and takes care of a sequence of mechanical action, rather than to the conditions of its inception or the sequel of its conclusion. A mind imbued with the logic of this machine process does not by habitual proclivity or with incisive effect attend to these alien matters that have no meaning within the horizon of that logic. The creative augmentation of material objects is a matter lying without the scope of the machine's logic.

As has already been remarked, the principle (habit of thought) that the quantity of material fact is constant is necessarily of ancient derivation and long growth. Taken in a presumptive sense, and held loosely as a commonplace of experience, it must have come up and attained some force very early in the workmanlike experience of the race. And the closer the application to the work in hand, the more consistently would this principle of common sense approve itself; so that it should, as indeed is sufficiently evident, be well at home among the habitual generalisations current in the days of handicraft; although it does not seem to have been generally accepted at that time as a principle necessarily having a universal application,—as witness the ready credence then given to theological dogmas of creation and the like. The habits of accountancy that came on under the price system, as the scope of the market grew larger with the growth and diversification of handicraft, seem to have had a great effect in extending and confirming the habitual acceptance of such a theorem. A strict balance, a running equilibrium of the quantitative items involved, is the central fact of the accountant's occupation. And this habit of scrutiny and balancing of quantities, and a meticulous tracing out and accounting for any apparent excess or deficiency in the sums handled, pervades the community at large, though in a less pronounced fashion, as well as that fraction of the population employed in trade. The discipline of the handicraft system in this respect gains incontinently in scope and vigour as the growth of that technological system, with its characteristic business management, goes forward.

When presently the machine technology comes forward this habitual preconception touching the invariability of material quantity finds new applications and new refinements of application, with the outcome that its guidance of men's thinking grows ever more inclusive and more peremptory. But it is not until half a century after the Industrial Revolution that the principle may be said finally to have gained unquestioning acceptance as a theorem universally binding on material phenomena. By that time—about the second quarter of the nineteenth century—the unqualified validity of this theorem had become so unmitigated a matter of course as to have fairly shifted from the ground of empirical generalisation to that of metaphysical thesis. Men of science then quite ingenuously set about proving the law of the Conservation of Energy by appeal to experiments and reasoning that proceeded with absolute naïveté on the tacit assumption of the theorem to be proven.

In its bearing on the growth of institutions the machine technology has yet scarcely had time to make its mark. Such institutional factors as, e. g., the common law are necessarily of slow growth. A system of civil rights is not only a balanced scheme of habitual responses to those stimuli at whose impact they take effect; it is at the same time a scheme which has the sanction of avowed common consent, such as will express itself in rating these institutional elements as facts of immemorial usage or as integrally inherent in the nature of things from the beginning. Such civil institutions take shape as prescriptive custom, and matters of habit which so are supported by broad grounds of authenticity and correlation with other elements of a prescriptive scheme of things will adapt themselves only tardily to any change in the situation or to any new bias in the drift of discipline. What happened in the matter of civil rights under the system of handicraft is an illustration in point. There need be little question but the eighteenth century scheme of Natural Rights was an outcome of the protracted discipline characteristic of the era of handicraft, and an adaptation to the exigencies of daily life under that system.

The scheme of Natural Rights, with its principles of Natural Liberty and its insistence on individual self-help, was well adapted to the requirements of handicraft and the petty trade, whose spirit it reflects with admirable faithfulness. But it was of slow growth, as any scheme of institutions must be, in the nature of things. So much so that handicraft and the petty trade had been in effectual operation some half-a-dozen centuries, in ever increasing force, before the corresponding system of civil rights and moral obligations made good its pretensions to rule the economic affairs of the community. Indeed, it is only by the latter half of the eighteenth century that the system of Natural Rights came to passable maturity and finally took rank as a secure principle of enlightened common sense; and by that time the handicraft system was giving way to the machine industry. And even then this result was reached only in the most advanced industrial community of Europe, where the discipline of handicraft and trade had had the freest scope to work out its natural bent, with the least hindrance from other dominant interests at variance with its schooling.[1]

So it has come about that while the system of Natural Rights is an institutional by-product of workmanship under the handicraft system and is adapted to the exigencies of craftsmanship and the petty trade, it never fully took effect in the shaping of institutions until that phase of economic life was substantially past, or until

[1] All this, of course, neither ignores nor denies the substantial part which the *jus gentium* and the *jus naturale* of the Roman jurists and their commentators have played in the formulation of the system of Natural Rights. In point of pedigree the line of derivation of these legal principles is doubtless substantially as set forth authentically by the jurists who have spent their competent endeavors on that matter. So far as regards the English-speaking communities this pedigree runs back to Locke, and through Locke to the line of jurists and philosophers on whom that great scholar has drawn; while for the promulgation of the like system of principles more at large the names of Grotius, Pufendorf, Althusius doubtless have all the significance commonly assigned them. See pp. 290–293 above.

the new era, of the machine industry and the large business brought on by the new technology, had come to rule the economic situation. So that hitherto the work of the machine industry has been organised and conducted under a code of legal rights and business principles adapted to the state of the industrial arts which the machine industry has displaced. Latterly, it is true, the requirements of the machine technology, in the way of large-scale organisation, continuity of operation, and interstitial balance of the industrial system, have begun to show themselves so patently at variance with these business principles engendered by the era of handicraft as to throw a shadow of doubt on the adequacy of these "Natural" metaphysics of natural liberty, self-help, free competition, individual initiative, and the like. But, harsh as has been the discrepancy between the received system of economic institutions on the one side and the working of the machine technology on the other, its effect in reshaping current habits of thought in these premises has hitherto come to nothing more definitive than an uneasy conviction that "Something will have to be done about it." Indeed, so far is the machine process from having yet recast the principles of industrial management, as distinct from technological procedure, that the efforts inspired in responsible public officials and public-spirited citizens by this patent discrepancy have hitherto been directed wholly to regulating industry into consonance with the antiquated scheme of business principles, rather than to take thought of how best to conduct industrial affairs and the distribution of livelihood in consonance with the technological requirements of the machine industry.

It is true, among the workmen, and particularly among those skilled workmen who have been trained in the machine technology and are exposed to the full impact of the machine's discipline, uncritical habitual faith in this institutional scheme is beginning to crumble, so far as regards that principle of Natural Rights that vests unlimited discretion in the owner of property, and so far as regards property in the material equipment of industry. But this is about as broad a proposition of such a kind as current facts of opinion and agitation will bear out, and this inchoate break with the received habitual views touching the dues and obligations of discretion in industrial matters is extremely vague and almost wholly negative. Even in those members of the community who are most directly and rigorously exposed to its discipline the machine process has hitherto wrought no such definite bias, no such positive habitual attitude of workmanlike initiative towards the conventions of industrial management as to result in a constructive deviation from the received principles.[1]

On the other hand the business principles engendered by the habit of mind that gave rise to the system of Natural Rights has had grave consequences for workmanship under the conditions imposed by the machine industry. As has been shown in some detail in the foregoing chapter, the individualistic organisation of the work, coupled with the personal incidence of the handicraft technology, and the stress thrown on price rating and self-help by the ever increasing recourse to bargain and sale ("free contract") under that system, led in

[1] Unless the "Syndicalist" movement is to be taken as something sufficiently definite in its principles to make it an exception to the rule.

the end to the habitual rating of workmanship in terms of the price it would bring. Then as always workmanlike efficiency commanded the approval of thoughtful men, as being serviceable to the common good and as a substantial manifestation of human excellence; and at the same time, then as ever, efficient work was a source of comfort and complacency to the workman. But under the teaching of the price system efficiency came to be rated in terms of the pecuniary gain.

With the advent of the machine industry this pecuniary rating of efficiency gained a new impetus and brought new consequences for technology as well as for business enterprise. Typically, the machine industry runs on a large scale, as contrasted with handicraft, and it involves a relatively wide and exacting division of labour between workmanship and salesmanship. Under the conditions of large ownership implied in this modern industrial system the workmen no longer have, or can have, the responsibility of the pecuniary management of the industrial concern; on the other hand the same conditions of large ownership and extensive business connections require the businessmen in charge to delegate the immediate oversight of the plant and its technological processes to other hands, and to devote their own energies to the pecuniary management of the concern and its transactions. Hence it follows that as the machine system and the highly specialised business enterprise that goes with it reach a larger scale and a higher degree of elaboration the businessmen in charge are, by training and by progressive limitation of interest, less and less competent to take care of the technological exigencies of the machine system. But at the same time the discretion in technological matters still rests in their hands by force of their ownership. So that, while the responsibility of technological discretion still rests on them, and cannot be fully delegated to other hands, the exigencies of business enterprise and of the training which it involves will no longer permit them to meet this responsibility in a competent fashion.

The businessmen in control of large industrial enterprises are beginning to appreciate something of their own unfitness to direct or oversee, or even to control, technological matters, and so they have, in a tentative way, taken to employing experts to do the work for them. Such experts are known colloquially as "efficiency engineers" and are presumed to combine the qualifications of technologist and accountant. In point of fact it is as accountants, capable of applying the tests of accountancy in a new field, that these experts commend themselves to the businessmen in control, and the "efficiency" which they look to is an efficiency counted in terms of net pecuniary gain. "Efficiency" in these premises means pecuniary efficiency, and only incidentally or in a subsidiary sense does it mean industrial efficiency,—only in so far as industrial efficiency conduces to the largest net pecuniary gain. All the while the businessmen retain the decisive superior discretion in their own incompetent hands, since all the while the whole matter remains a business proposition. The "staff organisation," in which vests the superior control of these technological affairs, consistently remains an organisation of worldly wisdom, business enterprise—not of technological proficiency,—a state of things not to be remedied so long as industry is carried on for business profits.

Meantime the workmen of all kinds and grades—labourers, mechanics, operatives, engineers, experts—all imbued with the same pecuniary principles of efficiency, go about their work with more than half an eye to the pecuniary advantage of what they have in hand. The attitude of the trades-unions towards their work and towards the industrial concerns in whose employ their work is done illustrates something of the habitual frame of mind of these men, who are avowed experts in the matter of workmanship.

Latterly many inconveniences have beset the community at large as well as particular sections and classes of the industrial community, due in the main to a consistent adherence to these business principles in the management of industrial affairs. The capitalist-employers, on the one hand, have gone on the full powers with which the modern institution of ownership and its broad implications has vested them; with the result that the public at large, investors, consumers of industrial products, users of "public utility" agencies serving such needs as light, fuel, transportation, communication, amusement, etc., feel very much aggrieved; as do also and more particularly the workmen with whom the capitalist-employers do business on the lines laid down by the authentic business principles involved in the discretionary ownership of the industrial plant and resources. On the other hand the workmen, resting their case on the same common-sense view that the individual is a self-sufficient economic unit who owes nothing to the community at large beyond what he may freely undertake "for a good and valuable consideration in hand paid,"—the workmen stand likewise on the full powers given them by the current institutions of ownership and contractual discretion, and so work what mischief they can to their employers and to the public at large always blamelessly within the rules of the game as laid down of old on the pecuniary principles of business discretion, and in the light of such sense as their training has given them with regard to efficiency in the industries that have fallen into their hands. And then the "money power" comes in as a third pecuniarily trained factor, with ever increasing force and incisiveness, to muddle the whole situation mysteriously and irretrievably by looking after their own pecuniary interests in a fashion even more soberly legitimate and authentic, if possible, than the workmen's management of their own affairs.

Of course, all this working at cross purposes is not altogether due to trained incapacity on the part of the several contestants to appreciate the large and general requirements of the industrial situation; perhaps it is not even chiefly due to such inability, but rather to an habitual, and conventionally righteous disregard of other than pecuniary considerations. It would doubtless appear that a trained inability to apprehend any other than the immediate pecuniary bearing of their manœuvres accounts for a larger share in the conduct of the business-men who control industrial affairs than it does in that of their workmen, since the habitual employment of the former holds them more rigorously and consistently to the pecuniary valuation of whatever passes under their hands; and the like should be true only in a higher degree of those who have to do exclusively with the financial side of business. The state of the industrial arts requires that these several factors should cooperate intelligently and without reservation, with an eye single to the exigencies of this modern wide-sweeping technological system; but their habitual addiction to pecuniary rather than technological standards and considerations leaves them working at cross purposes. So also their (pecuniary) interests are at cross purposes; and since these interests necessarily rule in any pecuniary culture, they must decide the line of conduct for each of the several factors engaged.

These discrepancies, obstructive tactics and disserviceable practices are commonly deplored and are presumably deplorable, and they doubtless merit extensive discussion on these grounds, but their merits in this bearing do not properly come into consideration here. The matter has been brought in here not with any view of defence, denunciation or remedy, but because it is a matter of grave consequence as regards the training given by business experience to these men in whose hands the current scheme of institutions has placed the technological fortunes of the community. And whether these pecuniary tactics and practices that fill so large a place in the attention and sentiments of this generation come chiefly of a lack of insight into current technological exigencies, or of a deliberate choice of evils enforced by the pecuniary necessities of the case, still their disciplinary value as bearing on the sense of workmanship taken in its larger scope will be much the same in either case. Habituation to bargaining and to the competitive principles of business necessarily brings it about that pecuniary standards of efficiency invade (contaminate) the sense of workmanship; so that work, workmen, equipment and products come to be rated on a scale of money values, which has only a circuitous and often only a putative relation to their workmanlike efficiency or their serviceability. Those occupations and those aptitudes that yield good returns in terms of price are reputed valuable and commendable,—the accepted test of success, and even of serviceability, being the gains acquired. Workmanship comes to be confused with salesmanship, until tact, effrontery and prevarication have come to serve as a standard of efficiency, and unearned gain is accepted as the measure of productiveness.

Efficiency conduces to the common good, and is also a meritorious and commendable trait in the person who exercises it. But under the canons of self-help and pecuniary valuation the test of efficiency in economic matters has come to be, not technological mastery and productive effect, but proficiency in pecuniary management and the acquisition of wealth. Both in his own estimation and in the eyes of his fellows, the man who gains much does well; he is conceived to do well both as a matter of personal efficiency and in point of serviceability to the common good. To "do well" in modern phrase means to engross something appreciably more of the community's wealth than falls to the common run. But since gains, and hence efficiency, are conceived in terms of price, it follows that the man, workman or businessman, who can induce his fellows to pay him well for his services or his goods is accounted efficient and serviceable; from which it follows that under this canon of pecuniary efficiency men are conceived to serve the common good somewhat in proportion as they are able to induce the community to pay more for their services than they are worth.

The businessman who gains much at little cost, who gets something for nothing, is rated, in his own as well as in his neighbours' esteem, as a public benefactor indispensable to the community's welfare, and as contributing to the common good in direct proportion to the amount which he has been able to draw out of the aggregate product. It is perhaps needless to call to mind that of this character are the main facts in the history of all the great fortunes;[1] although the current accounts of their accumulation, being governed by pecuniary standards of efficiency and serviceability, dwell mainly on the services that have inured to the community from the traffic with which the great captains have interfered in their quest of gain. The prevalence of salesmanship, that is to say of business enterprise, and the consequent high repute of the salesmanlike activities and aptitudes in any community that is organised on a price system, is perhaps the most serious obstacle which the pecuniary culture opposes to the advance in workmanship. It intrudes into the most intimate and secret workings of the human spirit and contaminates the sense of workmanship in its initial move, and sets both the proclivity to efficient work and the penchant for serviceability at cross purposes with the common good.

But under the conditions engendered by the machine technology the scope of this pecuniary standard of workmanship has been greatly enlarged. On the whole the

[1] Cf., e. g., Anna Youngman, *The Economic Causes of Great Fortunes*, especially ch. vi; R. Ehrenburg, *Grosse Vermögen;* Ida Tarbell, *History of the Standard Oil Company.*

machine industry calls for a large-scale organisation, increasingly so as time has passed and the machine process has come more fully to dominate the industrial situation. By the same move initiative and discretion have come to vest in those who can claim ownership of the large material equipment so required, and the exercise of such initiative and discretion by these owners is loosely proportioned to the magnitude of their holdings. Smaller owners have the same freedom of initiative and discretion, in point of legal and conventional competency,—such freedom and equality between persons being of the essence of Natural Rights; but in point of practical fact, as determined by technological and business exigencies, there is but small discretion left such smaller holders. Initiative and discretion in modern industrial matters vest in the owners of the industrial plant, or in such moneyed concerns as may stand in an underwriting relation to the owners of the plant; such discretion is exercised through pecuniary transactions; and these pecuniary transactions whereby the conduct of industry is guided and controlled are entered into with a view to gain in terms of price. It is but a slight exaggeration to say that such transactions, which govern the course of industry, are carried out with an eye single to pecuniary gain,—the industrial consequences, and their bearing on the community's welfare, being matters incidental to the transaction of business. In every-day phrase, under the rule of the current technology and business principles, industry is managed by businessmen for business ends, not by technological experts or for the material advantage of the community. And in this control of industrial affairs the smaller businessmen are in great part subject to the discretion of the larger.[1]

By ancient habit, handed down from the days of handicraft and petty trade, this pecuniary management is conventionally conceived to be directed to the production of goods and services, and the businessman is still conventionally rated as a producer and his gains accepted as a measure of his productive efficiency. In conventional speech "producer" means the owner of industrial plant, not the workmen employed nor the mechanical apparatus about which they are employed.[2] The "producers," "manufacturers," "captains of industry," whose interests are safeguarded by current legislation and by the guardians of law and order are the businessmen who have a pecuniary interest in industrial affairs; and it is their pecuniary interests that are so safeguarded, in the naïve faith that the material interests of the community at large coincide with the opportunities for gain so secured to the businessmen.

It has already been spoken of above that the processes of industry are bound in a comprehensive system of give and take, in such a manner that no considerable fraction of this industrial system functions independently of the rest. The industrial system at large may be conceived

[1] Cf. a paper "On the Nature of Capital" in the *Quarterly Journal of Economics*, November, 1908.

[2] As late as Adam Smith's time "manufacturer" still retained its etymological value and designated the workman who made the goods. But from about that time, that is to say since the machine process and the business control of industry have thoroughly taken effect, the term no longer has a technological connotation but has taken on a pecuniary (business) signification wholly; so that the term now designates a businessman who stands in none but a pecuniary relation to the processes of industry.

as a comprehensive machine process, the several sub-processes of which technologically inosculate and ramify in what may be conceived as a network of elements working in a moving equilibrium, none of which can go on at its full productive efficiency except in duly balanced correlation with all the rest. This characterisation will strictly apply only so far as the machine technology has taken over the various branches of industry, but it applies in a loose though by no means idle fashion also as regards those elements of the industrial system in which the machine technology has not yet become dominant. In so far as the industrial system is of this character it will also hold that the business management of any one branch or line or parcel of industries will have its effect on the rest, primarily and proximately on those other branches or lines with which the given parcel stands in immediate relations of give and take, through the market or more directly through technological correlation,—as, e. g., in the transportation system. Business management which affects a large section of this balanced system will necessarily have a wide-reaching effect on the working of the system at large. Such business control of industry, as has just been remarked above, is exercised with a view to pecuniary gain; but pecuniary gain in these premises comes from changes, and apprehended changes, in the efficiency of the various industrial processes that are touched by such control, rather than from the work-day functioning of the several items of equipment involved. The changes which so bring gain to these larger businessmen may be favourable to the effective working of industry, but they may also be unfavourable; and the opportunities for gain which they afford the larger businessmen may be equally profitable whether the disturbance in question is favourable or unfavourable to industrial efficiency. The gains to be derived from such disturbance are proportioned to the magnitude of the disturbance rather than to its industrial productiveness. It should follow, of course, that if the machine technology should come so to dominate the industrial situation as to bind all industry in a rigorously comprehensive balanced process, the material fortunes of the community would come to rest unreservedly and in all details in the hands of those larger businessmen who hold the final pecuniary discretion.

In qualification of this broad proposition it is to be noted that, while the gains of the superior rank of businessmen accrue in the manner indicated,—by means of disturbances which may indifferently be favourable or unfavourable to industry,—yet in the long run it is necessarily true that the gains which so inure to the pecuniary magnates must be derived from the net product of industry and will in the long run be larger in the aggregate the more productive the community's industry is. What makes business profitable to the businessmen is, after all, their usufruct of the community's industrial efficiency. In the long run nothing can accrue as income to the pecuniary magnates more than the surplus product of industry above the subsistence of the industrial community at large. But so long as the magnates have not come to a working arrangement on this basis and "pooled their interests" the proposition as formulated above appears to be adequate to the facts,—that the gains of these larger businessmen are a function of the magnitude of the disturbances which they create rather than of their productive effect.

It should also follow, and so far as the above characterisation holds it does follow, that the current pecuniary organisation of industry vests the usufruct of the community's industrial proficiency in the owners of the industrial equipment. Proximately this usufruct of the industrial community's technological knowledge and working capacity vests in the detail owners of the equipment, but only proximately. At the further remove it vests only in the businessmen whose command of large means enables them to create and control those pecuniary conjunctures of industry that bring about changes in the market value and ownership of the equipment.

Breinigsville, PA USA
23 March 2011
258281BV00002B/72/A

9 781596 058934